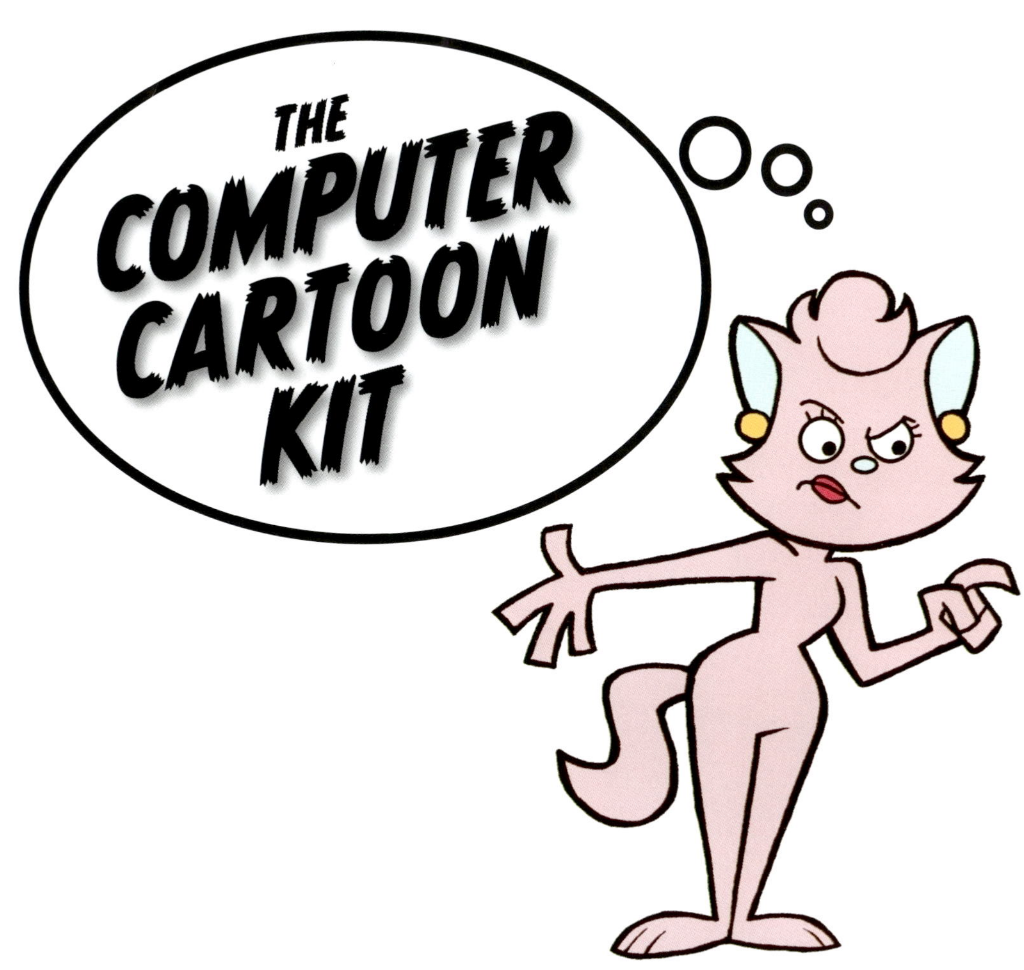

THE COMPUTER CARTOON KIT

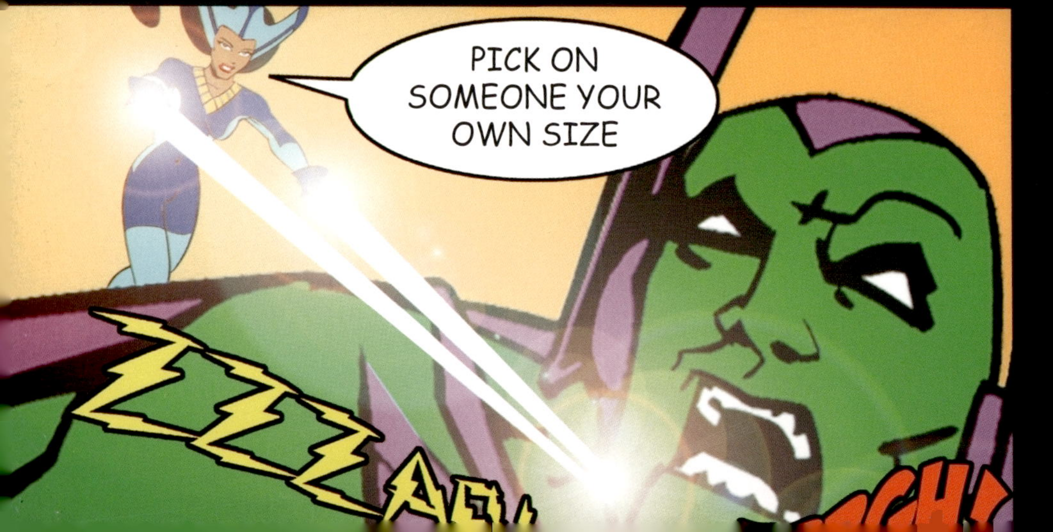

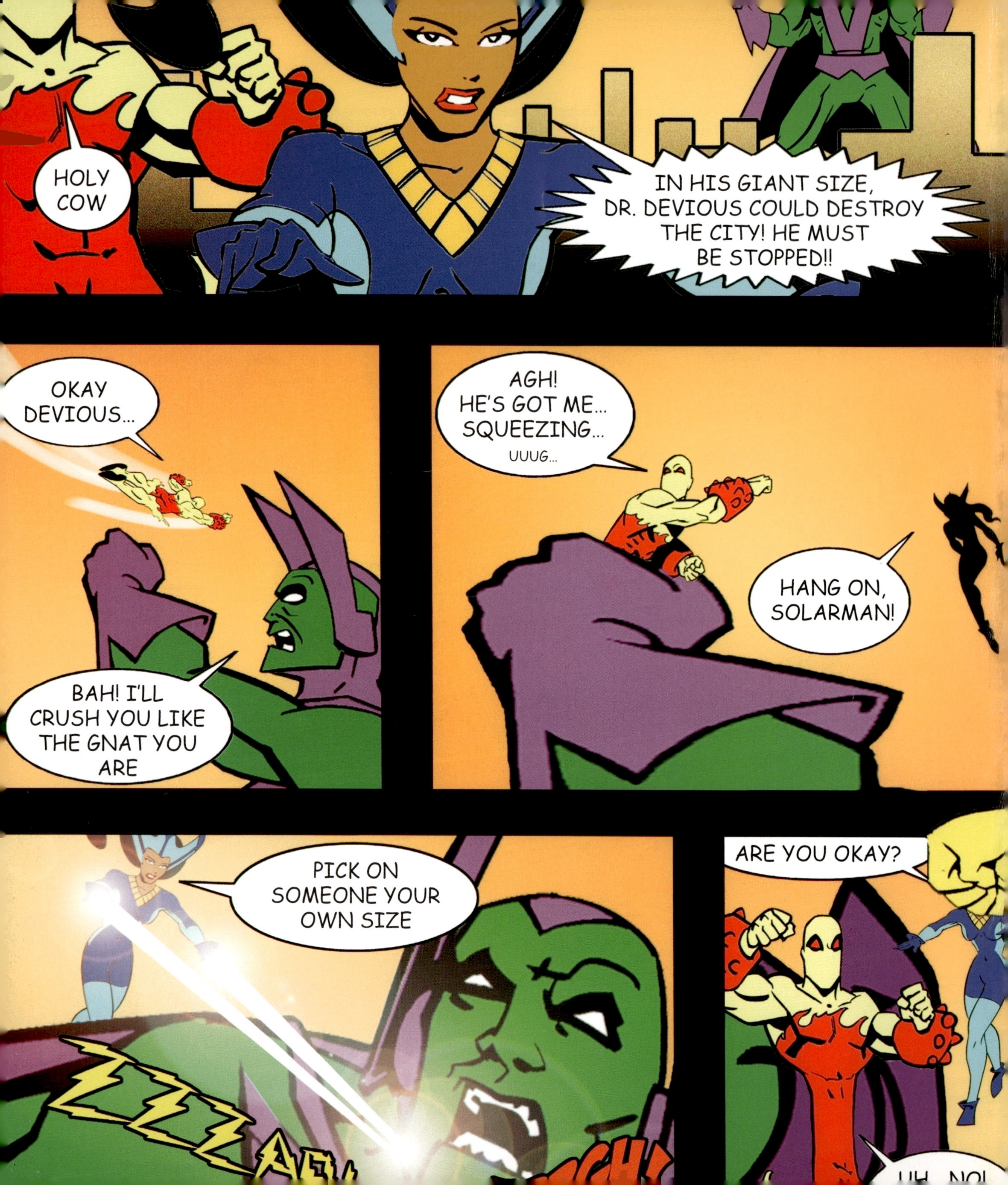

HOLY COW
IN HIS GIANT SIZE, DR. DEVIOUS COULD DESTROY THE CITY! HE MUST BE STOPPED!!
OKAY DEVIOUS...
BAH! I'LL CRUSH YOU LIKE THE GNAT YOU ARE
AGH! HE'S GOT ME... SQUEEZING...
UUUG...
HANG ON, SOLARMAN!
PICK ON SOMEONE YOUR OWN SIZE
ZZZ
AGH

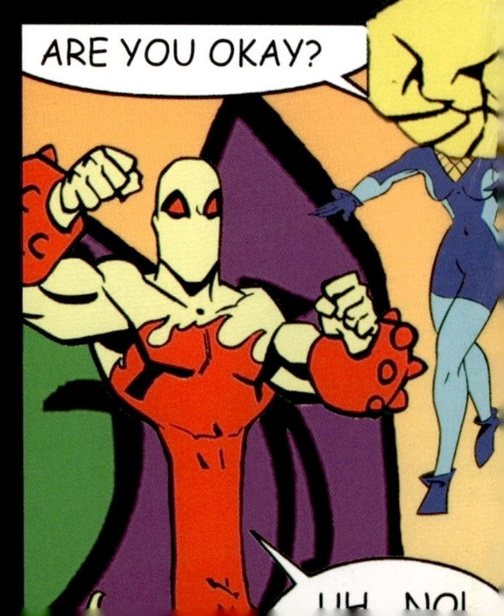

ARE YOU OKAY?
UH, NO!

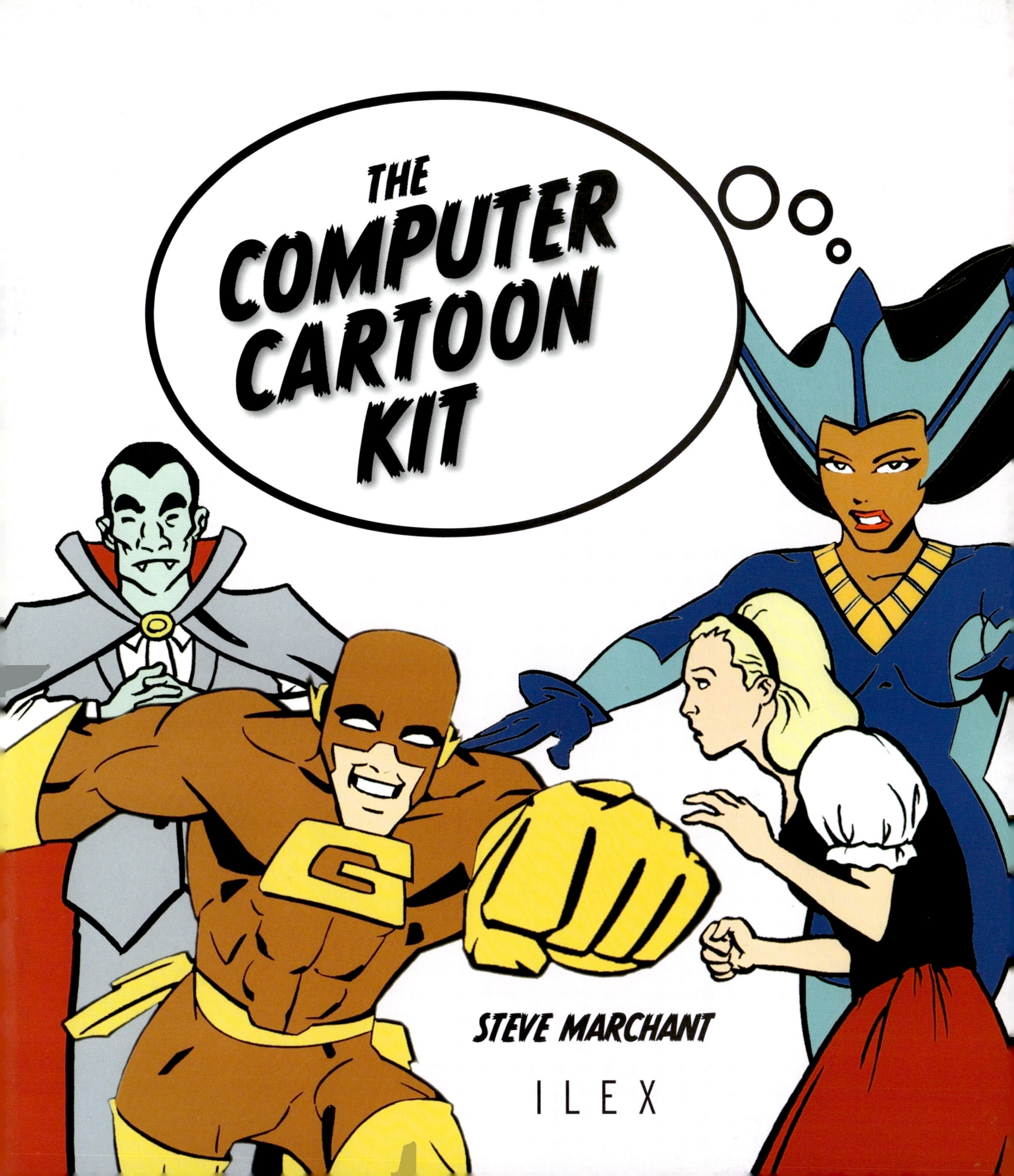

THE COMPUTER CARTOON KIT
STEVE MARCHANT
ILEX

Computer Cartoon Kit

First published in the United Kingdom in 2006 by
I L E X
The Old Candlemakers
West Street, Lewes
East Sussex
BN7 2NZ

I L E X is an imprint of The Ilex Press Ltd
Visit us on the web at:
www.ilex-press.com

Copyright © 2006 The Ilex Press Limited

This book was conceived by
ILEX Cambridge, England

ILEX Editorial, Lewes:
Publisher: Alastair Campbell
Creative Director: Peter Bridgewater
Managing Editor: Tom Mugridge
Editor: Adam Juniper
Art Director: Julie Weir
Designer: Chris and Jane Lanaway
Design Assistant: Kate Haynes

ILEX Research, Cambridge:
Development Art Director: Graham Davis
Technical Art Editor: Nicholas Rowland

British Library Cataloguing-in-Publication Data
A catalogue record for this book is available from the British Library

ISBN 10 – 1-904705-86-3
ISBN 13 – 978-1-904705-86-4

Printed and bound in China

For more information on this title please visit:
www.web-linked.com/myocuk

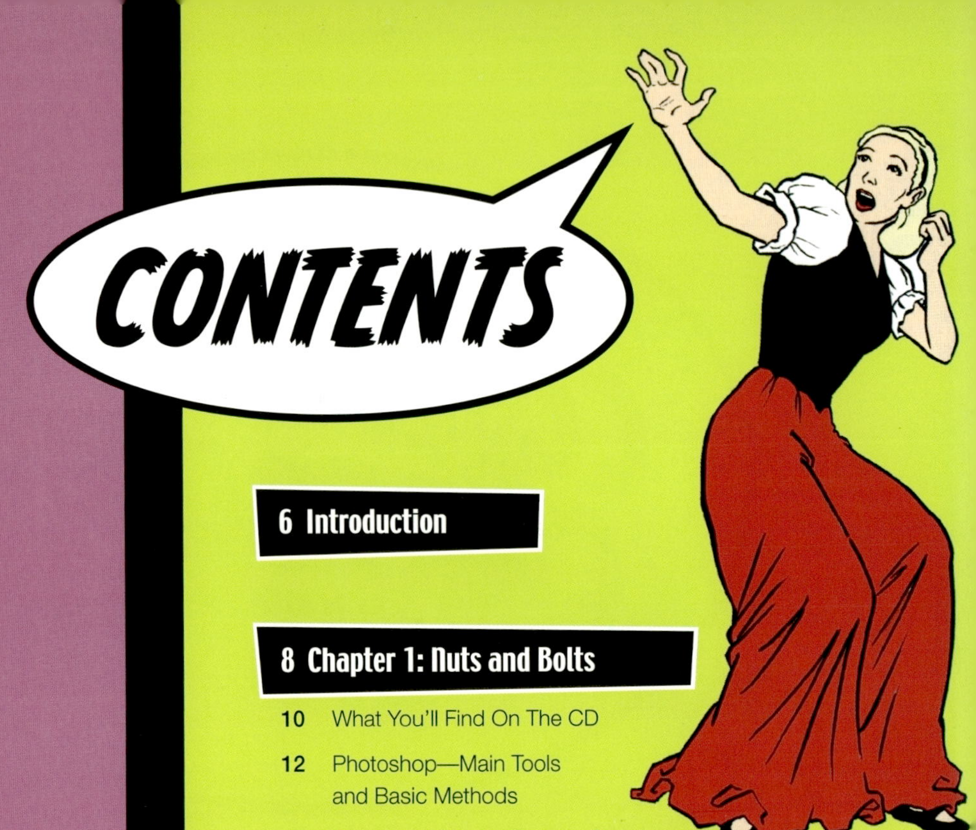

Contents

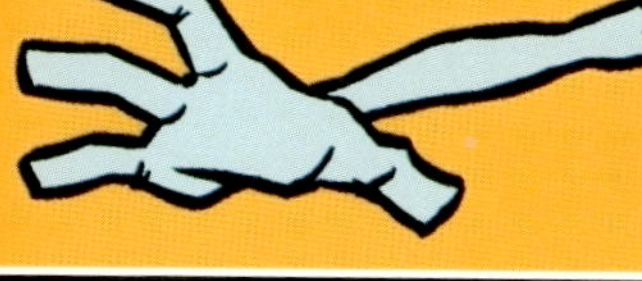

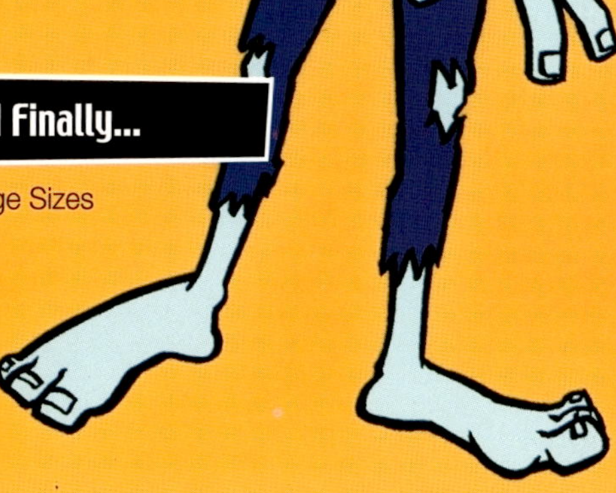

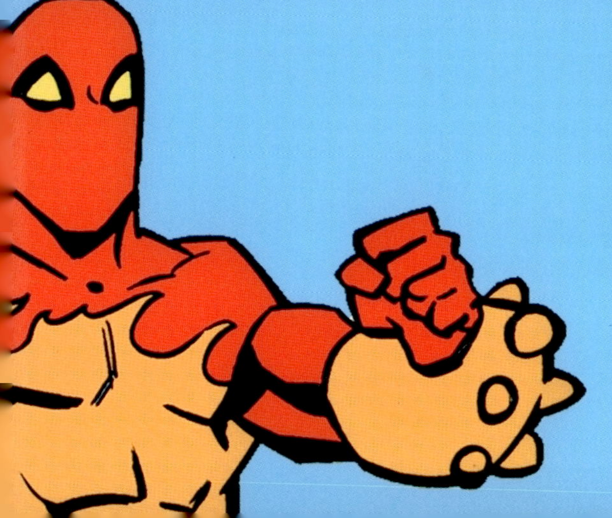

Introduction

The Computer Cartoon Kit, with its accompanying CD containing images by some of today's top talents, will allow you to quickly create your own cartoons and comic strips, utilizing methods that will be explained, step-by-step throughout the book. Anyone with a rudimentary grasp of basic computer skills should be able to learn how to bring their ideas to life on the screen and the printed page. Cartoons are used to inform, to entertain, and to pass comment on world events. They are all around us—on the internet, on television, food packaging, bus stop ads, even on the clothes we wear. Cartoons take varied forms around the world, but the key ingredients remain the same: pictures —sometimes simple, sometimes immensely complex—with the possible addition of embedded text to enhance their meaning. Whether created with a mouse or drawn with a pencil, it's safe to say they are here to stay. With the exception of animated film, the most popular use of cartoons is in comic strips, either in your newspaper, or in comic books. While a single cartoon may only require an explanatory caption—or none at all— comic strips usually contain dialogue and sound effects embedded within each picture frame, allowing the reader to enjoy artwork and writing virtually simultaneously. "Comics" were so-called because the earliest versions were mostly humorous collections. But comics and cartoons have equally been used to portray tales of action, romance, historical events, everyday lives, even grief and suffering. How will you use *The Computer Cartoon Kit*?

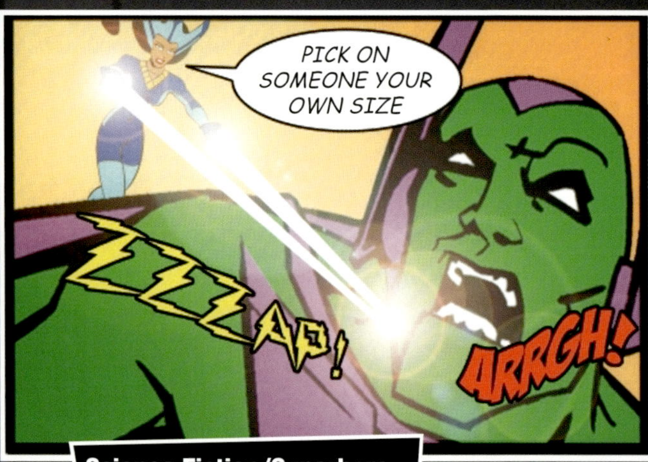

Science Fiction/Superhero

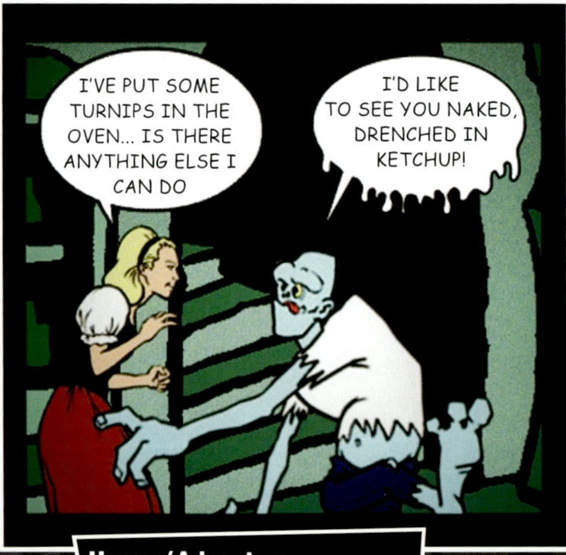

Horror/Adventure

We've provided pictures grouped into four broad categories: Science Fiction/Superhero; Horror/Adventure; Slice of Life/Romance; Humor/Funny Animal. These categories represent the most popular genres used in cartoons and comic strips. If you haven't been fanatical about comics for most of your life, you might want to acquaint yourself further with these genres by looking on the internet, or browsing in your nearest comics shop.

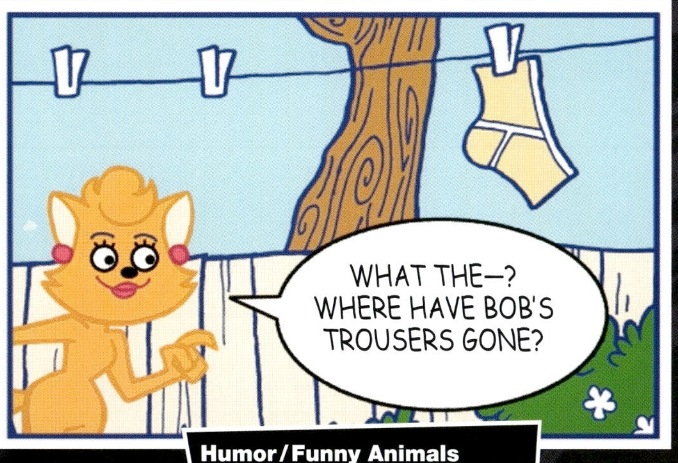

Humor / Funny Animals

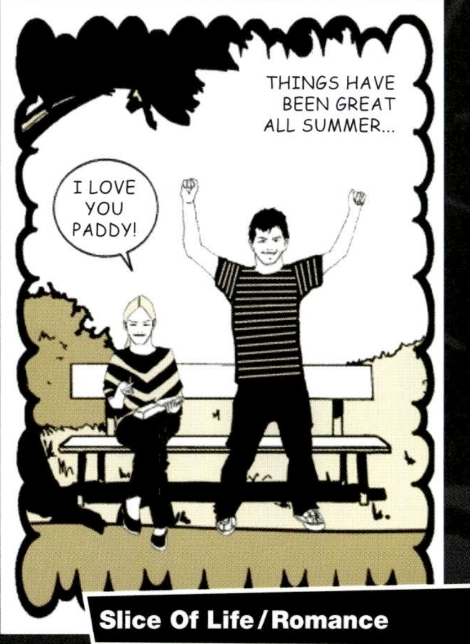

Slice Of Life / Romance

Here, then, are a few signposts toward some of the best examples of each category…

For science fiction and superheroes, the work of one man towers above that of his peers and of those who came later: Jack Kirby. Kirby's kinetic artwork brought a bold dynamism to the characters he cocreated with Stan Lee at Marvel Comics in the 1960s, and his influence is felt to this day. As well as designing and illustrating such famous stalwarts as the *Silver Surfer*, the *X-Men*, and the *Fantastic Four*, Kirby threw his own ideas into the storytelling mix, leading him to write and draw his famous *Fourth World* series for DC Comics.

The most infamous and influential horror comics were those produced by EC Comics in the 1950s. *Vault of Horror*, *Tales From The Crypt*, and *The Haunt Of Fear* mesmerized readers with their gory tales of grisly ghouls, illustrated by luminaries such as Wally Wood, Jack Davies, and "Ghastly" Graham Ingels. These are the horror comics that were banned from Britain in the 1950s, and eventually disappeared from American shelves. Often reprinted and freely available today, they continue to exert a major influence on practitioners of comics' dark arts.

Romance had all but died as a genre by the 1980s, when Jaime Hernandez launched *Locas* (Spanish for "Crazy Women") in the comic *Love & Rockets*. *Locas* has—at first glance—the look of a 1960s romance comic, but Hernandez' story lines have a wit and sophistication that is totally up to date. The misadventures of Maggie, Hopey, and their friends, as they navigate gigs, gangs, jobs, and relationships have resonated with legions of fans around the world.

Calvin & Hobbes was a popular newspaper comic strip that ran for only 10 years before its creator, Bill Watterson, decided to bring it to a close, leaving behind a body of work that represents one of the finest humor strips in the world. Calvin is a six-year-old boy whose hyperactive imagination brings his toy tiger Hobbes to life as a walking, talking comedy foil. Together, they get into a series of hilarious scrapes, matched by Watterson's subtly dynamic cartooning and mastery of comical expressions. Book collections and websites abound dedicated to this wonderful strip.

The Computer Cartoon Kit supplies you with images and techniques to produce your own cartoons and strips, but only you can supply the necessary ideas and imagination. Hopefully, our recommendations might lead you further into the exciting and diverse world of comics; take our word for it, it's a great place to be.

1 Nuts and Bolts

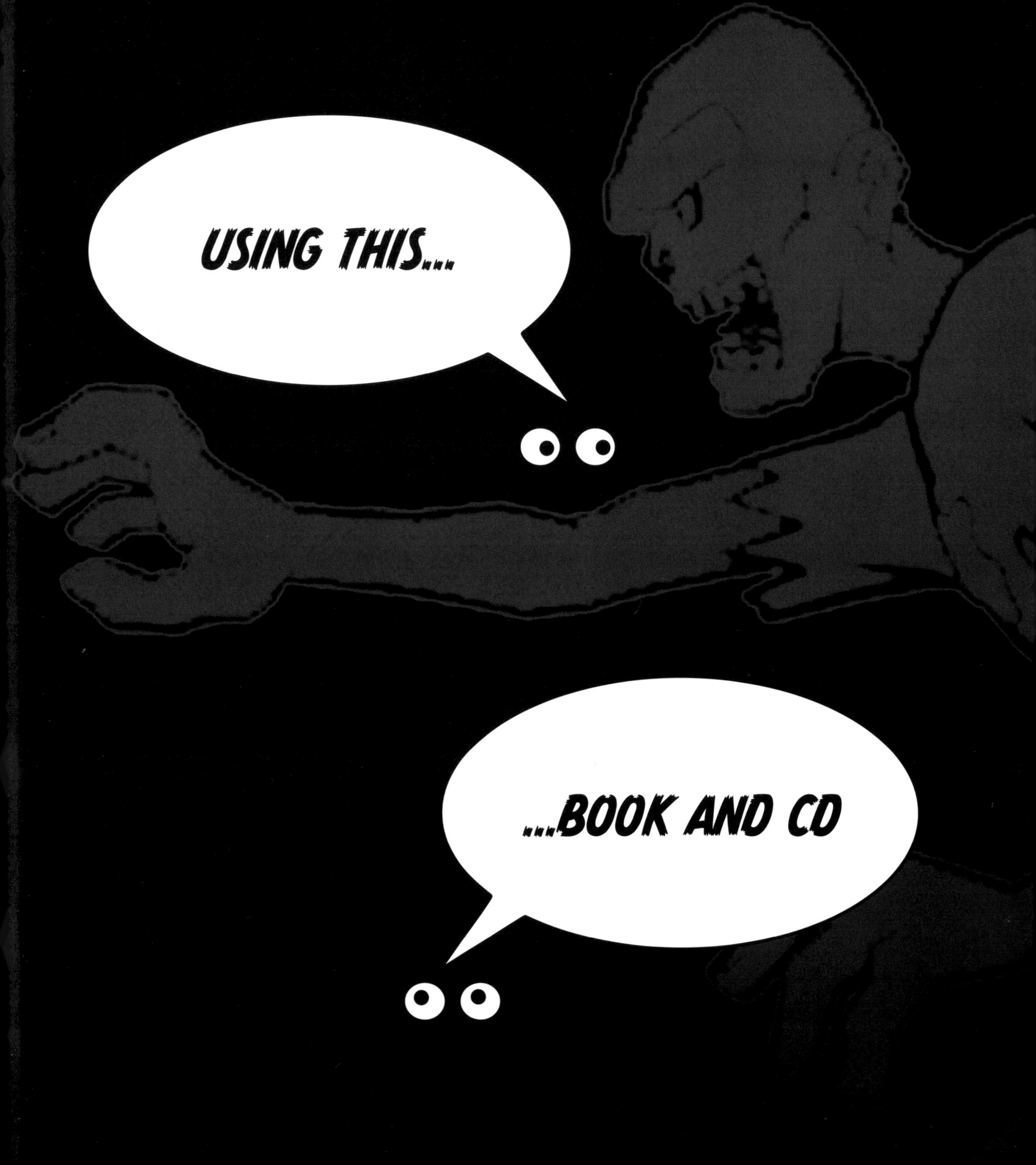

USING THIS...
...BOOK AND CD

What You'll Find On The CD

The Computer Cartoon Kit comes with a selection of images on disc, encompassing four broad genres: Science Fiction/Superhero; Horror/Adventure; Slice Of Life/Romance; and Humor/ Funny Animals.

   Within each category, you'll find a selection of characters, poses, and environments, additional tools, and a range of facial expressions that can all be combined and re-combined ad infinitum. Thanks to the magic of Photoshop Elements, they can also be cropped, resized, flipped around the other way, or distorted—they are at your service to realize a multitude of ideas.

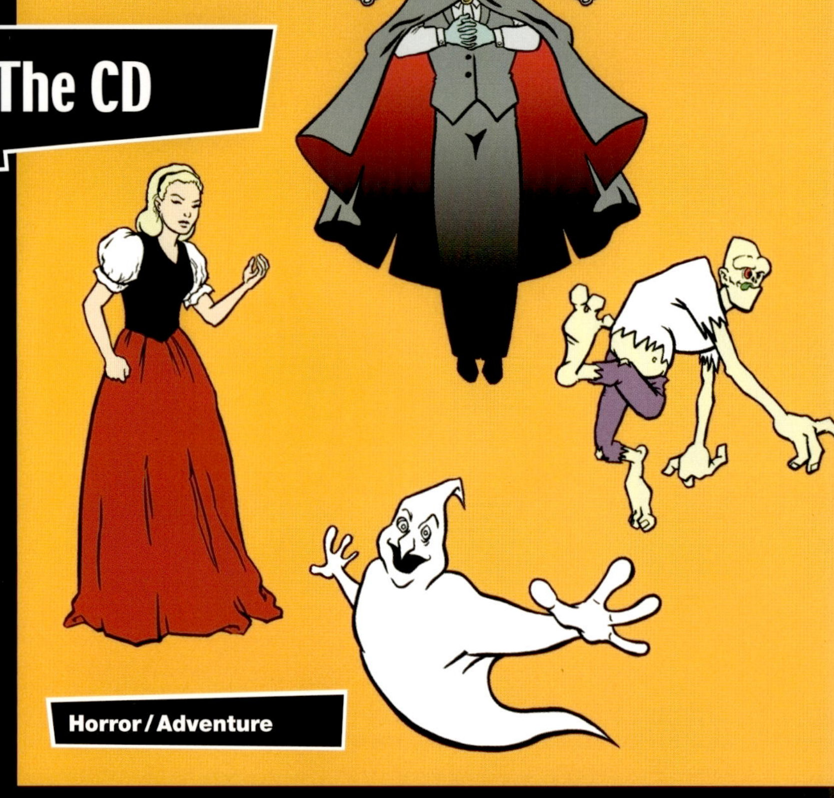

Horror / Adventure

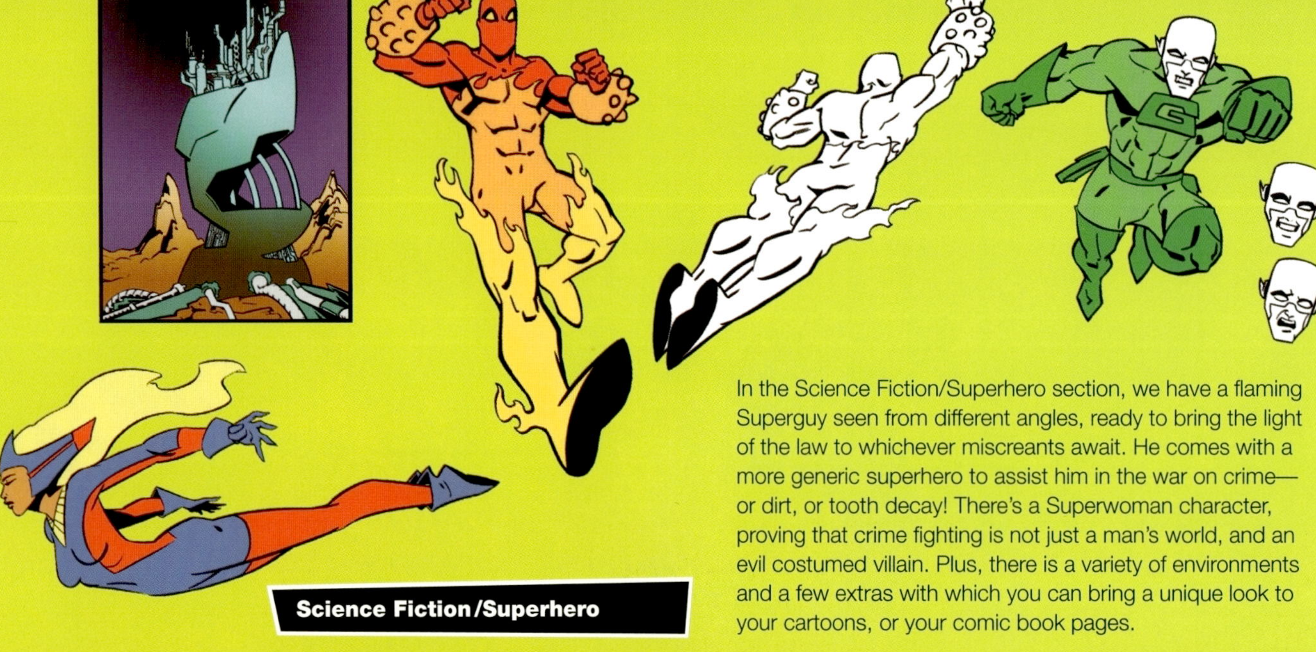

Science Fiction/Superhero

In the Science Fiction/Superhero section, we have a flaming Superguy seen from different angles, ready to bring the light of the law to whichever miscreants await. He comes with a more generic superhero to assist him in the war on crime—or dirt, or tooth decay! There's a Superwoman character, proving that crime fighting is not just a man's world, and an evil costumed villain. Plus, there is a variety of environments and a few extras with which you can bring a unique look to your cartoons, or your comic book pages.

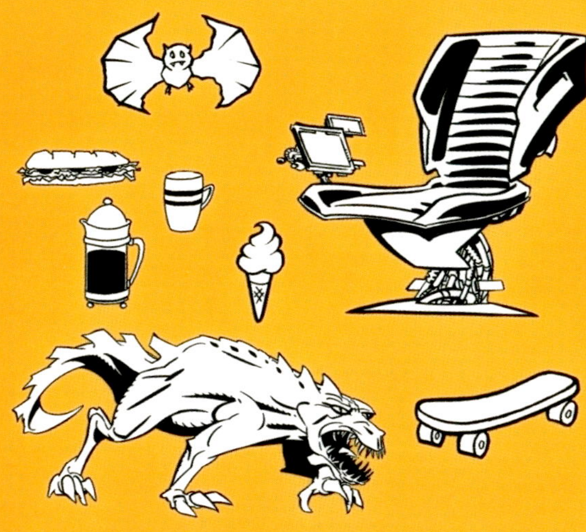

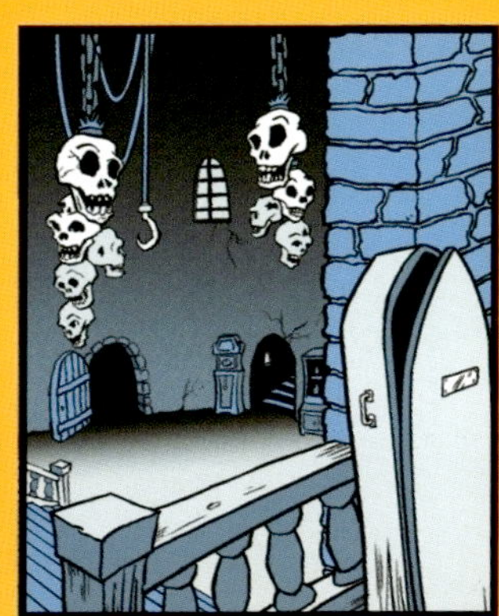

The Horror / Adventure section features Dracula, who is happy to stand in as any vampire Count you may require. He comes with a fearful woman who may not be all she seems, and a selection of ghosts and zombies. Some atmospheric backgrounds will give these characters an appropriately gloomy setting, and a selection of accoutrements will help to create a suitably creepy setting.

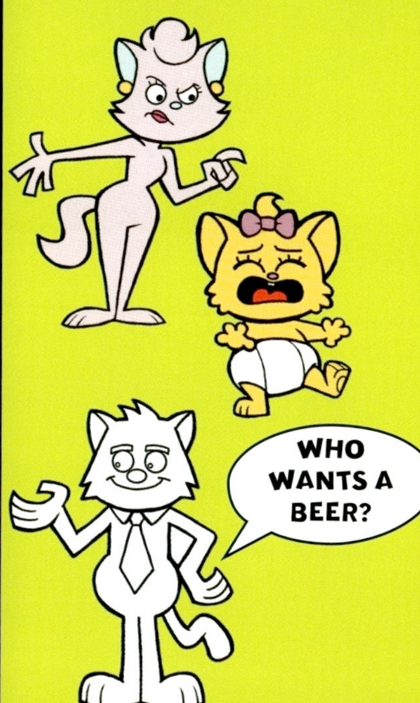

Humor / Funny Animals

People often expect cartoons to be funny, or populated by anthropomorphic animals, so we have a selection of these too, in our Humor/Funny Animals section, along with a great choice of expressions and backgrounds.

In addition, you'll find word balloons and sound effects with which to liven up your work.

Of course, these images are just the beginning, the basic building blocks that should enable you to come up with many and varied ways of telling a story or simply illustrating a point. In the coming pages, we'll be showing you how to manipulate these pictures, or sections of them, in order to make them dance to your tune.

Slice Of Life / Romance

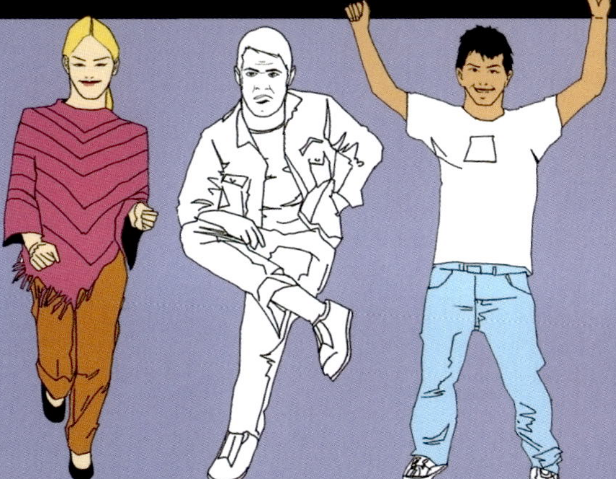

Our selection of Slice Of Life/ Romance images should provide you with ample opportunity to tell those everyday tales that need to be told of ordinary folk living ordinary—and extraordinary—lives. Young people standing, walking, sitting, talking, and a bunch of everyday settings should give you the raw material you'll need to tell of life's great ups and downs.

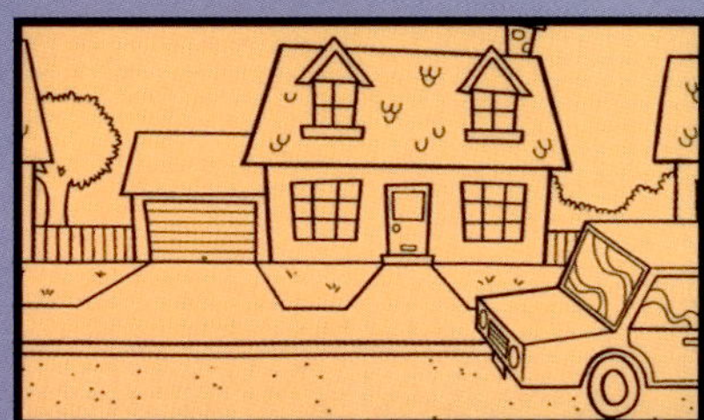

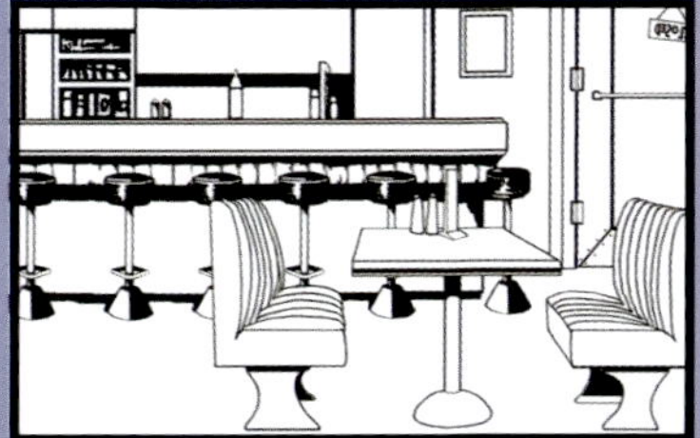

Photoshop: Main Tools and Basic Methods

Photoshop Elements can open in one of three modes—Editor, Creator, and Organizer—and it's Editor that we will be using throughout this book. Upon opening Editor for the first time, you will be confronted by a bewildering array of tools and menus. Some will be useful for our purposes, but others are mostly for photographers, graphic designers, and other specialized users.

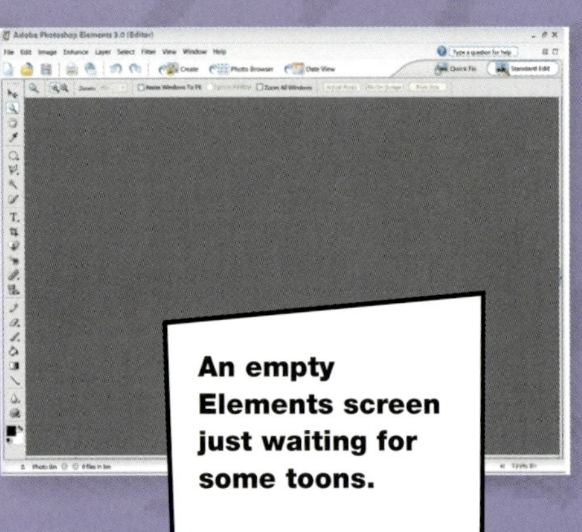

An empty Elements screen just waiting for some toons.

Menu bar

1 The Menu bar runs across the top of your screen. We'll make the most use of File, Edit, Image, Layer, Select, Filter, and Window. Throughout the book, you'll get instructions for using many of these commands.

Shortcuts

2 Beneath the Menu bar are shortcuts, the most useful of which are: Create new file, allowing you to create a blank document to a specific size; Open file, which lets you quickly access your images; Undo, when you accidentally make a wrong move; Redo, if you change your mind again, and Save. Choose PSD if you wish to continue working on your picture later, or TIFF for a fine-quality archive file, suitable for printing.

Toolbox

3 At the side of the screen is the Toolbox. It's used in conjunction with the Options bar below the Shortcuts. This provides alternatives and settings for the tool you choose.

A The Move tool lets you "grab" a selected portion of your picture and reposition it or carry it over to another document.

B The Zoom tool magnifies part of an image.

C The Hand tool moves a magnified image around inside its window.

D The Eyedropper selects a color contained in any part of any open image.

Next we have our Selection tools. In different ways, these allow you to select one part or several parts of an image to fill with color, distort, move, or work on in any other way, to the exclusion of the rest of the image.

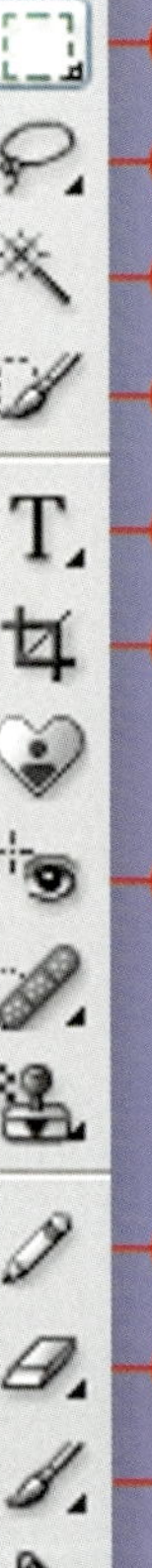

File   Edit   Image   Enhance   Layer   Select   Filter   View   Window   Help

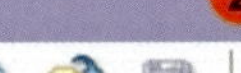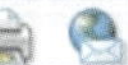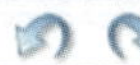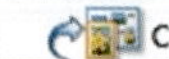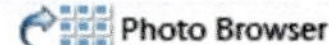 Create   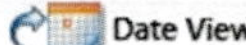 Photo Browser   Date View   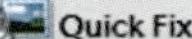 Quick Fix   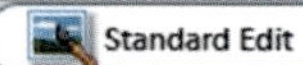 Standard Edit

E The Rectangular Marquee tool enables you to select a rectangular area by clicking, holding, and dragging the mouse. To deselect, simply click once within the selected area.

F Clicking the Lasso tool displays all three variations in the Options bar, and they all work in a similar way, allowing you to trace around an area of your image to make a selection.

G The Magic Wand selects any enclosed area of the same color. How far it interprets a color as "the same" depends on the Tolerance box on the Options bar. A low Tolerance will only select adjacent pixels of the exact same shade; a higher Tolerance will be less discriminating and select a larger area.

H The Selection Brush lets you fill in your own area to be selected. To deselect, you must go to Select > Deselect on the Menu bar at the very top.

I The Text tool is covered in greater depth later in this book (*see page 16*).

J The Crop tool lets you trim an image to the area you require. Simply click, drag, and press Enter on your keyboard. Modify the area to crop via the tiny handles around the bounding box.

K The Red Eye Removal tool and the Spot Healing Brush are only useful to cartoonists suffering from red eyes and spots. The Clone/Pattern Stamp is best left to more advanced users.

L The Pencil and Brush tools enable you to draw directly onto your on-screen image in a wide variety of line thicknesses and styles. Changing the Mode from Normal to any of the other pull-down options will send you into a terrifying universe from which there is no return.

M The Eraser works like its real-life equivalent, with the options of changing its shape and size.

N The Paint Bucket instantly fills any enclosed or selected area with color. Its Tolerance setting affects how far it spreads, and is generally best left at around 120.

O The Gradient tool fills with a gradual blend from one color to another. Simply click in an enclosed or selected area, drag across, and release.

P The Line/Shape tool is not very intuitive. It creates a solid shape or line of color by clicking and dragging.

Q The Blur and Sponge tools will not be of much use to us.

R At the bottom of the Toolbox are windows showing the last two colors that you have used. A new color can be selected by clicking on the foreground window; switch to the previous color by clicking on the tiny arrows. The whole toolbox can be dragged elsewhere onto the screen by grabbing it at the top.

4 The bottom of the screen contains the Photo Bin; this is where Elements stores pictures you might minimize as you work. It can be pulled up or down like a drawer.

5 The Palette Bin down the right side works in the same way, storing detachable palettes accessed from Window on the Menu bar.

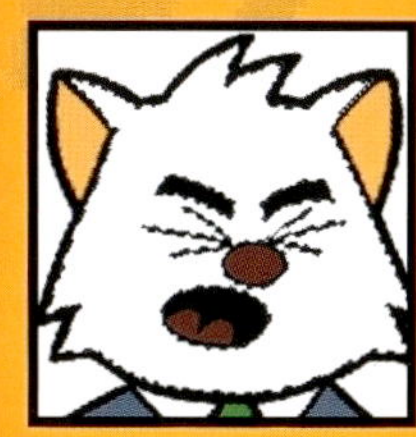

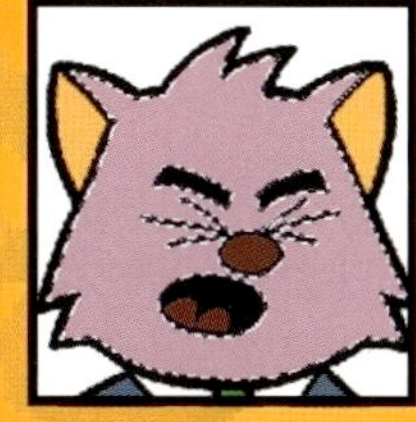

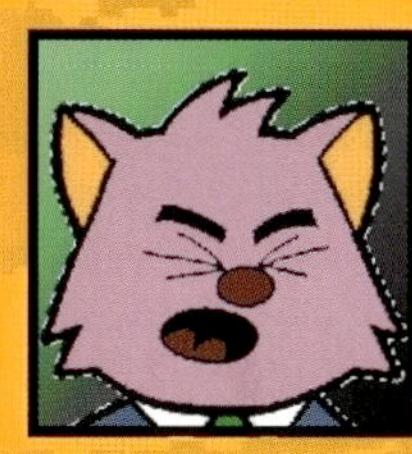

The Paint Bucket tool can change a lot in just moments.

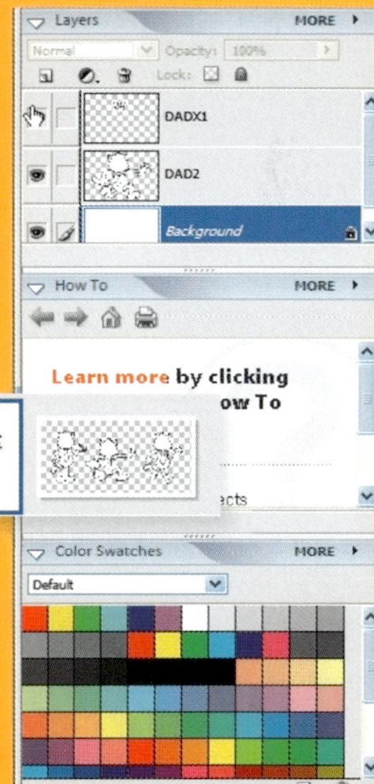

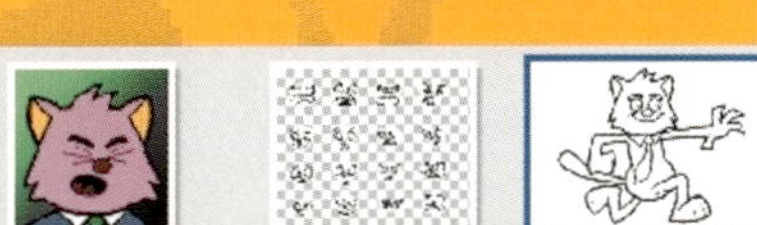

4

Each tool can be refined in the Tool options bar.

Creating A Simple Cartoon Panel

Here's where you find out just how easy it is to create cartoons using the images supplied on the CD. Let's imagine that you wish to create a Halloween picture, perhaps a vampire, in a spooky old castle, with a zombie, and—cliché alert!—a screaming woman.

1 Search the Horror folder on the CD for the Castle Interior image and open it. You may wish to crop the image to use just part of it.

Next, choose one of the several Dracula figures available.

Choose a Zombie, and a Woman, and color all images as you wish. Check out our "coloring" section (*page 26*) for full instructions. Have all four pictures open in Photoshop.

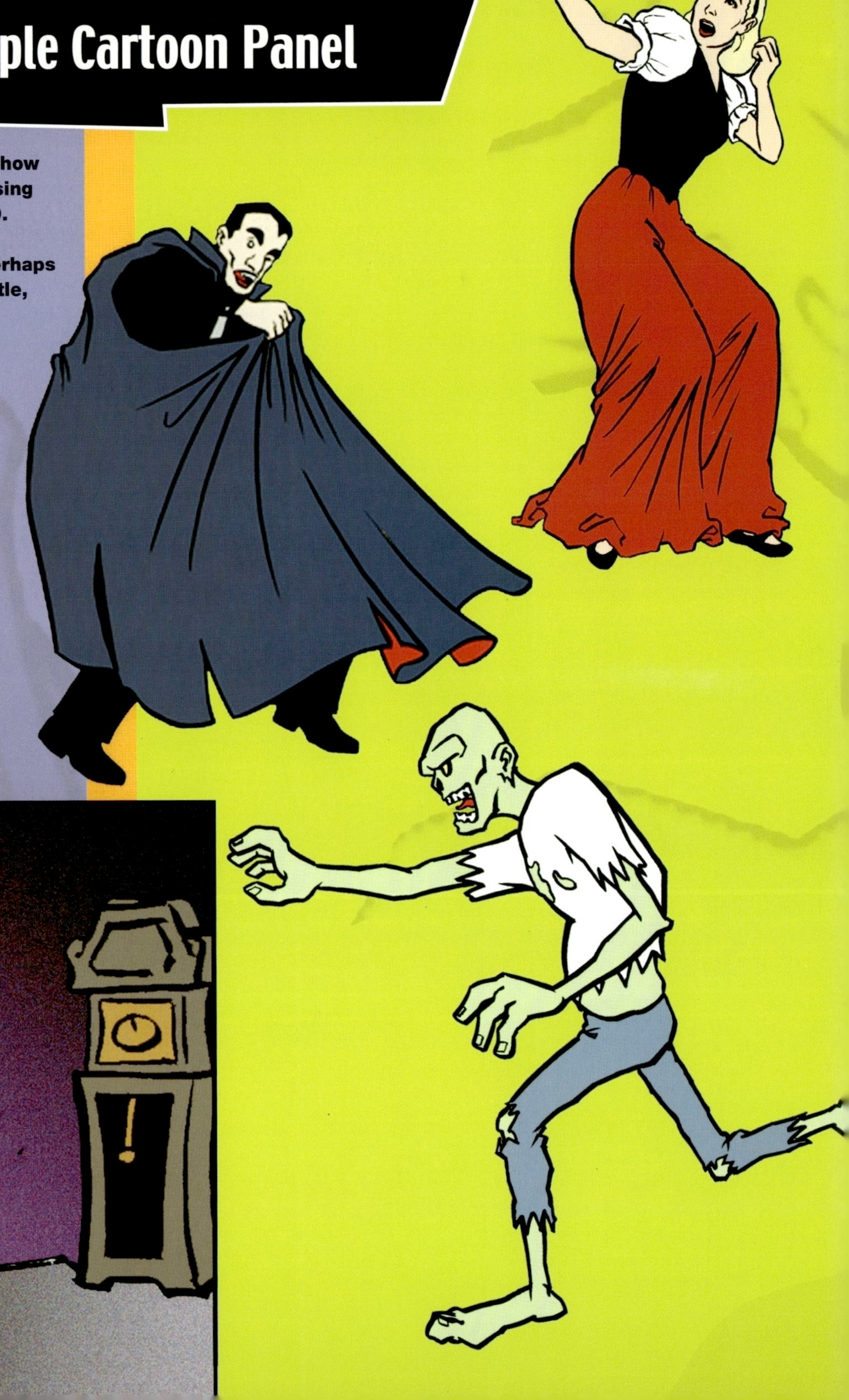

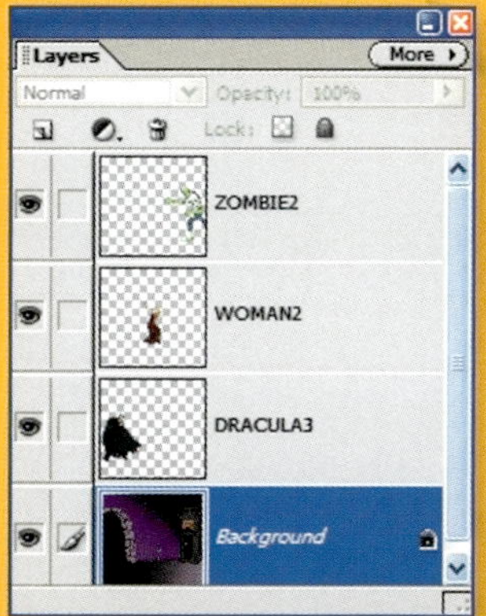

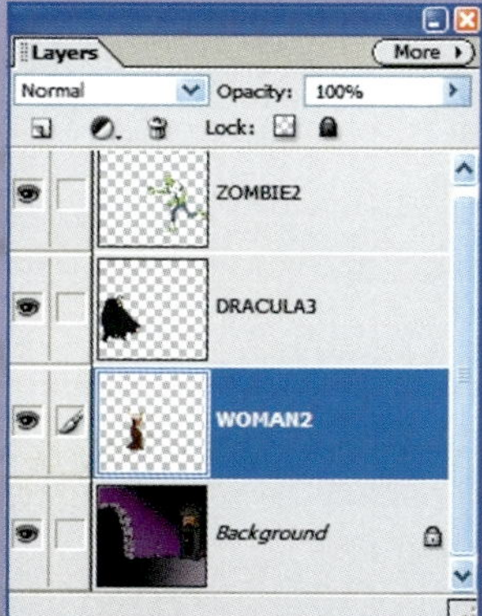

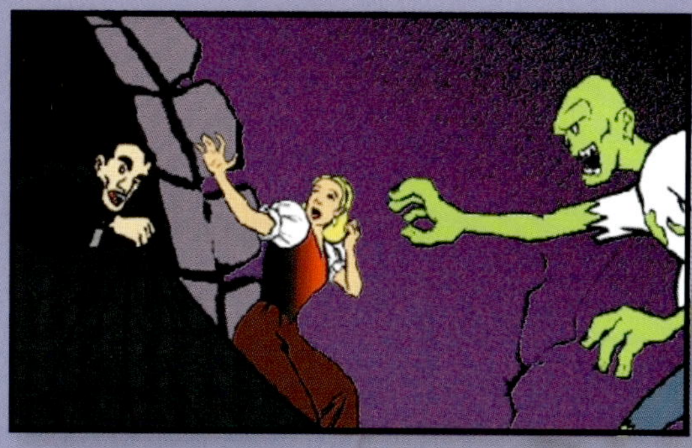

3 The Layers palette will now show that the Castle Interior now has four layers, including your background and three characters. By clicking on each of these layers, you can use the Move tool to reposition the characters wherever you want them in the scene.

Here's the clever part: by clicking, holding, and dragging on any of the characters' layers in the palette, you can drag them above and below each other, allowing you to overlap the characters in your picture.

4 Now Dracula can appear to be behind the Woman, urging the Zombie on toward their terrified captive. To heighten the drama, you may wish to group the characters closer together and eliminate part of the empty castle background. Using the Crop tool, you can frame your panel any way you like. At this point, go to Layers>Flatten Image on the top menu bar.

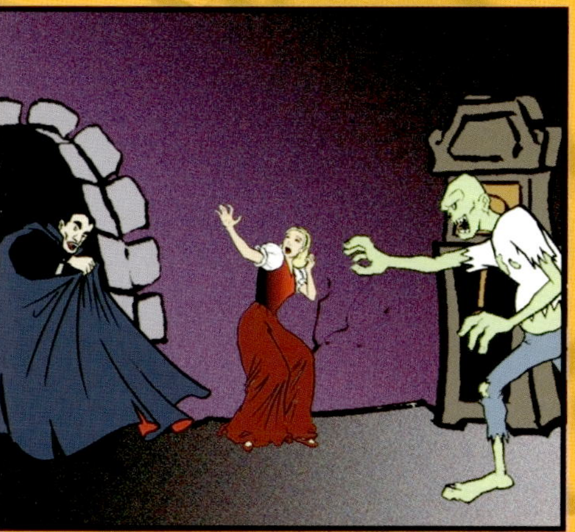

2 Next, open the Layers palette; you'll see that each image of a figure is comprised of two layers; a plain background, with the picture floating on a layer above. Click on the Dracula layer in the palette. Now, using the Move tool, click on the picture, hold down the button, and drag him over onto the Castle Interior background. Aaagh! Horrifying— he's way too big! Click Undo and go to our Resizing section on page 26 for advice on quickly and simply resizing images. After resizing Dracula, repeat this process with the Monster and the Woman, and drag them all onto the background.

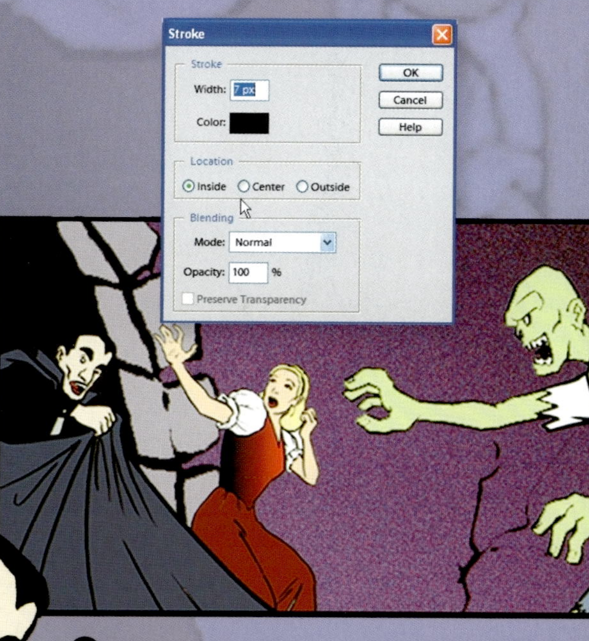

5 As a final touch, choose Select All from the menu. Then make sure that black is chosen as your foreground color. Next, go to Edit, and choose Stroke. Enter a width of 7 pixels, and check the box marked Inside. When this is applied, you will get a nice black border around your panel. Save as a TIFF or a JPEG, and your work is done.

Adding Text and Balloons

In the early days of comics, text and dialogue were often included in separate blocks of text beneath each picture, a tradition still employed in the popular British newspaper strip *Rupert the Bear*. However, as you will most likely wish to use speech balloons within the picture itself, here's how to use the Text facility in Photoshop Elements and the balloons included on your CD.

1 As with hand-drawn and lettered cartoons, you'll need to create the text first and then fit the balloon around it. So, here's a picture of a rather stern-looking man. Perhaps he's saying:

"Yes, this is a gun in my pocket, and no, I'm not pleased to see you!"

Let's put the dialogue into the frame.

Before we begin, open the Layers palette from the top menu bar (Window > Show Layers). Then, ensure that you've selected black as your foreground color.

3 Make sure that the central Alignment box is selected on the top bar, so that your type will be easier to place into a balloon.

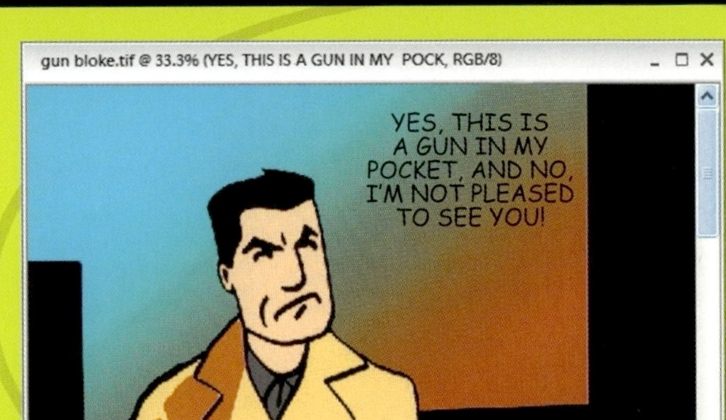

4 Now, click in the area where you want the finished balloon to appear, and type away, breaking the lines every so often so that the overall shape of the text roughly mimics the shape of a speech balloon. At this point, you can adjust the size of the font, and the "leading"—the distance between each line. Simply highlight the text and alter the settings at the top bar. It's best to keep these settings the same for each balloon in the same comic strip.

2 Next, take a look at your picture and find some area of "dead space" near the character who's speaking. That's where we'll place the dialogue. Click on the Text tool in the toolbox, and then choose your font from the top bar. You'll probably want one that resembles hand-lettering and doesn't look too "mechanical." For our purposes here, we're using Comic Sans, which comes pre-installed on most computers. See the later section on Fonts (*see page 40*) for more ideas.

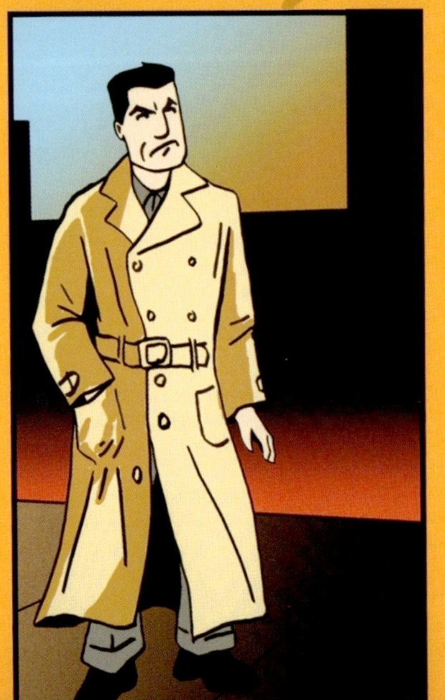

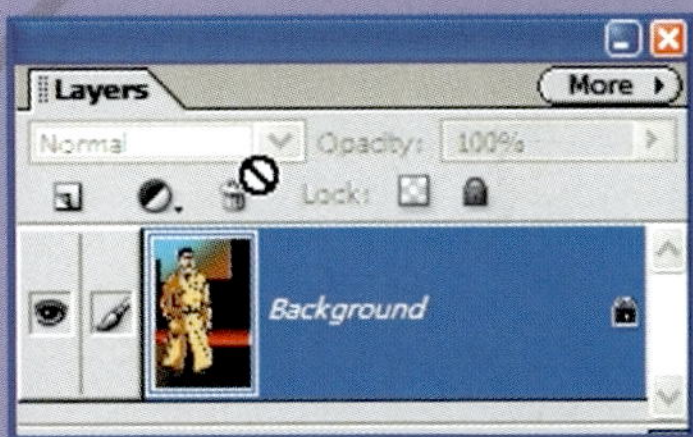

5 You'll see that your text appears as Layer 1 in the Layers palette; it is, in effect, floating above your picture, which will be labeled Background. By pressing Enter (↵) on the numeric side of your keyboard, or by clicking on another tool in the toolbox, you finish the typing, and you'll see that it now has a name in the Layers palette. To go back in to correct a spelling, or to add more type, simply click on Text and then click back on your dialogue to continue. You can also embolden certain words by highlighting them and clicking Bold from the menu on the top bar, or in the Character palette. But don't overdo it.

7 No matter; the bounding box around your text allows you to stretch and distort your balloon to fit. Drag the handles to adjust it to the correct shape and size. When you're satisfied, hit Enter (the regular one) or click on an innocuous tool (such as Magnify) and the balloon will remain in that shape. If you need to reposition the speech balloon slightly you can use the Move tool on both text and balloon layers.

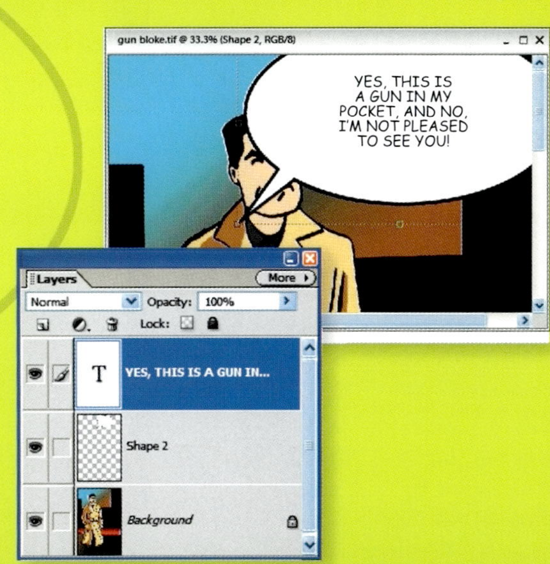

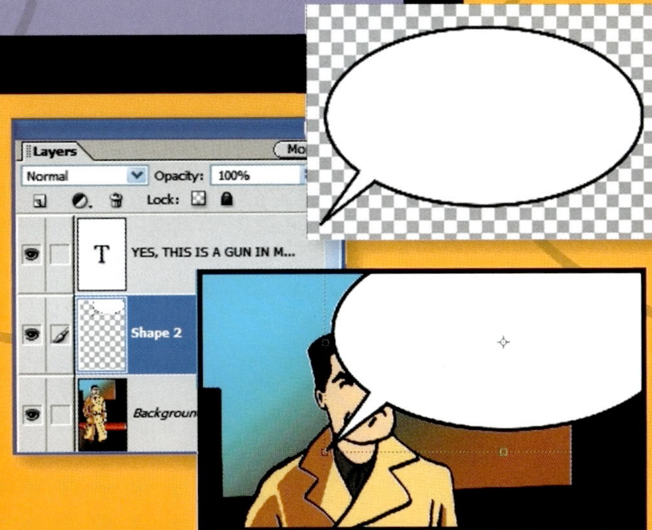

6 With our dialogue complete, we now need to add a balloon from the selection on the disc.

Drag it over to your picture and place it above the text. You'll see that it's listed in your Layers palette as Layer 1; click on this and drag the layer down the palette so that it sits above the Background layer—when you let go, it will now sit below the text (and will probably be the wrong size).

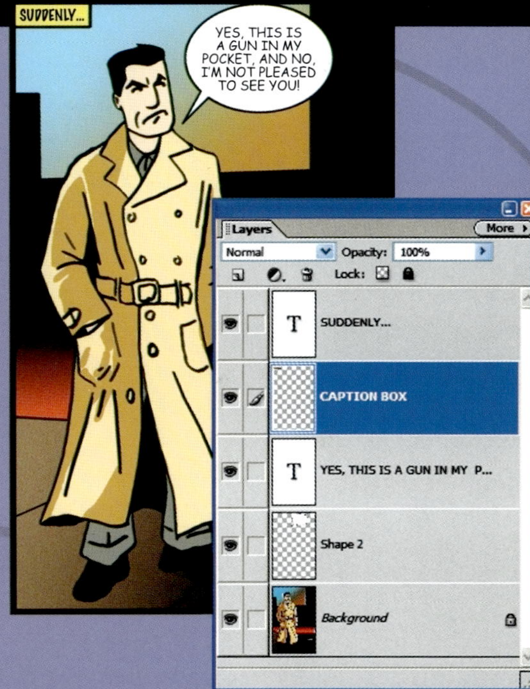

8 If your picture needs an additional caption, such as "Suddenly…," follow the same process as above, but instead of using a balloon, open a new layer (Layer > New), move it below the text, and use the Line tool to draw a box beneath. You can even fill it with a light color if you wish.

2 All in the Frame

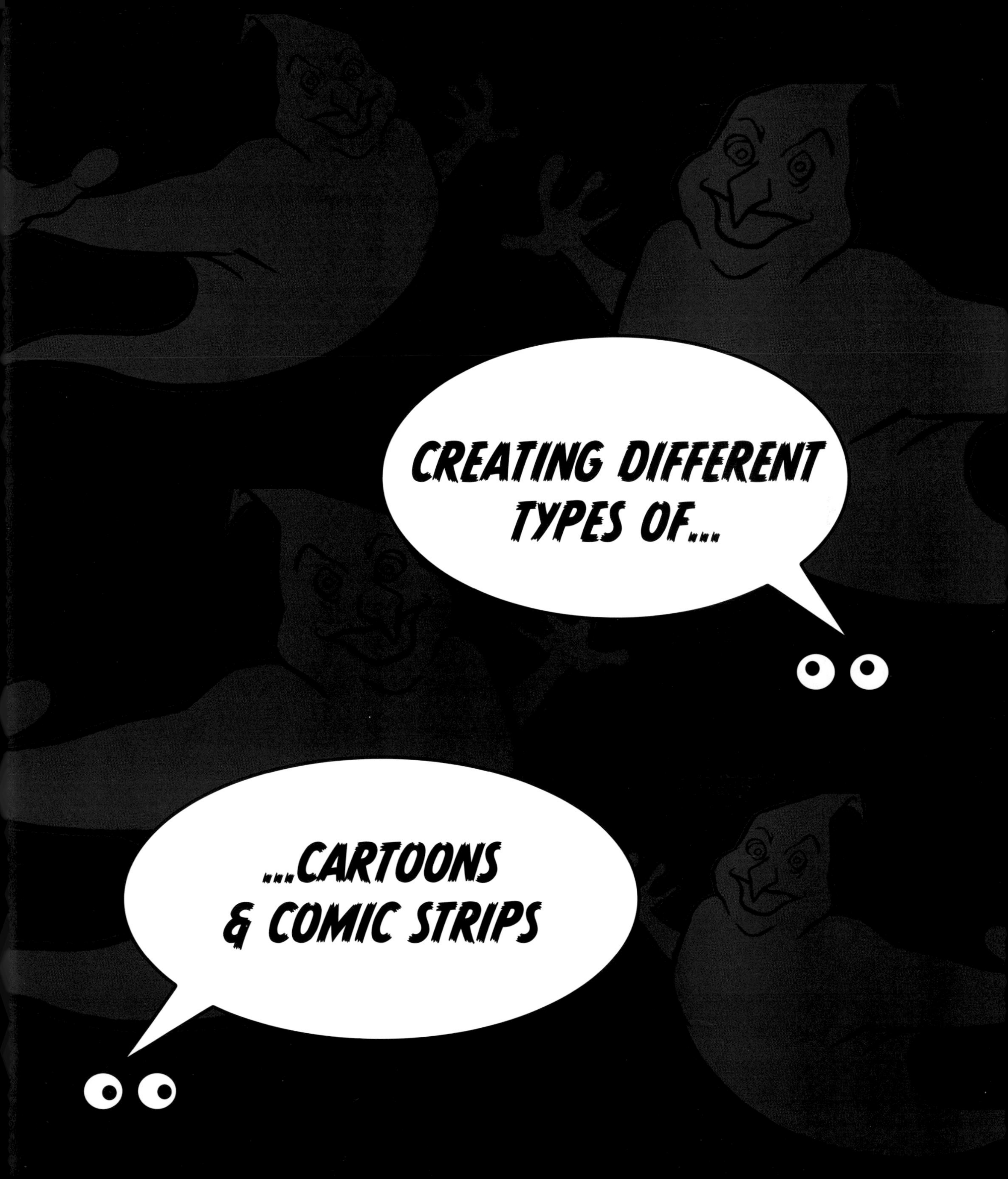

CREATING DIFFERENT TYPES OF...
...CARTOONS & COMIC STRIPS

Panel Composition: Composing Interesting Pictures

In this section, we'll be taking a look a how you might create really eye-catching panels using the images on the disc. You are recommended to attempt these only after you are fully conversant with constructing simple pictures; you'll also need to check out the Resizing section on page 26 unless you are already familiar with the process.

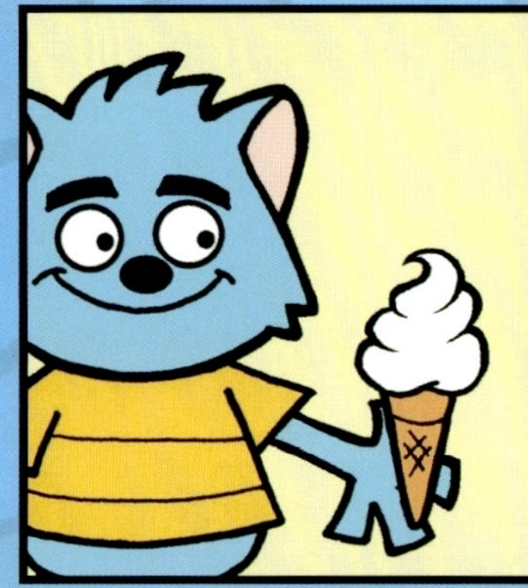

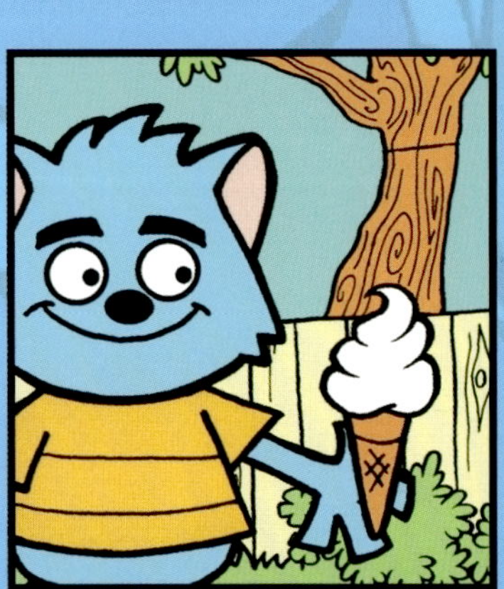

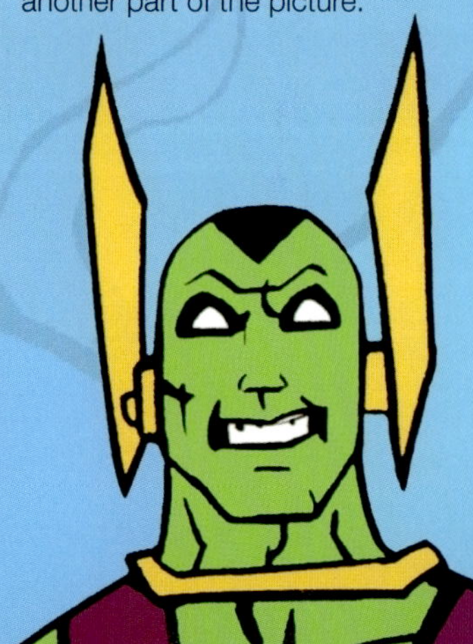

In composing your panels, you need to concentrate on one simple question: what is the main point of interest in the picture? If someone is holding an ice cream cone and talking about how delicious it is, then we need to clearly see that ice cream cone —it needs to have its own part of the picture and not be obscured by another object, by a word-balloon, or be "hidden" within another part of the picture.

If we view the arrangement of our panel as simple shapes, we can clearly see how this operates.

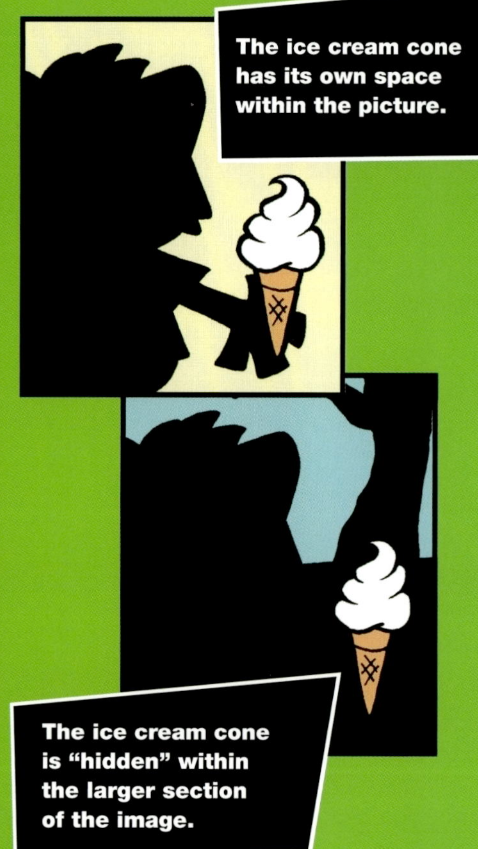

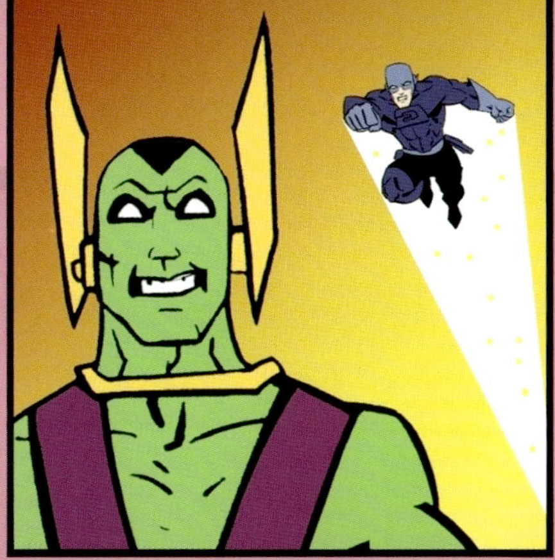

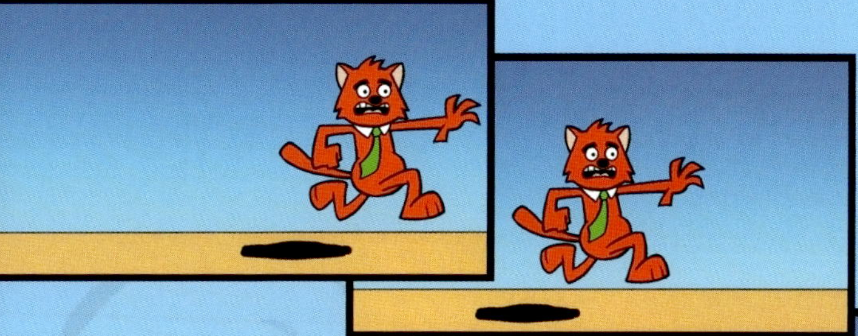

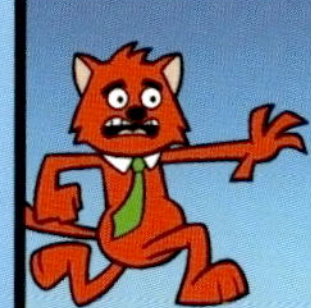

Sometimes an element of the background might be important—in which case, although seemingly far away, it should be clearly seen.

Also, if characters should appear to be in a hurry, having them apparently about to leave the panel works better than placing them dead center. Placing a running character to the left of the panel makes it look as though he has just arrived at his destination.

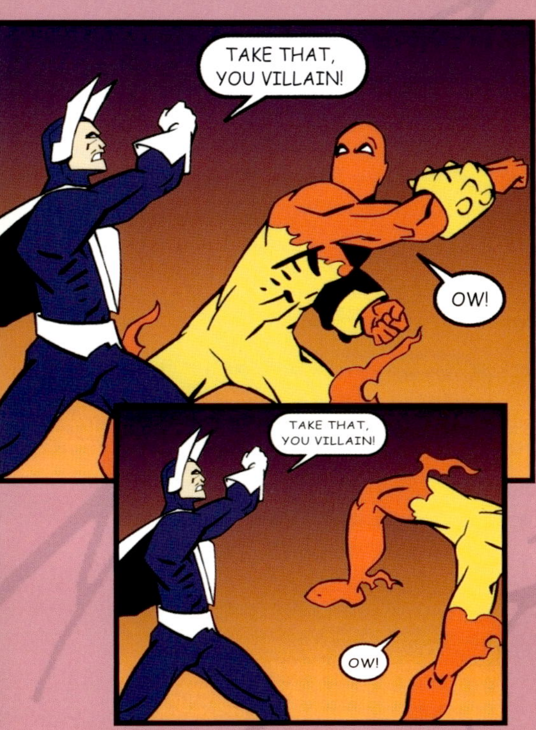

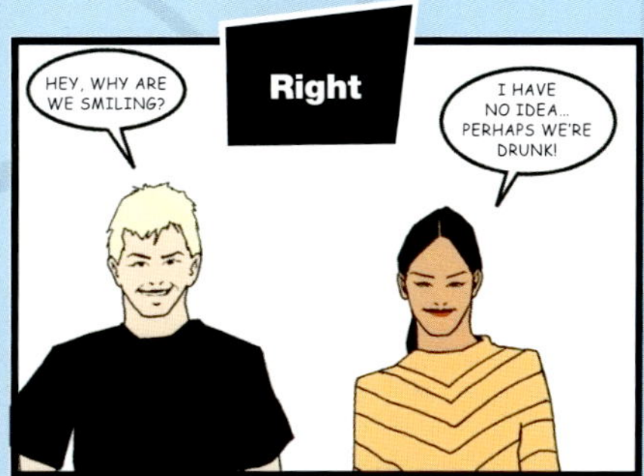

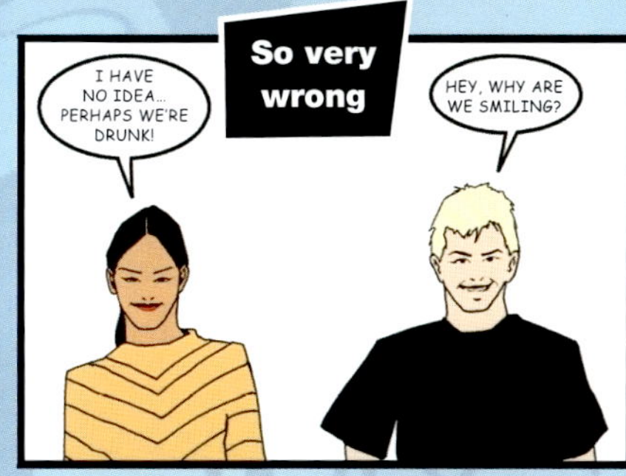

You should always remember that, in the western world, we read from left to right. This means that someone reading the word balloons in your work will automatically read the left balloon in your picture first. Because of this, if two or more people are meant to be speaking in the same panel, they should be placed in "speaking order" as you compose the picture. For further tips, see the section on Balloon Placement.

Panels with symmetrical composition—equally balanced shapes at either side—convey a quality of stillness; perfect for a scene of two people talking or relaxing together, but to show characters slugging it out in a good old-fashioned fist-fight, a more off-balance arrangement imparts a sense of dynamism. The reader's mind gets a sense of movement in what is actually a still image.

Before you even attempt to start resizing and moving images, it's a great idea to rough out your designs on paper, making sure everything will look okay in the finished image. You don't need to draw any details, just simple stick-figures and shapes will give you enough of an idea of how the finished version might look, and of any elements that you might need to reconsider.

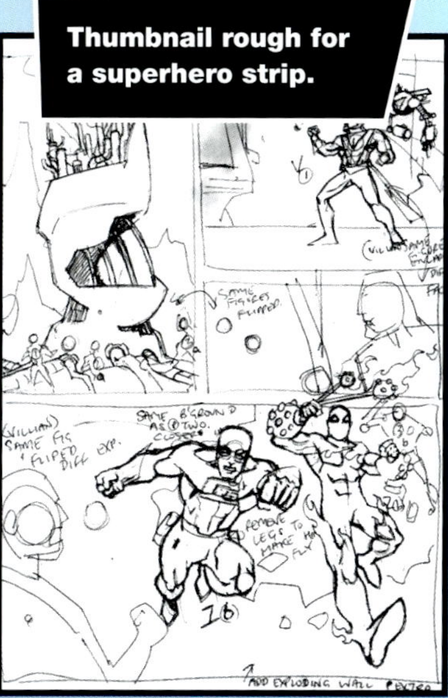

Page Composition

Having learned how to construct a panel, let's look at how to place a series of panels onto a typical comic-book-style page.

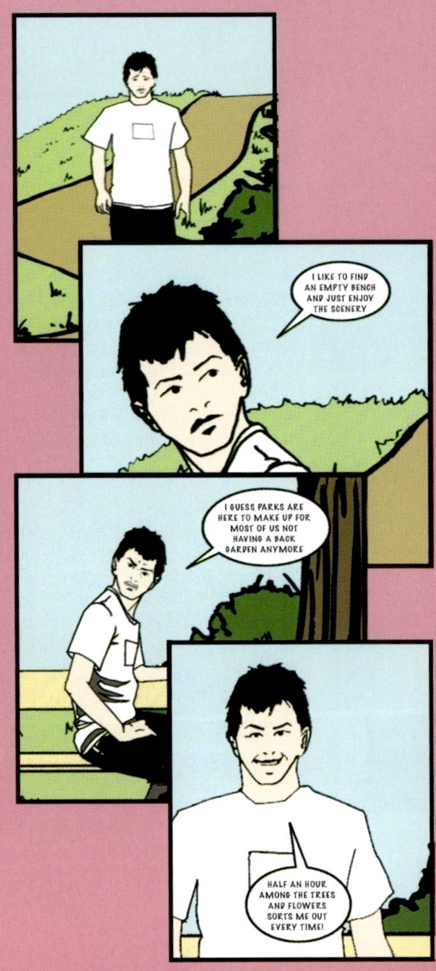

For demonstration purposes, we'll use four panels of equal size; a later section will show you how to be more adventurous, but it's best to start off simply until you get the hang of the process.

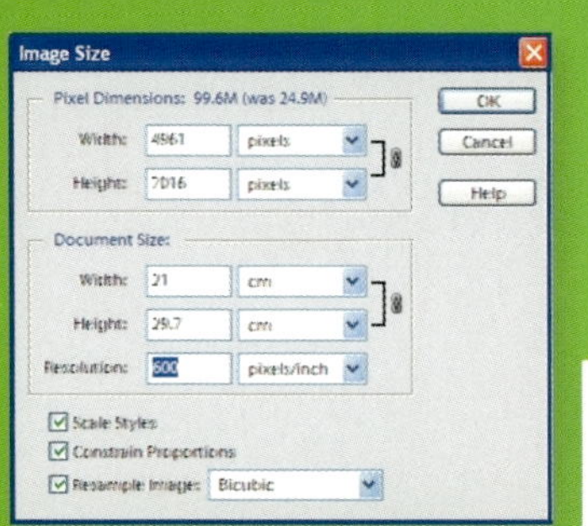

1 Open a blank letter sized document. The number of pixels per inch should match those of your panels. You can check this by going to Edit > Resize > Image Size, and altering if necessary. Next, you should open your Layers palette, and then we're ready to begin.

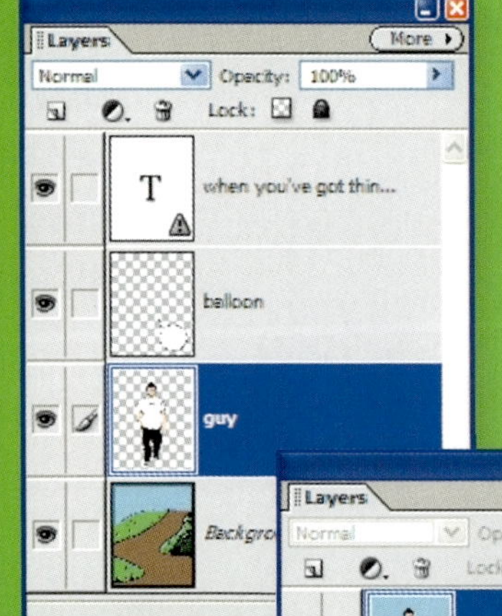

2 Click on your first panel, and flatten the image by going to Layers > Flatten Image from the top bar. This will ensure that you won't leave any part of your panel behind when it's moved onto the new page.

3 Repeat this step with all four panels. Then, using the Move tool, drag each panel onto the blank page. On the Layers palette, you'll see them numbered Layer 1, Layer 2, etc.

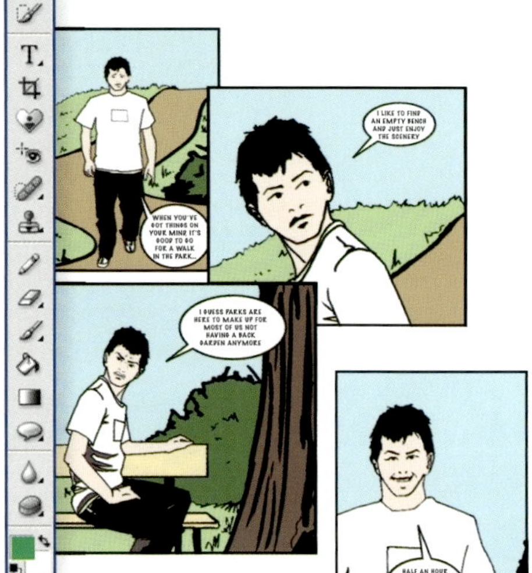

Slide pictures across to the new page with the Move tool.

4 By clicking on the appropriate layer in the Layers palette, you can use the Move tool to adjust the position of each panel relative to the others, and to the edge of your page. You will find that a funny box appears around the panel as it is moved to the new document; it'll disappear whenever you hold down the mouse button to move the panel, but amazingly reappear when you've finished. This box enables you to resize the panel by dragging the tiny handles around the side—ideal if one of your panels doesn't quite sit well with the rest. When they are all neatly grouped together, flatten the whole image and save it as Page 1, or whatever you choose.

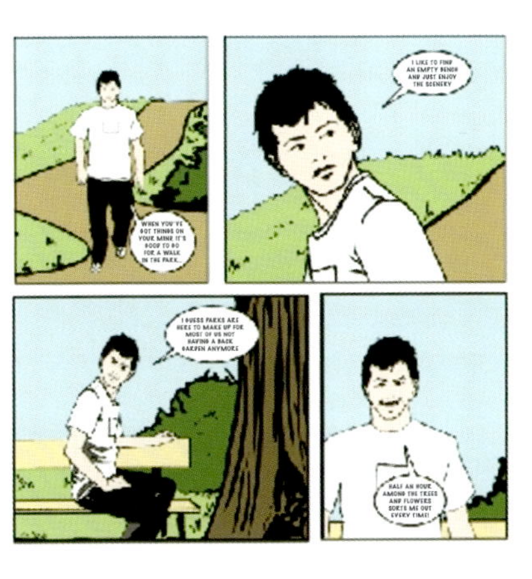

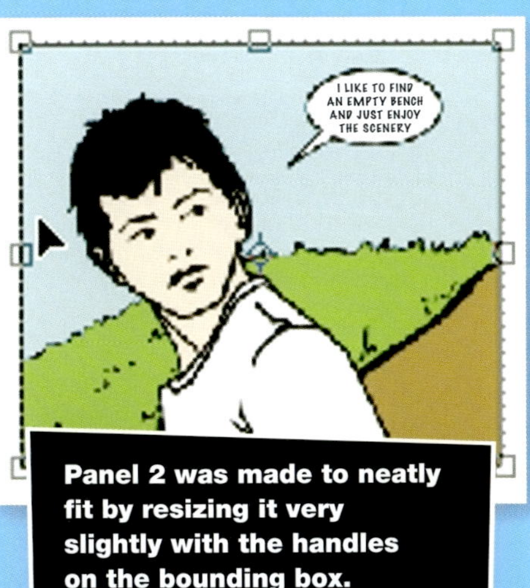

Panel 2 was made to neatly fit by resizing it very slightly with the handles on the bounding box.

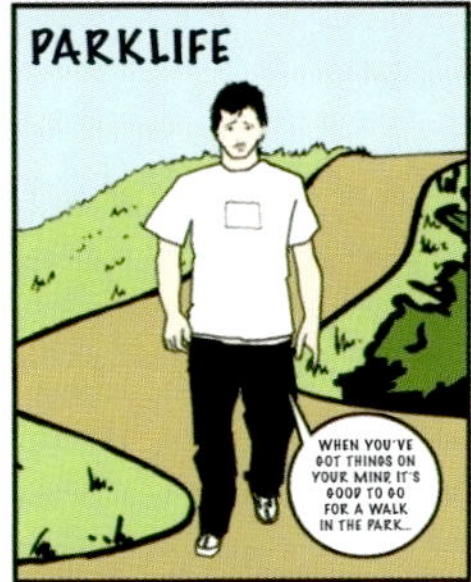

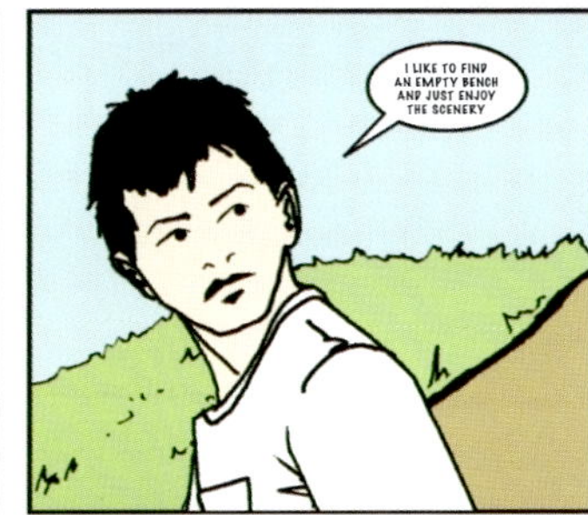

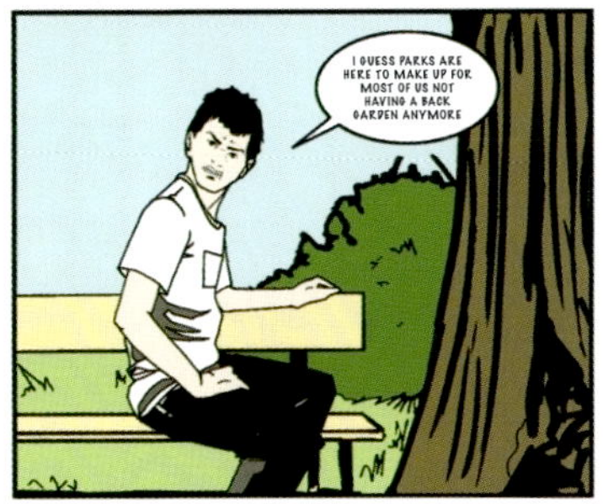

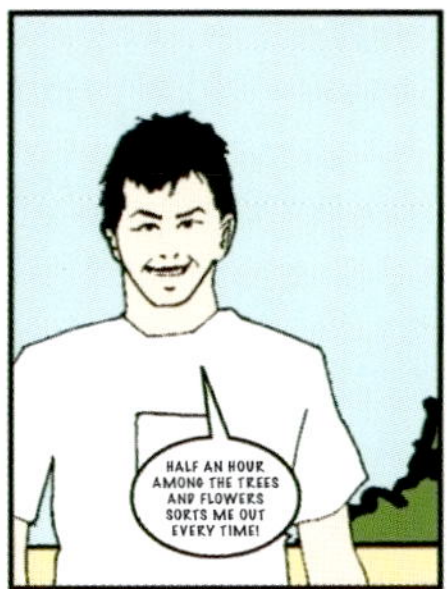

Final Touches

If there is a bit of dead space in your first panel, you might want to add a title. Choose a suitable font and type it over the top of the image. Similarly, if you want to "sign" your work, find a small place near the edge of either your first or last panel and repeat the process (obviously, your name should be smaller than the title, unless you're an egomaniac).

By highlighting the title or your name, you can change the color to contrast the background. Simply click on the colored box on the top menu bar and choose a new color.

Choosing Different Viewpoints

As we have already seen, using our images as supplied can create perfectly serviceable cartoons, but cropping the image adds a new dimension and can create a "Close-up" of a scene. Conversely, leaving the characters framed within a larger background gives us a "Long shot." These movie-making conventions, along with "Medium shot" and "POV" (point of view), can create different moods and tones and help improve your storytelling.

Close-ups are often used to show intense emotion.

However, they should be used sparingly, else your strip could resemble "Microscope Theater."

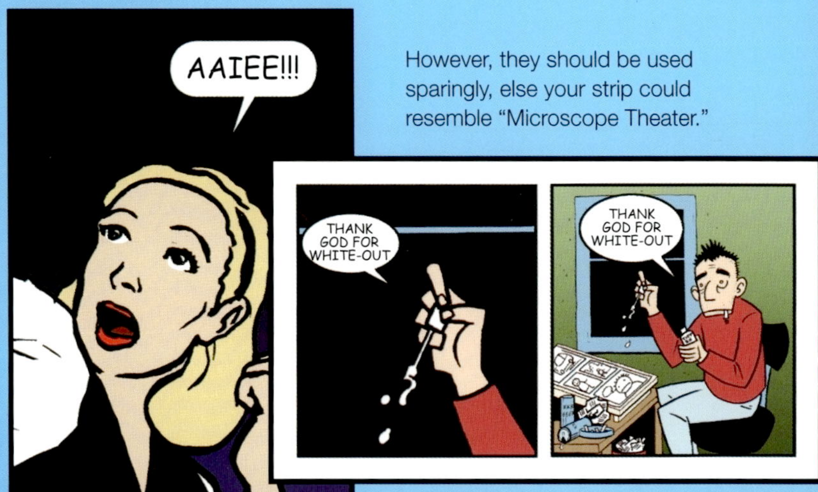

Close-ups are generally used to draw attention to a particular aspect of a scene, whether it's a person's face or a significant object or detail.

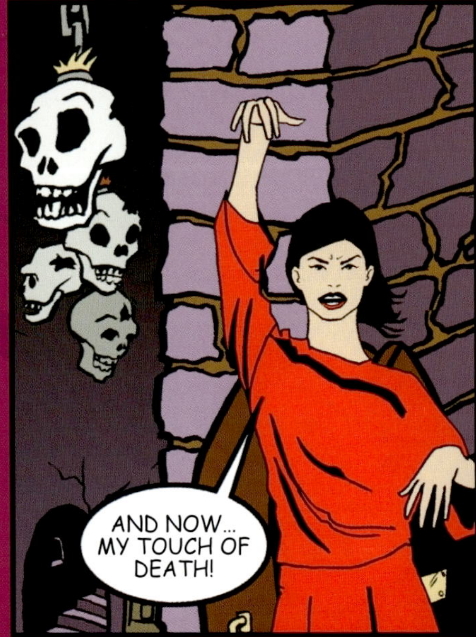

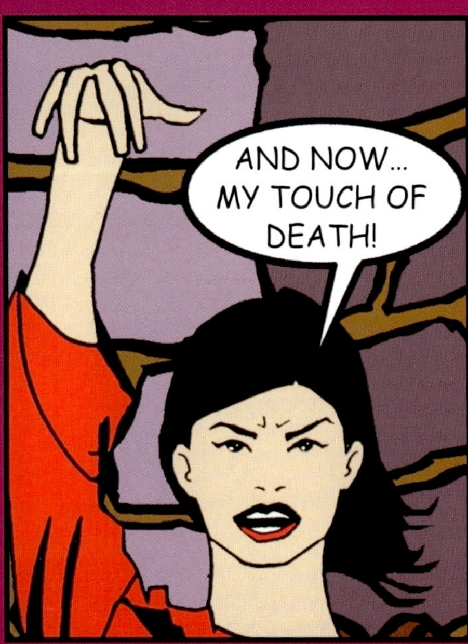

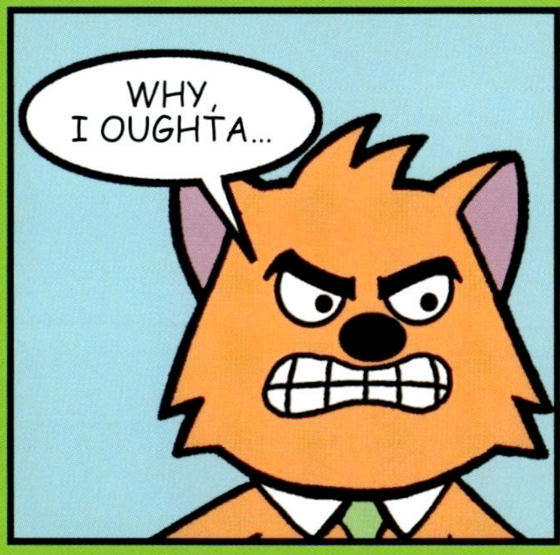

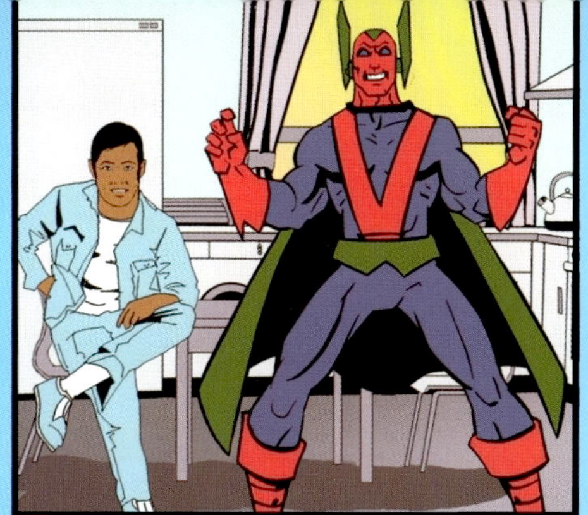

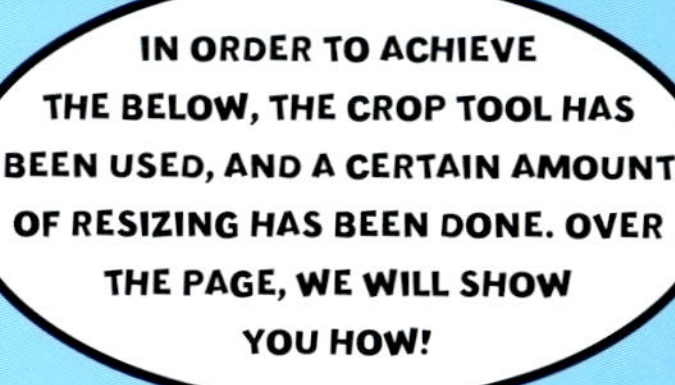

Another important thing to remember is that close-ups rarely work for single-panel cartoons. Without having previously seen the setting in more detail, a close-up will have no context for the reader—they won't have the information they need to understand what the picture is about or where the situation takes place. In this panel, for example, we have no idea who the character is angry with, or why.

This is a "Medium shot," including just enough information for the reader to know where the action is taking place; in this case, a suburban dining room.

Medium shots are the most common viewpoints used in comic strips, movies, and television, providing enough information about the scene, while cutting out any extraneous detail. They can give the impression that the reader is fairly close, perhaps in the same room or setting as the characters.

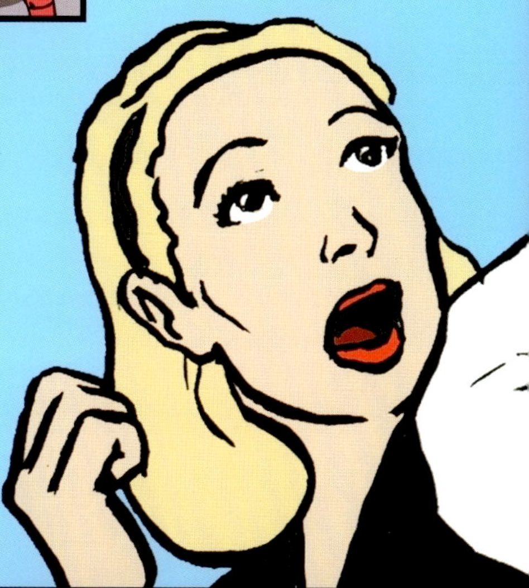

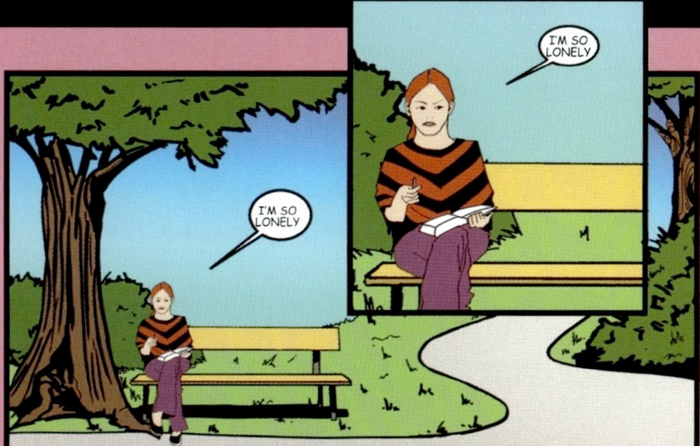

A "Long shot" means that we view the scene as though from a long way away from the characters. We can see more of the background, and get a better idea of where characters are in relation to their surroundings.

They establish a sense of place for subsequent panels, whether it's a busy street, an office, or a post-apocalyptic desert…. Such viewpoints are also useful for conveying a sense of loneliness or isolation.

At the Thumbnail stage, as you rough out your first ideas, it's worth pausing for a moment and considering what kind of viewpoints might best serve your pictures.

Typically, a strip might contain a long-shot at—or near—the beginning, to establish the scene, before moving into a series of varied viewpoints, with the occasional close-up where necessary.

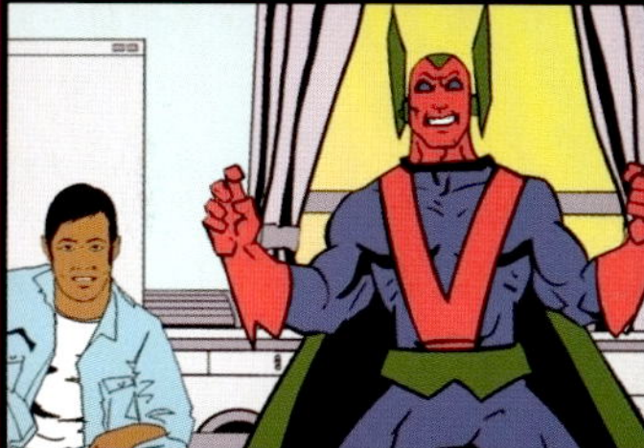

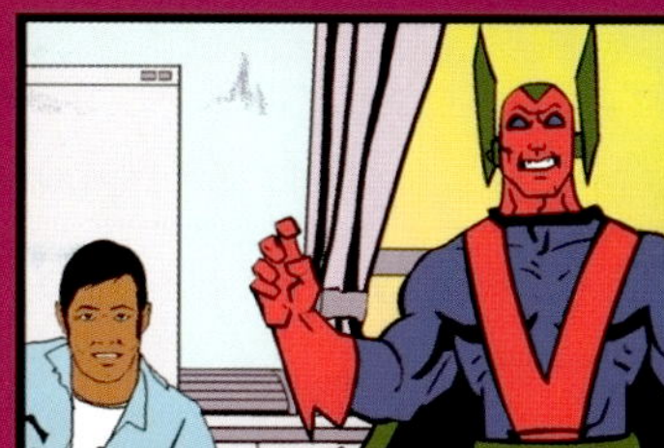

Resizing

Altering the size of your images— making them bigger or smaller to suit your purposes—is a fairly simple process. An important thing to remember is that it's best to color your images before you move and resize them, as coloring a much-reduced image can be extremely problematic.

You can also make use of the Flip Horizontal command (Image > Rotate > Flip Horizontal) which allows you to choose a "mirror image" version of any of our images, or cropped sections of them, effectively doubling—at least—the number available to you.

If you have already tried moving pictures onto a background, you'll have noticed that Photoshop Elements places a bounding box around them as you move them into place. By clicking and dragging on the box's handles, you can instantly enlarge or reduce the figure or object; you can also make it thinner or wider. However, you may find that when you are moving characters onto a background that has been cropped from a larger image, they may appear too large to use the bounding box handles. This is when we need to resize the characters before moving them.

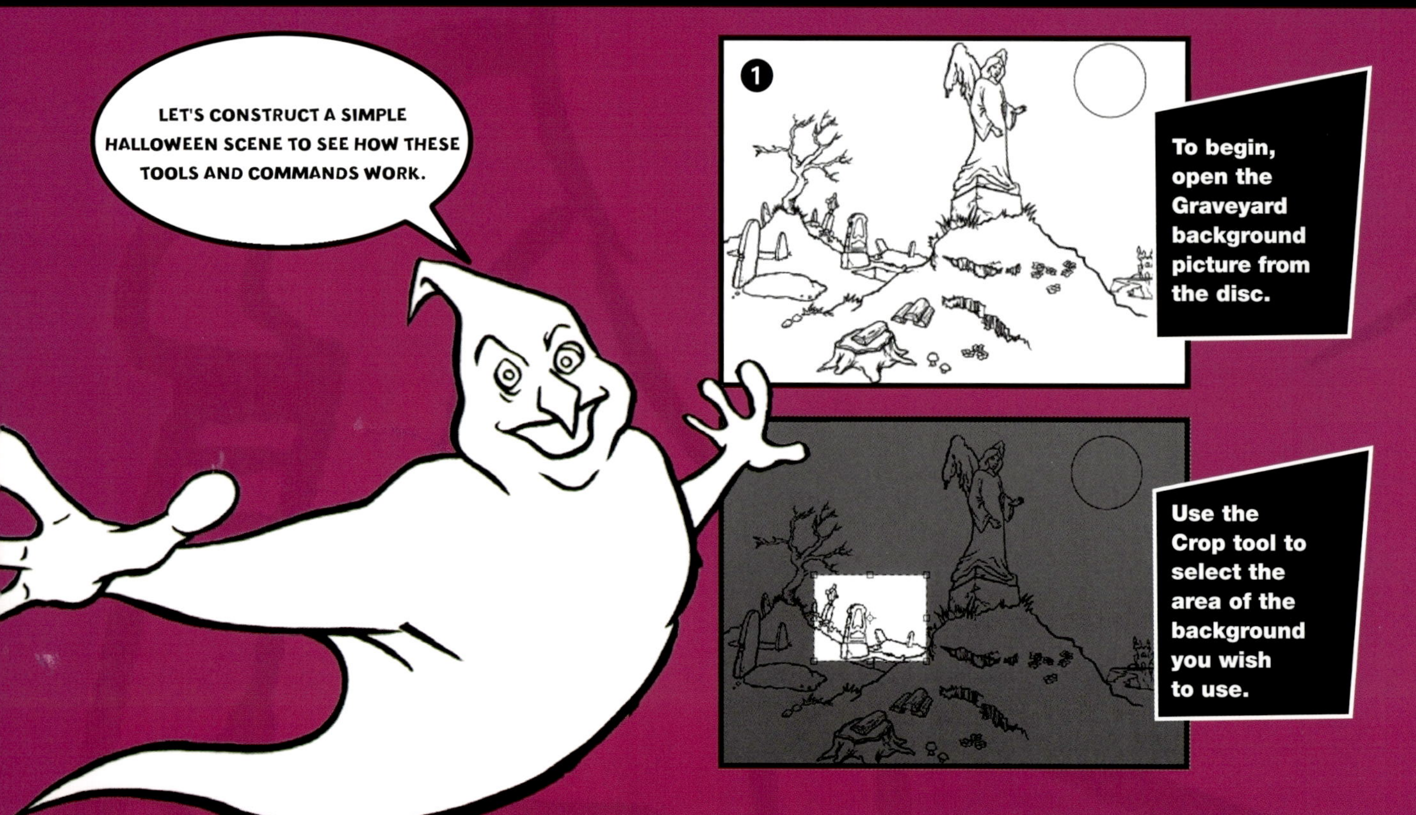

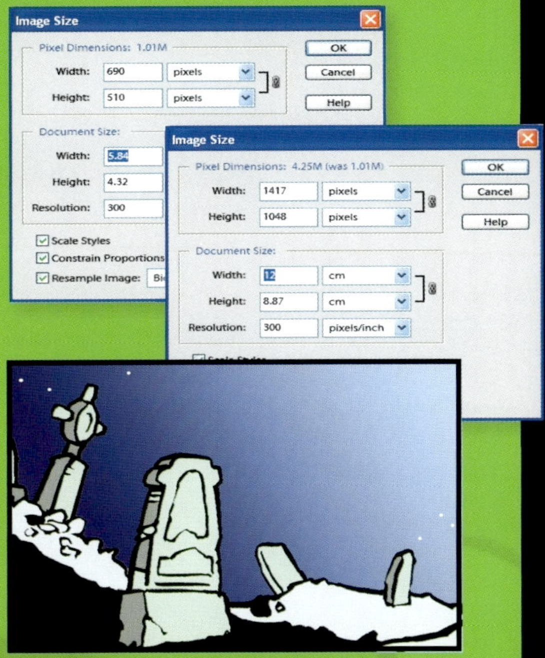

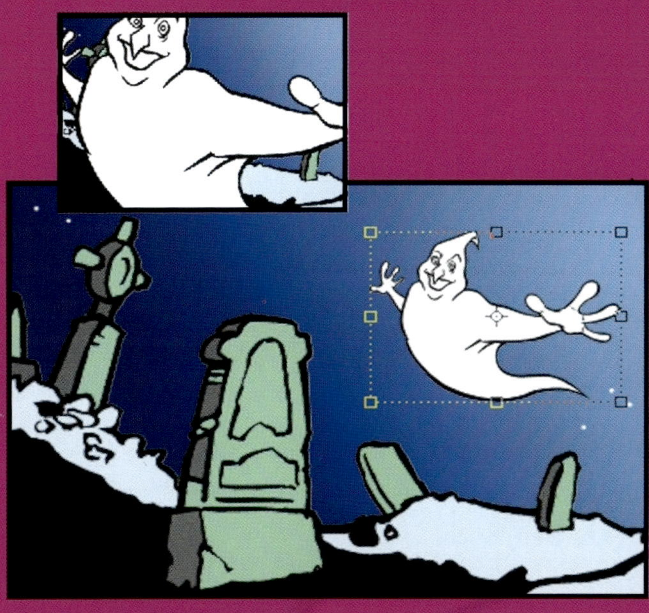

② You'll now be left with a part of your background that might be too small to be useful, so at the Menu bar, click on Image > Resize > Image Size and type higher values in the Document Size box, then click OK. Use Fit On Screen on the Options bar for the Magnifying Glass to make the image appear large enough to work on. Next, have fun coloring….

③ Now let's open a Ghost and drag him/her/it over onto our new background. AAAH! Scary! It's gigantic! Have no fear… here's how we make changes. Delete the layer containing the giant ghost (right-click on its layer in the Layers palette) and click again on the original Ghost's window. Then we can adjust its size by resizing from the Menu bar as before. If we now drag the ghost across again, it should easily fit onto the background, and we can use the bounding box to alter its position and size once more, if necessary.

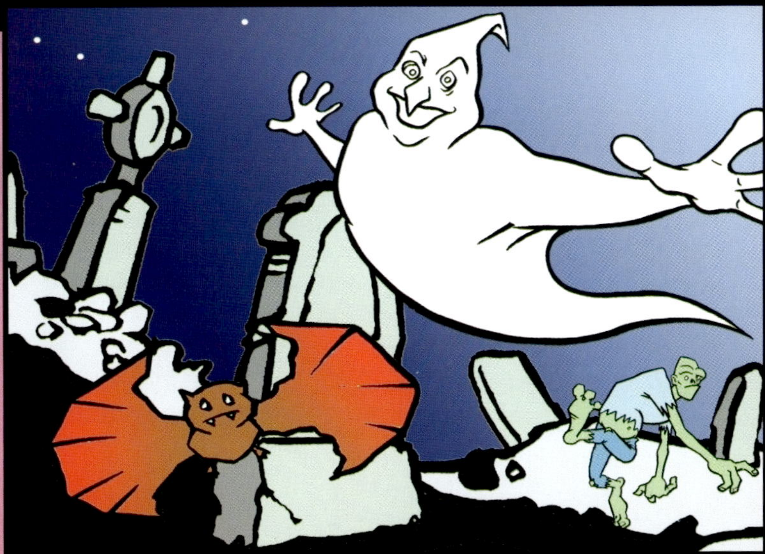

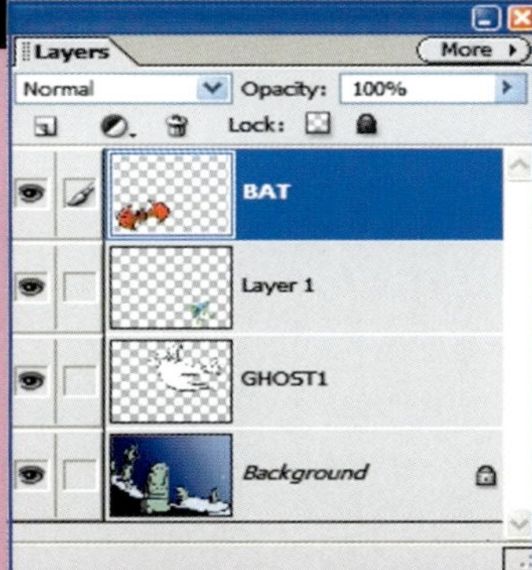

④ For a completely spooky graveyard, we can color a Zombie, shrink him, and place him in the background. A vampire bat completes the scene.

Coloring

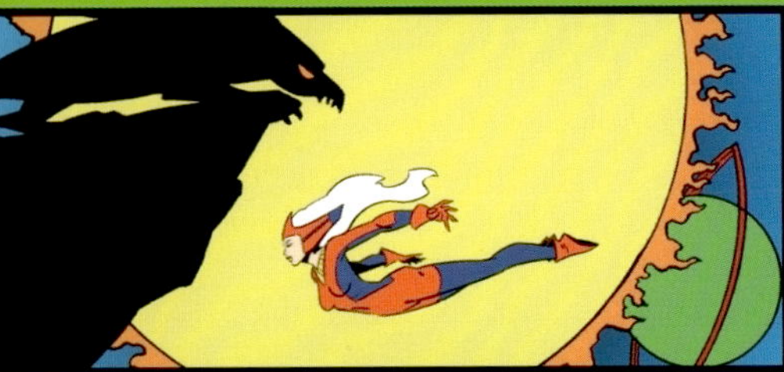

With Photoshop, you can quickly and easily add color to a black-and-white image. You can also add areas that blend one color into another, and subtly alter the final results before you finish your picture.

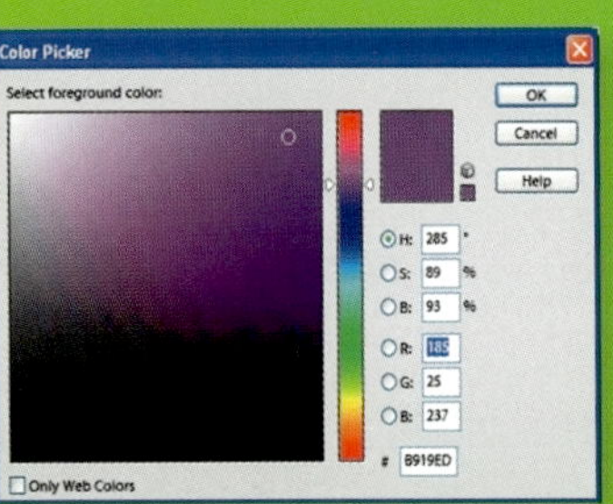

The Color boxes on the Toolbar are where we begin. By clicking on the foremost box, you will be presented with the Color Picker box that allows you to choose from millions of variations of any shade. Move the slider to select. When you choose your next color, the previous one will appear in the box behind, instantly available by clicking on the tiny switching arrows should you need it again. You can also use the Eyedropper tool to select colors from elsewhere in the image, or from any other image you may have open.

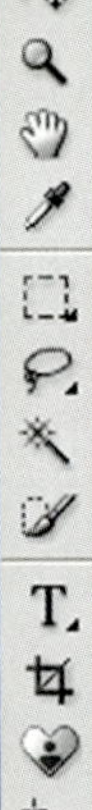

Using the Paint Bucket, you can instantly fill every enclosed space with color, just by clicking on it. Keeping the Tolerance fairly high in the Options menu will ensure that the color sits snugly against your black linework.

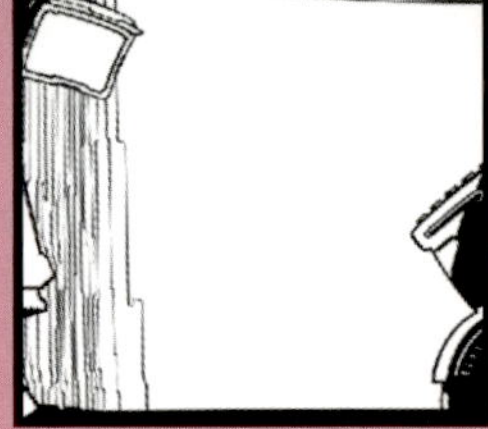

You can also use Gradient fills, blending two or more colors seamlessly together. For two colors, choose the ones you wish to use in both Color boxes; then, use the Magic Wand—or another selection tool—to select an area of your image. By dragging within the selected area, you will create a perfect blend between the two colors.

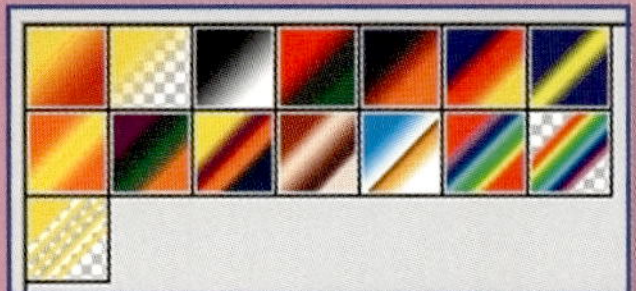

Photoshop also has many pre-set Gradients, accessed via the small arrow on the Options bar next to the colored gradient window.

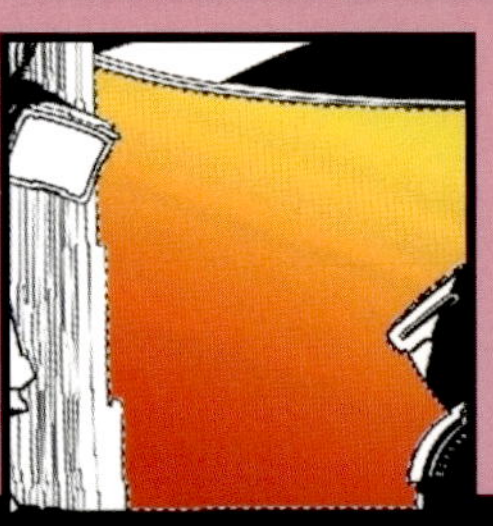

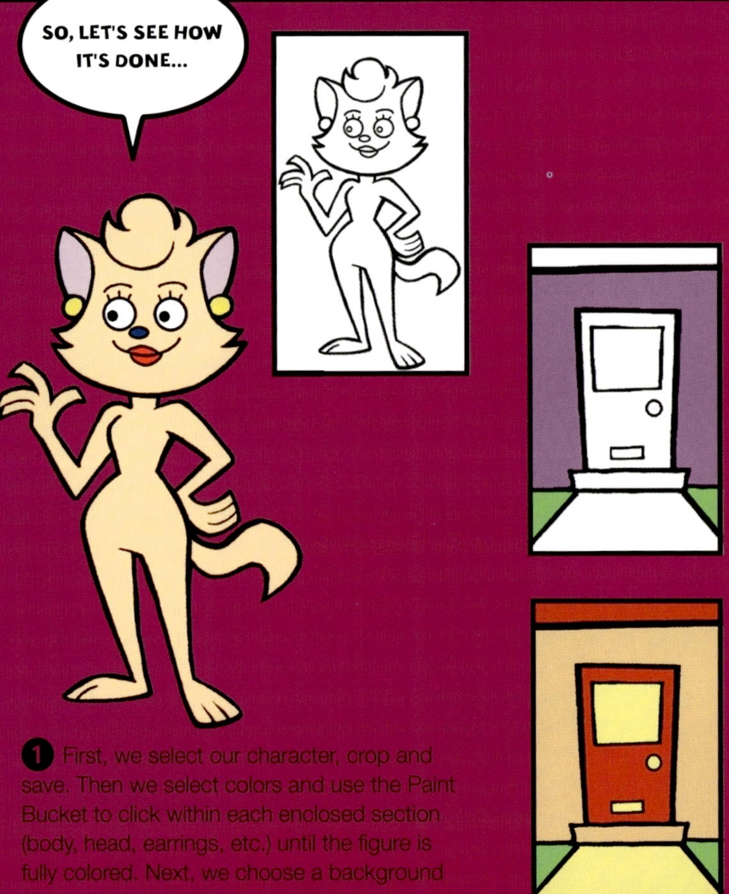

❶ First, we select our character, crop and save. Then we select colors and use the Paint Bucket to click within each enclosed section (body, head, earrings, etc.) until the figure is fully colored. Next, we choose a background picture and repeat the process.

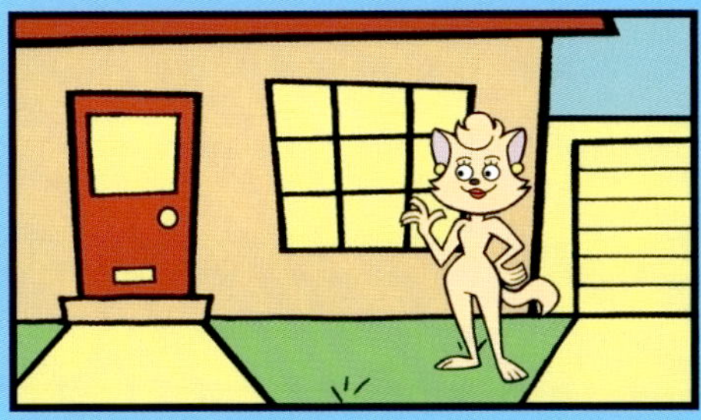

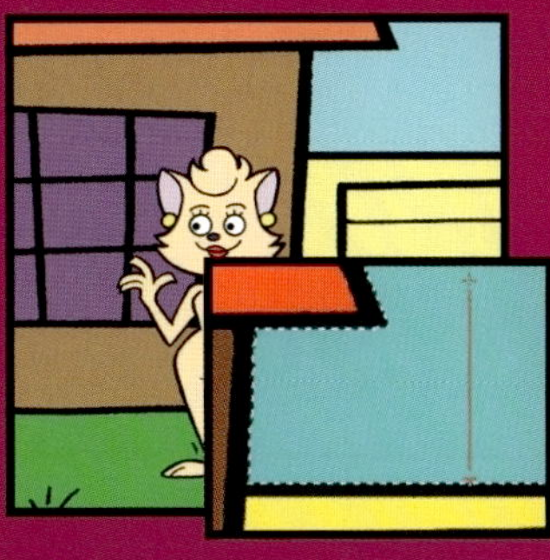

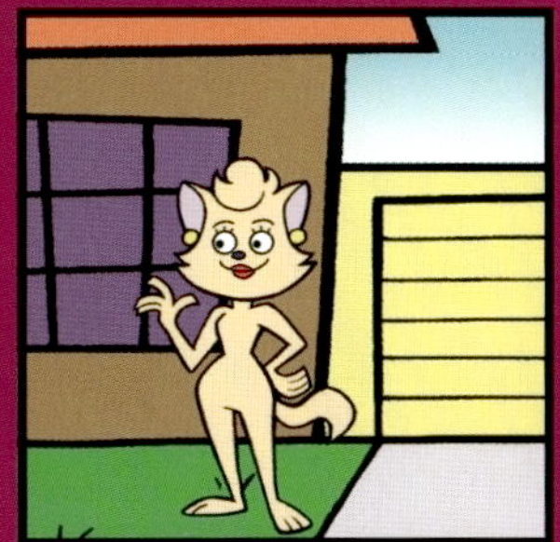

2 Using the Move tool, we place our character onto the background—and "Houston, we have a problem!" The color we chose for our character is too close to the color of the house, camouflaging her within the scene. The simple solution would be to go back in with the Paint Bucket and re-color parts of the picture, but we can be a bit more clever than that.

4 As a final touch, we can do something about that flat patch of blue sky. Use the Eyedropper tool to put the same blue in the Color box on the Toolbar, and switch it to the rear box by clicking on the tiny arrows. Select a lighter blue, and then use the Magic Wand to select the area of sky. By choosing the Gradient tool and dragging a line up through the selected area, the sky now loses its flat appearance and seems less solid than other parts of the picture.

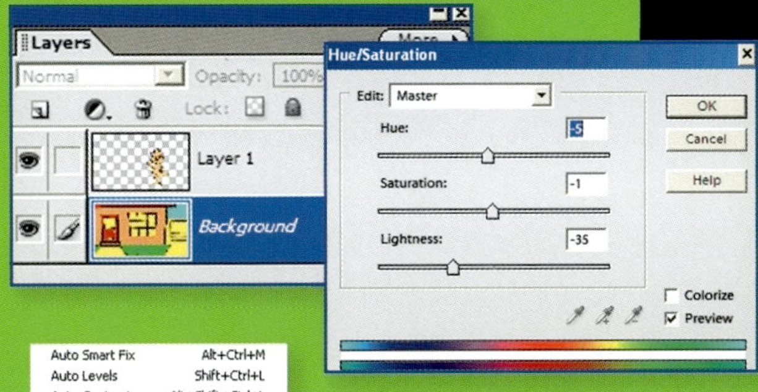

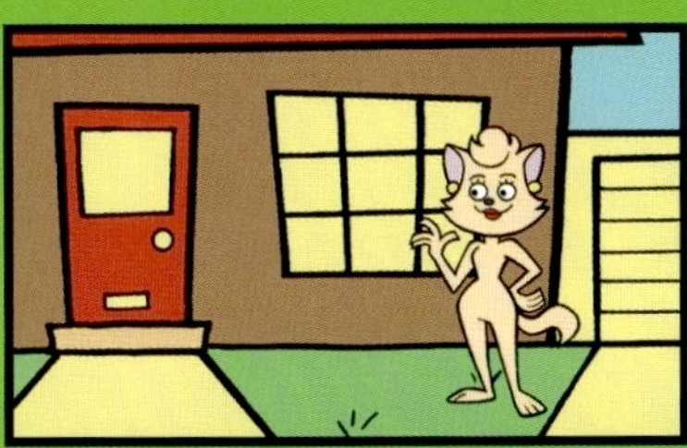

3 Dragging the Layers palette out of the Palette Bin, we need to ensure that the Background layer is highlighted. After selecting the side of the house, we can go to Enhance > Adjust Color > Adjust Hue/Saturation on the top Menu bar. By adjusting the sliders, we can subtly alter the color to a darker shade, allowing the character to be more noticeable in the picture, and use the same technique to alter other parts of the background if we wish.

Important!

We've seen how easy it is to use the Paint Bucket, but what if certain sections of your picture are not fully enclosed by a line? As we can see here, loose linework can create problems.

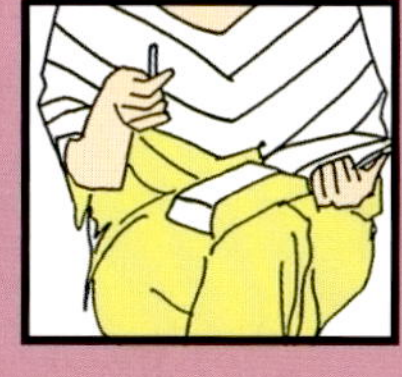

In order to separate the yellow trousers from the woman's sweater and book, we can Undo the color and go into the drawing with the Brush tool. To avoid going over any of the black lines, select the empty area first, and then paint the gaps in the linework with yellow. Deselect, and fill your trousers. Ho-ho.

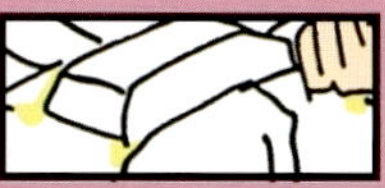

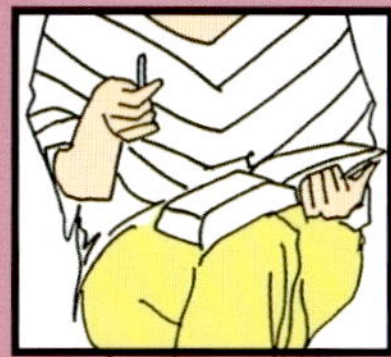

Altering Images

Our characters come with a range of expressions that can be moved onto the main figure. Simply select your chosen expression's layer in the palette and drag it into place with the Move tool.

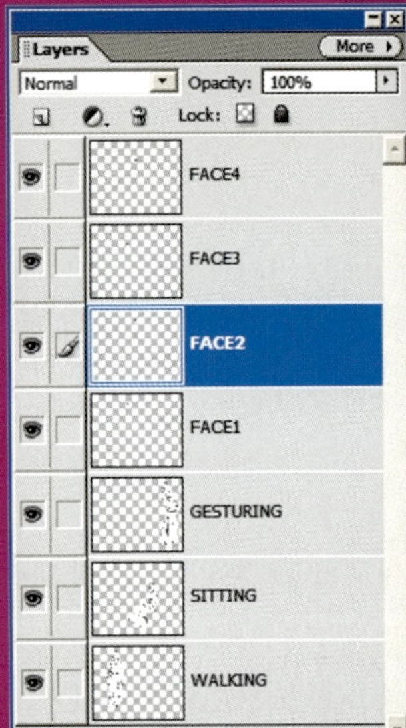

With the face in place, you'll want to ensure that it remains in place when it travels across to its destination—at the moment it is floating above the figure's layer. We can "seal" it in place by going to the Layers palette and clicking on the little eyes next to every layer we are NOT using, rendering them invisible. Next, go to Layers > Merge Visible, and the face will be "stuck" to the body until the next time you open the file.

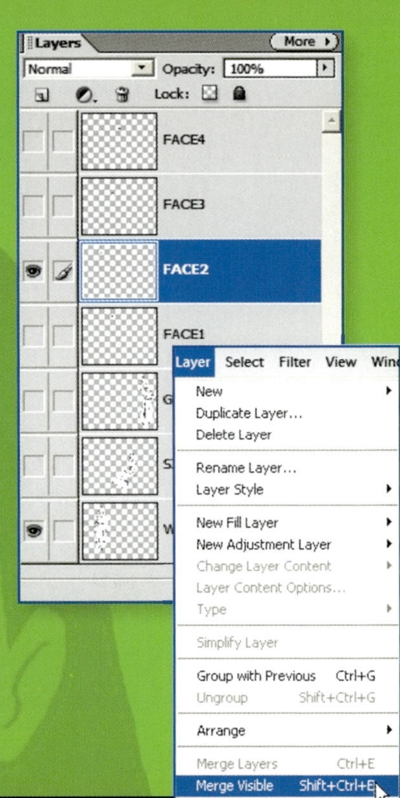

At this point, you can color the image, and crop it if necessary, ready to be dragged to a background.

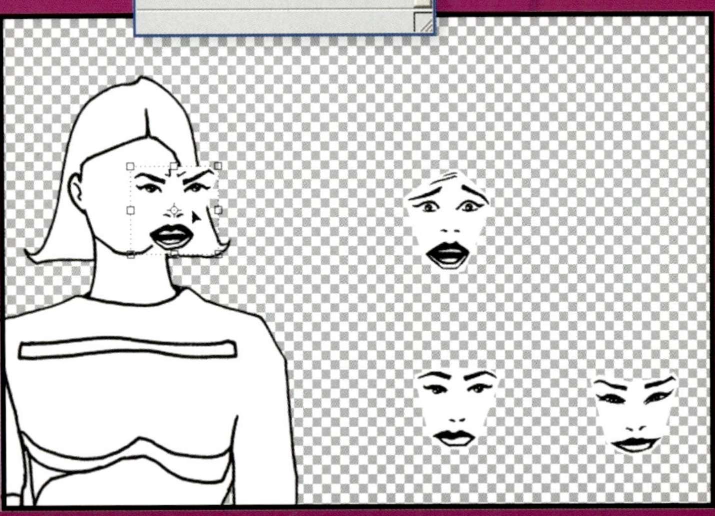

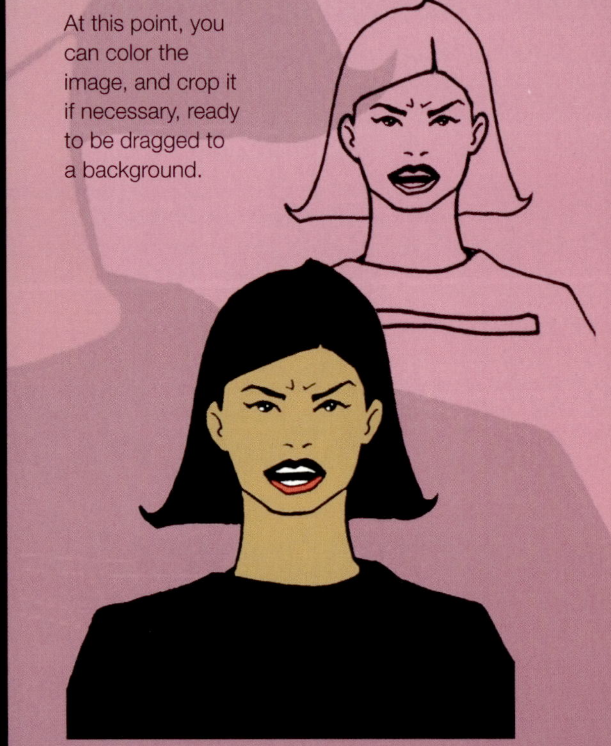

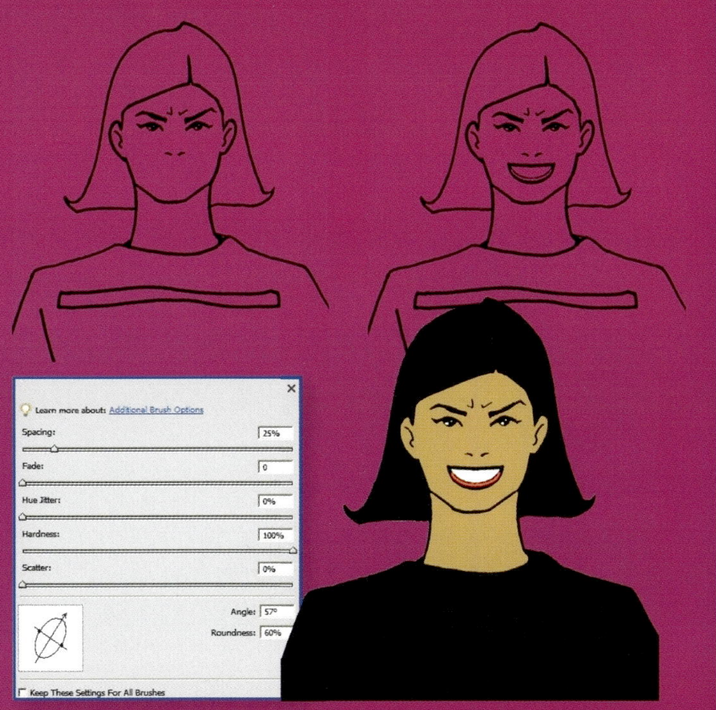

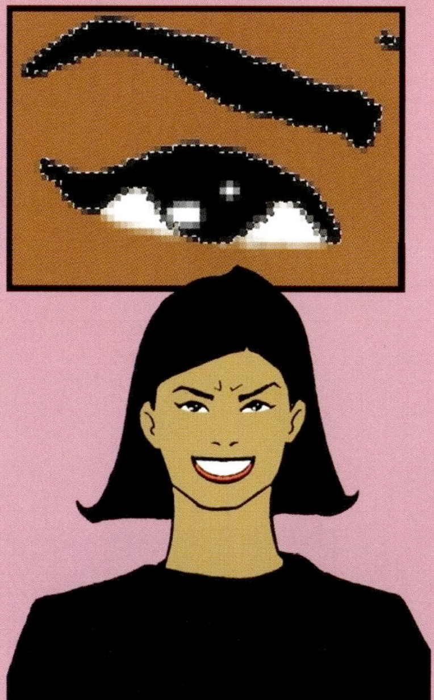

However, you might wish to alter certain details first, and you can accomplish this with the Brush tool. We recommend you attempt the following with a graphics pad and pen, as drawing with a mouse can yield unsatisfactory results.

Perhaps you'd prefer this woman to be smiling, so that the downward arch of her eyebrows will give the impression of an evil grin. First, you'll need to use the Brush tool to paint over the mouth with white. Next comes the re-drawing. Alter the size of the Brush to match the thickness of the other lines in the picture—you do this at the Size box on the Options bar. At More Options on the right-hand side, you can also alter the tip of the brush, making it more elliptical, like the tip of a drawing pen.

Carefully draw your new mouth directly onto the face, and add any other details if you so choose—glasses, maybe, or an unfortunate beard. After coloring, with this particular style of face, you have one further choice. Some cartoonists choose to show the whites of someone's eyes, especially if they will appear in close-up; others don't—it's a style choice. If you do wish to show them, here's how it can be done: simply click the Magic Wand on the face, so that the Brush will not affect the existing black lines; then magnify and draw in the whites of the eyes.

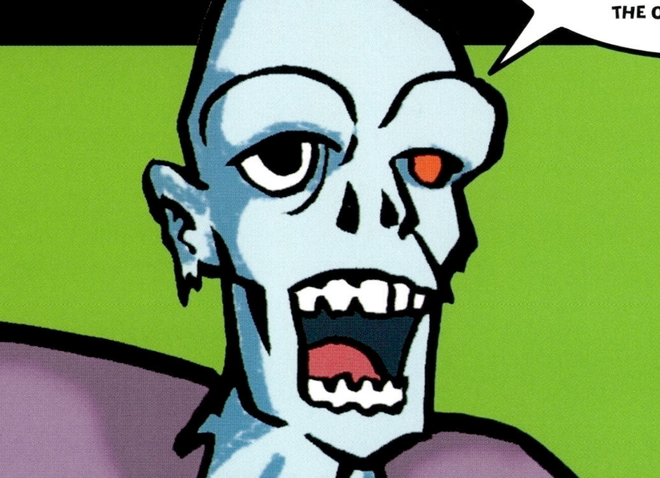

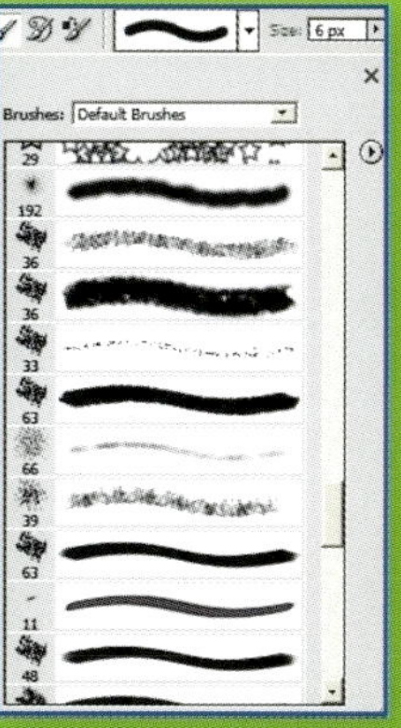

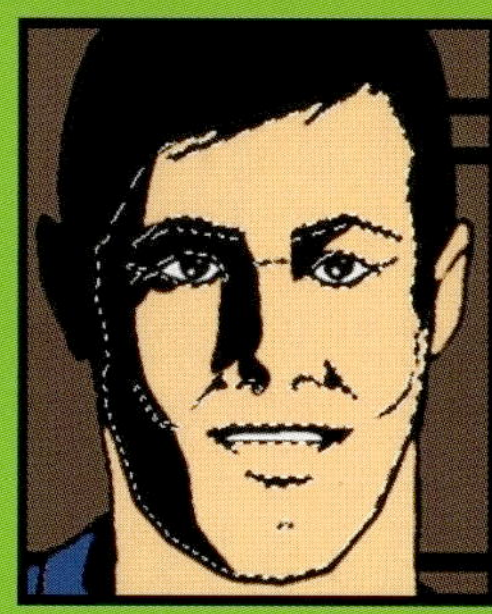

3 Variety is the Spice of Life

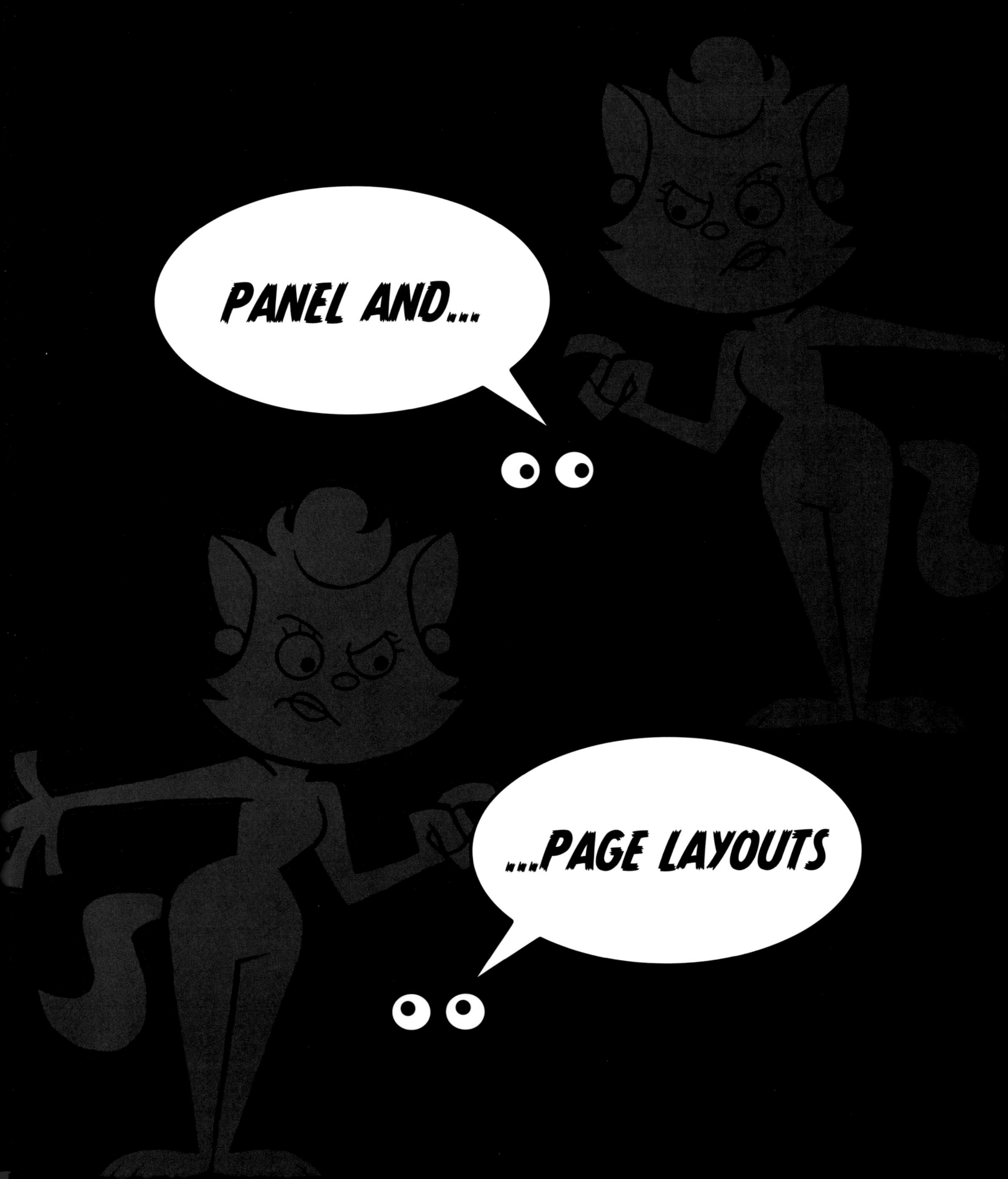

PANEL AND...
...PAGE LAYOUTS

Panel Shapes

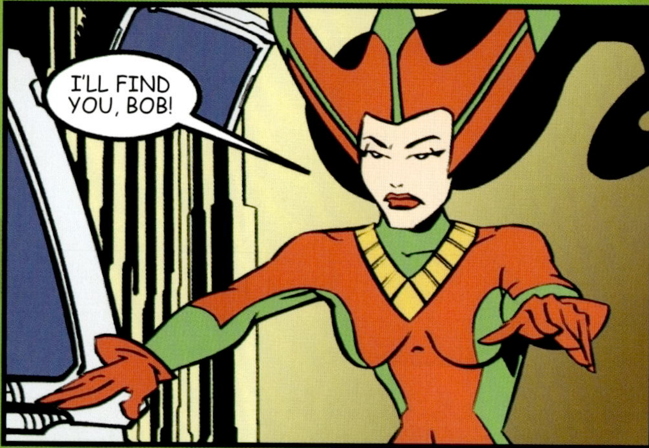

The standard shape for a comic strip panel is the rectangle, as this allows pictures to be easily arranged and read in rows, or "tiers." However, cartoonists occasionally employ other shapes—and sometimes none at all—for differing effects to enhance the story, gag, or selling point.

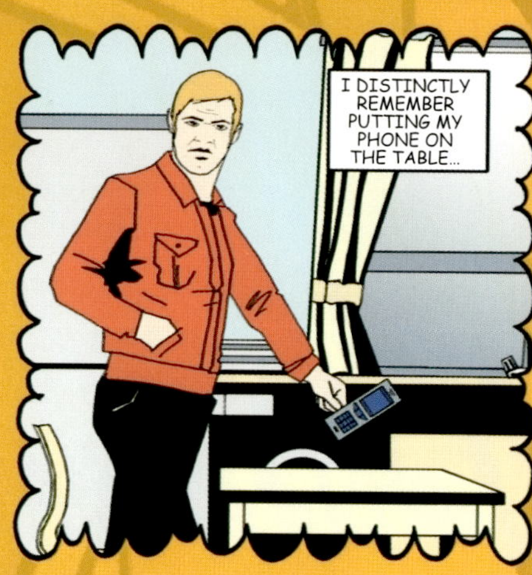

Cloud-like panel

A cloud-like panel is often used to show that this scene is a flashback to an earlier time, possibly a previously unseen part of the story. It can also be used to see what a character is thinking.

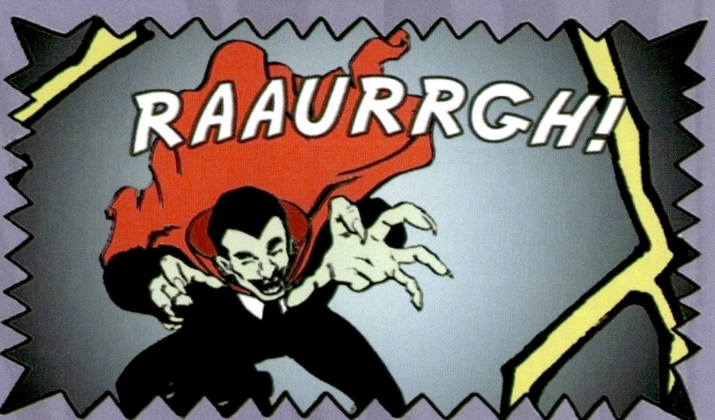

Jagged outline

A jagged outline can be used to highlight a startling, surprising, or explosive event—used sparingly, this is an effective device.

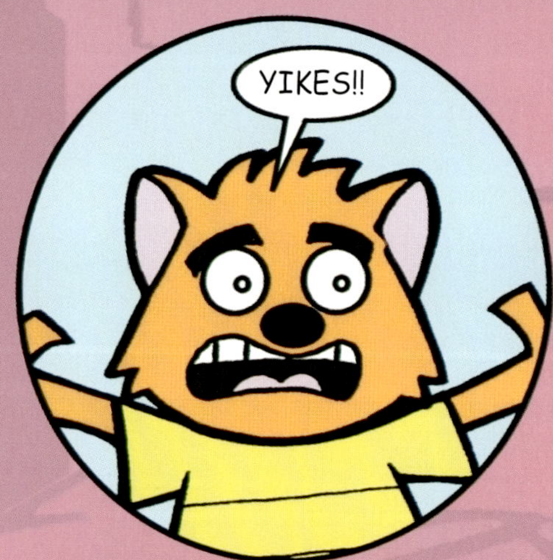

Circle

Sometimes, a circle is used for a close-up, or simply to add a little variety to the layout of the page.

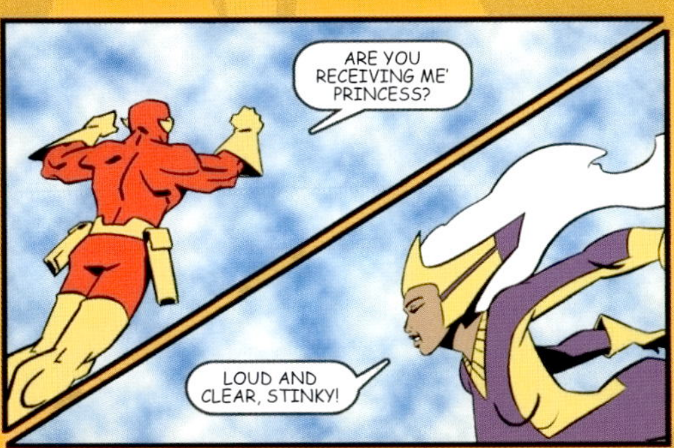

Split panel

A split panel can be used when you want to show characters in different settings experiencing some kind of closely related action—a phone call, for instance.

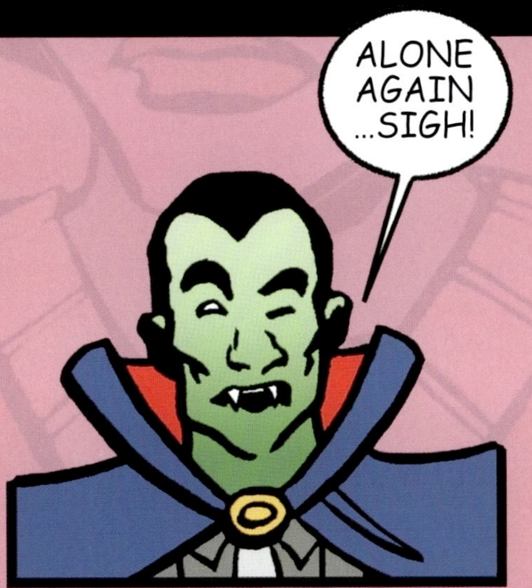

No panel border

Very occasionally, cartoonists use no panel border at all, except for a line cropping the bottom of the character if seen in close-up; this implies a sense of emptiness or infinity— our scene is momentarily unconstrained.

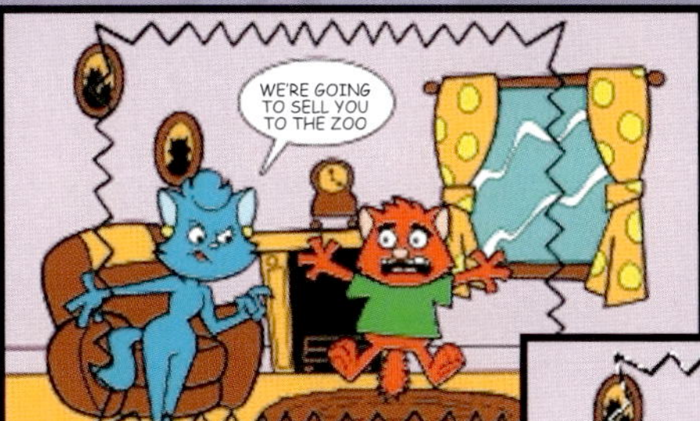

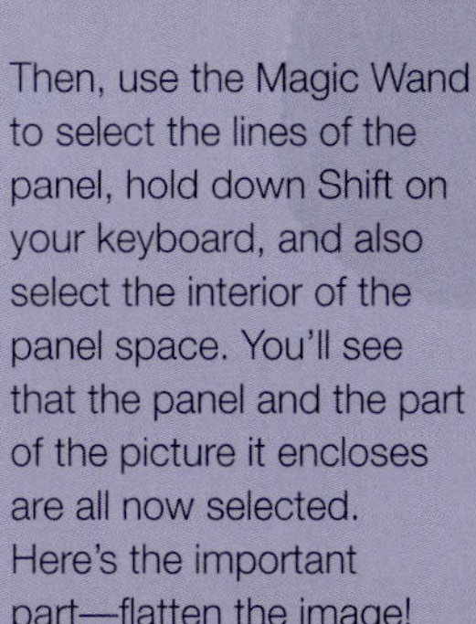

One way of creating panels is to work on a background image, crop, and add a black border, as shown in Creating a Simple Cartoon Panel (pages 14-15). Another way is to use the pre-drawn panels on the CD.

Add characters, color, and word balloons to a background as usual. Then open a panel shape and use the Move tool to drag it across to your picture. Use the handles on the bounding box to resize it to enclose all the elements of the picture that you want to be in your finished panel.

Then, use the Magic Wand to select the lines of the panel, hold down Shift on your keyboard, and also select the interior of the panel space. You'll see that the panel and the part of the picture it encloses are all now selected. Here's the important part—flatten the image! (Layer > Flatten Image).

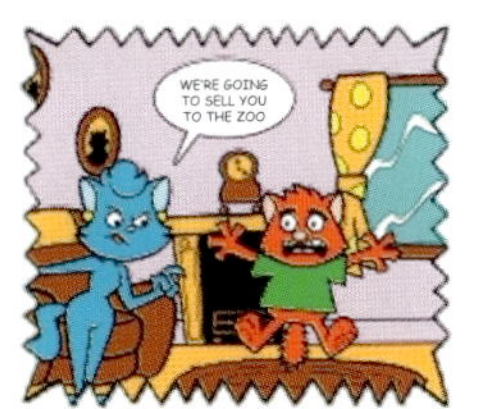

Open a new blank document. Drag the selected part of your picture across, and you'll see that it is now an enclosed panel on a new layer, ready to be put to further use.

If you wish to reuse your original picture, click on its title bar and go straight to Edit > Undo Flatten Image. Deselect the panel shape and then delete it by right-clicking on its name in the Layers palette.

Panels Per Page

There are no hard-and-fast rules about the number of panels one should place on a comic book page. However, it is worth considering the differing effects it can have on the reader.

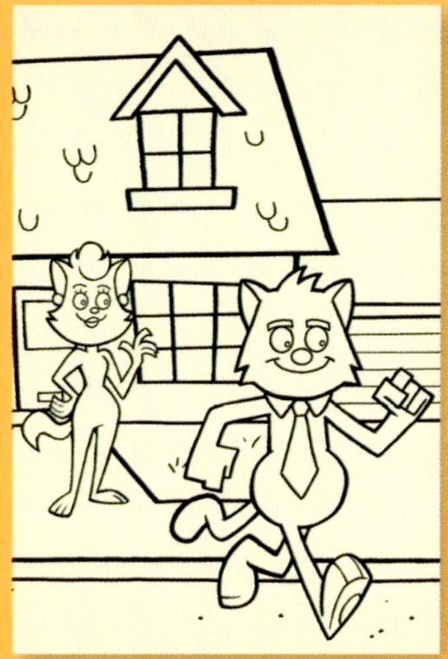

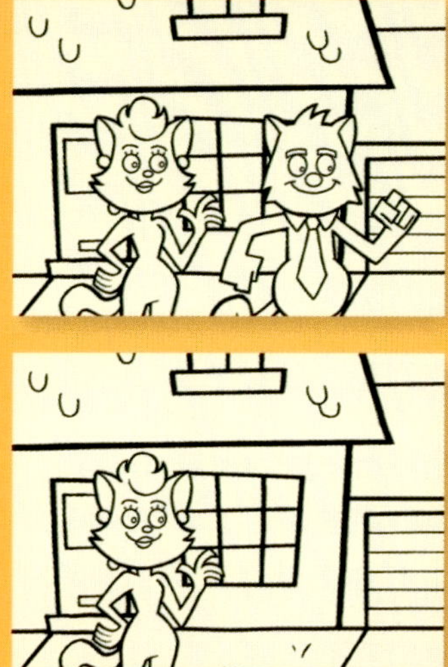

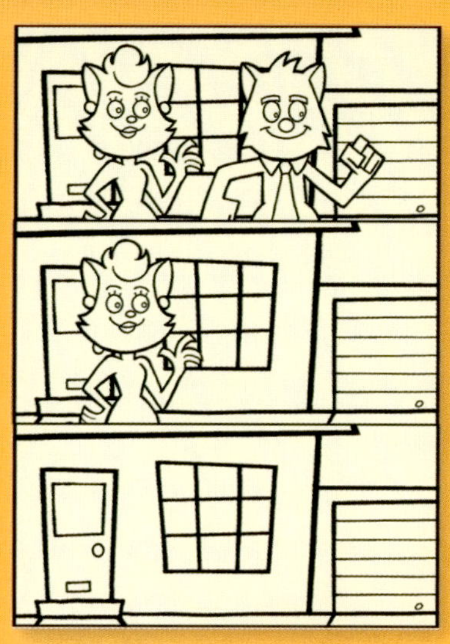

One single panel filling a whole page is usually known as a "splash page." Commonly, it is used at the start of a story, hitting the reader right between the eyes. It can also be used midway through a story to highlight an explosive scene or action. It might even be used at the very end, especially if you're leaving the reader with a suspenseful "cliffhanger" ending, to be continued in another installment. There is no reason why a comic book couldn't be totally comprised of full page panels, and this has been done before. One problem with this is that it does mean that you'll be giving the reader a very quick read indeed.

The same holds true of pages containing only two or three panels, though this could be useful if you want the reader to "speed up" while reading a particular part of a story—a fight scene, for example. Also, it's worth remembering that newspaper strips are often presented in two or three panels, precisely because they are not intended to engage a reader for more than a few seconds.

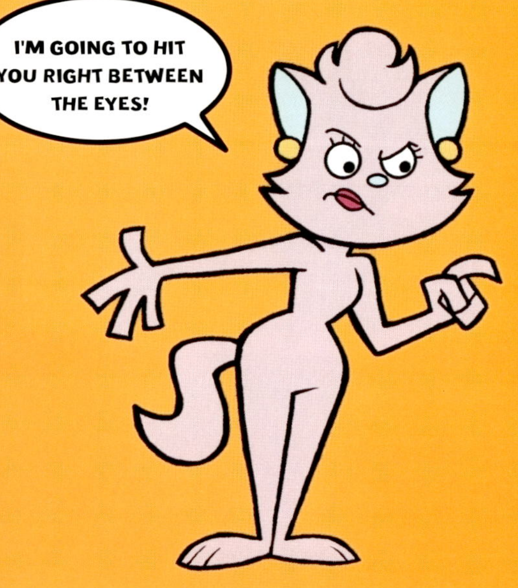

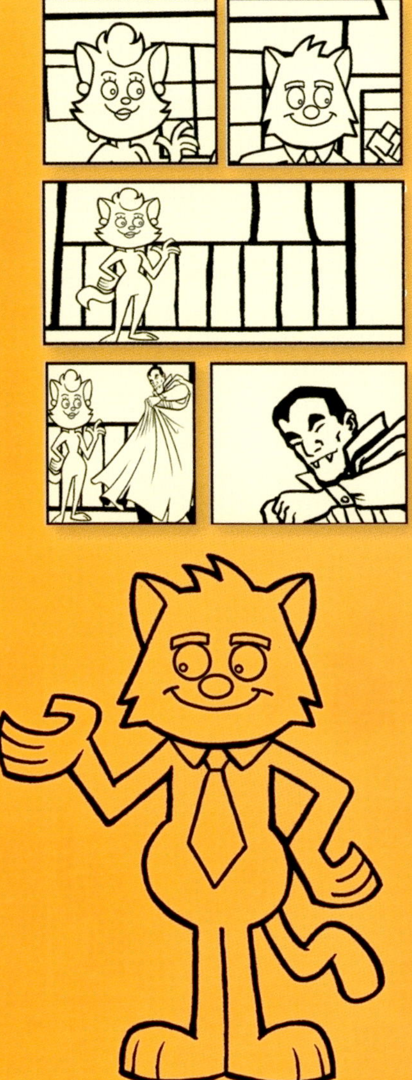

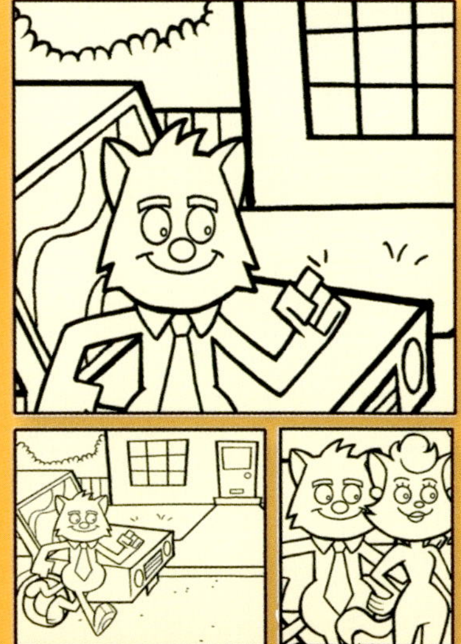

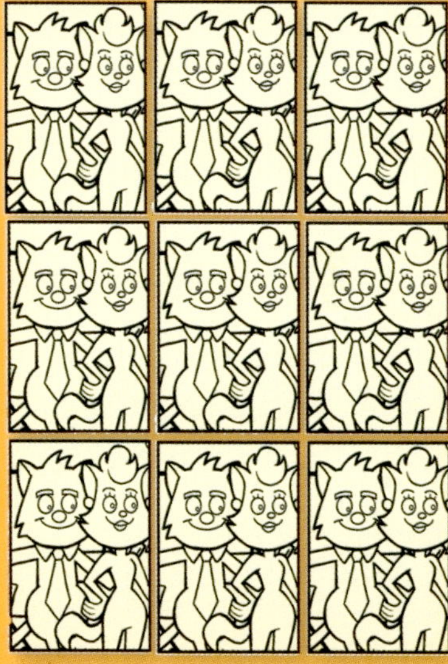

Generally, comic book pages contain anywhere between four and six panels per page. The size of each panel can vary, and sometimes a panel can occupy the whole width of a page—to establish a new setting for the characters, perhaps. A further variation on this tactic is to have one big panel taking up two-thirds of a page, with one or two beneath; this is a variation on the splash page technique.

Occasionally, you will see eight or nine panels per page being used in comics, or even more. This will slow the reader's experience, allowing them to become deeply immersed in a story. However, this means the panels may end up being printed quite small, meaning that details can be lost on the reader. With rare exceptions, comics that use this many panels on every page tend to actually be printed larger than the typical comic-book format, as can be seen in the hardbound editions common to European countries.

Balloon Placement

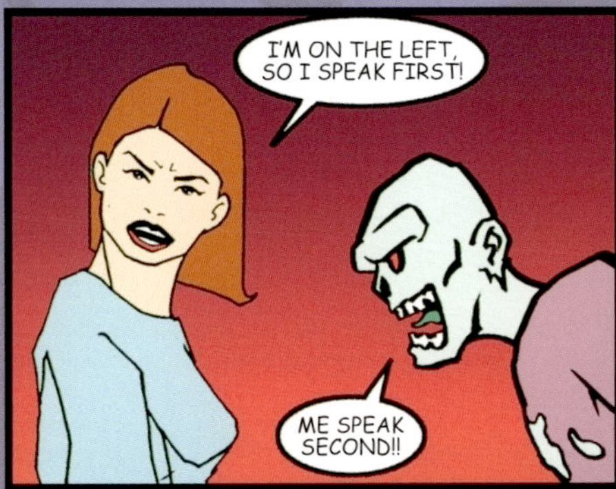

As we have seen, it's important to remember that, in most countries, people read from left to right—so the balloons in your pictures should be arranged to be read from left to right in sequence.

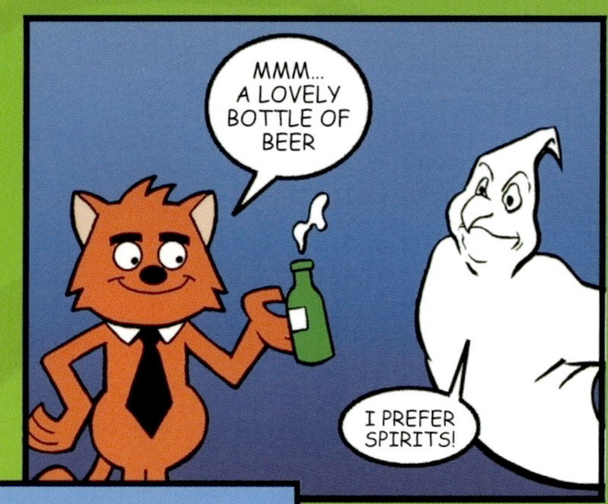

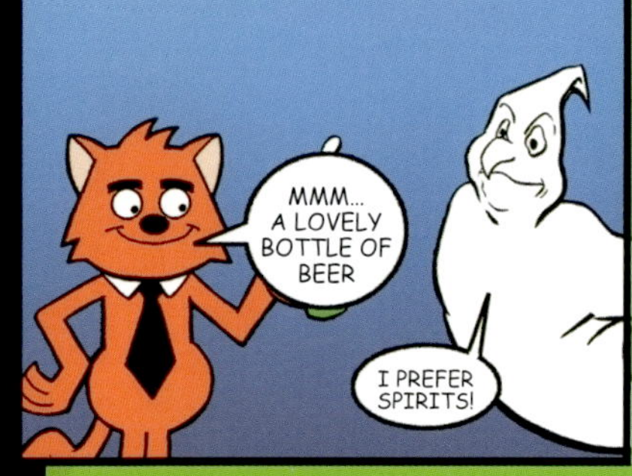

A vitally important thing to consider is that your word balloons should not cover an important part of the picture, such as another character's face, or the very thing under discussion.

But what if, in the same picture, someone speaks more than once? As well as reading from left to right, we also read from top to bottom—for example, when we read a newspaper column. So we can add the second comment by the first speaker below the first two balloons, and preferably slightly back to the left again.

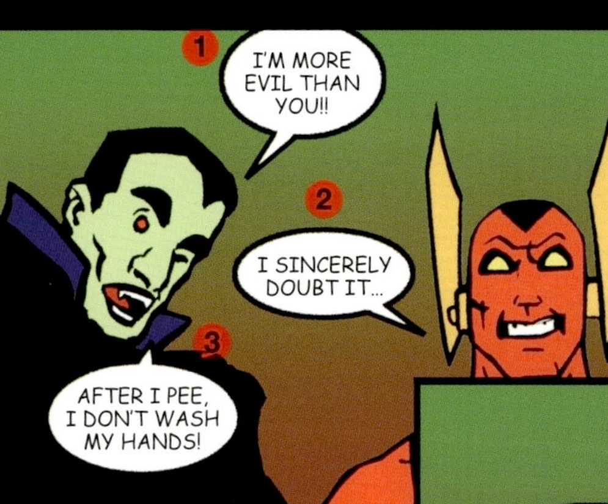

This logic dictates that, should the second speaker reply again in the same picture, his second balloon should be to the right of the third balloon. However, you can see that this overcrowds the panel—too many word balloons should be avoided.

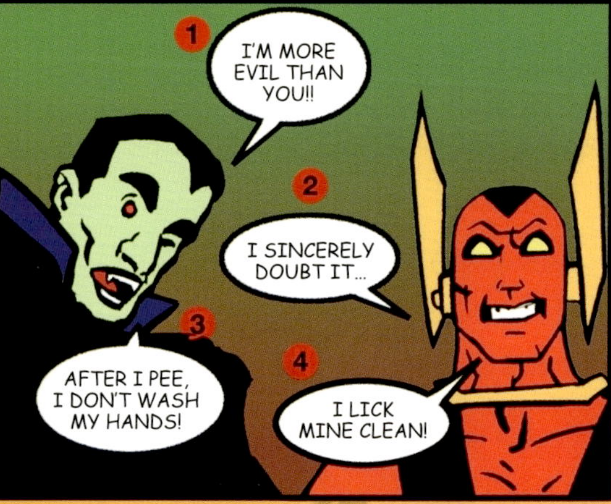

As well as the traditional oval-shaped word balloon, you'll no doubt be familiar with some of these other shapes, which can add nuances to how we interpret what is being said in a panel. The shapes shown here are included on your CD.

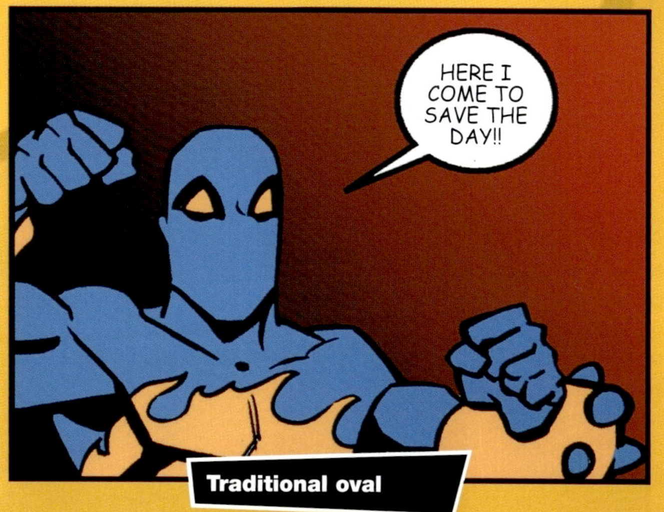

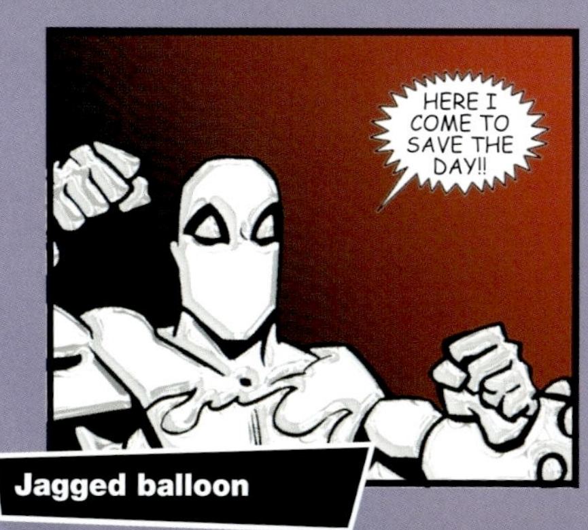

A jagged balloon can imply that something is being said in anger or urgency. It can also indicate an electronic voice, such as from a radio or a robot.

A balloon with a broken line indicates that someone is whispering.

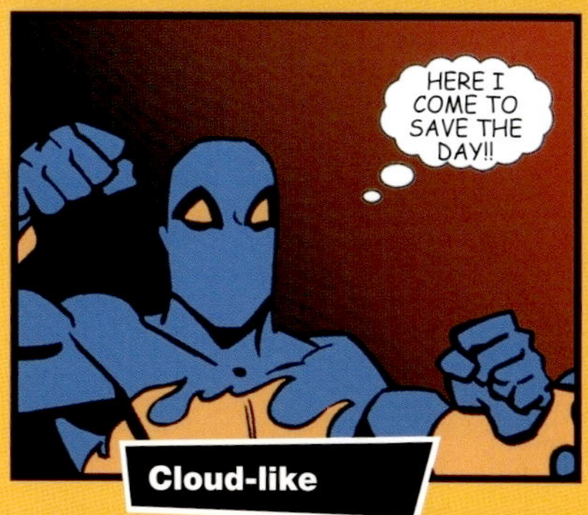

A balloon in the shape of a cloud, with trailing balloons leading to a character, tells us that these words are being thought, rather than spoken out loud.

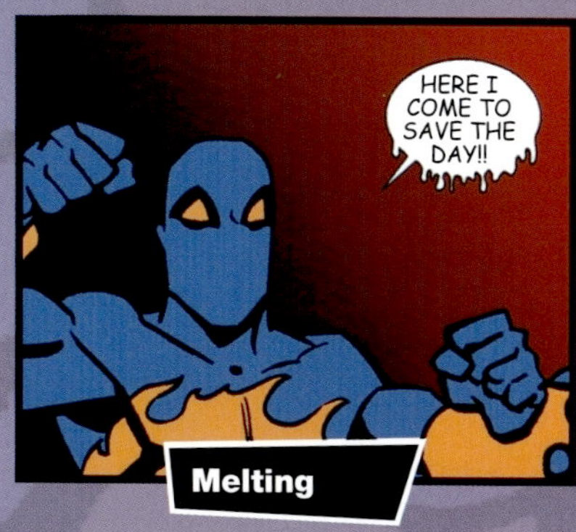

A balloon that appears to be melting can mean two things: either mortal dread, or that someone is being bitterly ironic.

Fonts

Until the mid-1990s, the lettering for comics and cartoons was written onto the original artwork by hand. Attempts by some publishers to print directly onto the word balloons and captions were mostly less than satisfying, as the rigid forms of letterpress printing were at odds with the more organic flow of the surrounding linework. The words stuck out like a sore thumb.

Even as computers became more sophisticated, for some years the choice of fonts available was limited to the traditional Times New Roman and mechanical sans-serif styles such as Arial and Impact—none of which looked good sitting in a word balloon. Then came Comic Sans, and the first indication that it was possible to have a typewritten font that resembled traditional hand-lettering.

Since then, professional lettering artists have been busy designing hundreds of fonts for many purposes, including the reproduction of their own hand-lettering style. Your computer has probably come with at least a couple, including the now ubiquitous Comic Sans, and Comix.

You are not limited to these, however. There are many websites full of free fonts that you can download and use right away. For the connoisseur, there are also sites that provide a wider range of styles for a small fee.

Do not underestimate the importance of choosing a font that does not distract the reader from the artwork; having spent so much effort creating your incredible images, you're not going to want to spoil the overall effect by using lousy lettering.

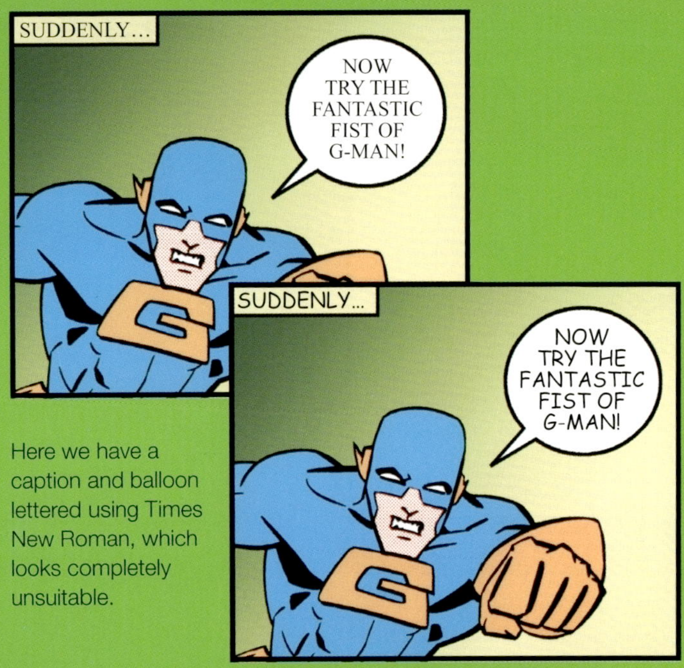

Here we have a caption and balloon lettered using Times New Roman, which looks completely unsuitable.

Using Comic Sans, we get a more organic look, as though lettered by hand, which sits better among the other hand-drawn lines in the panel.

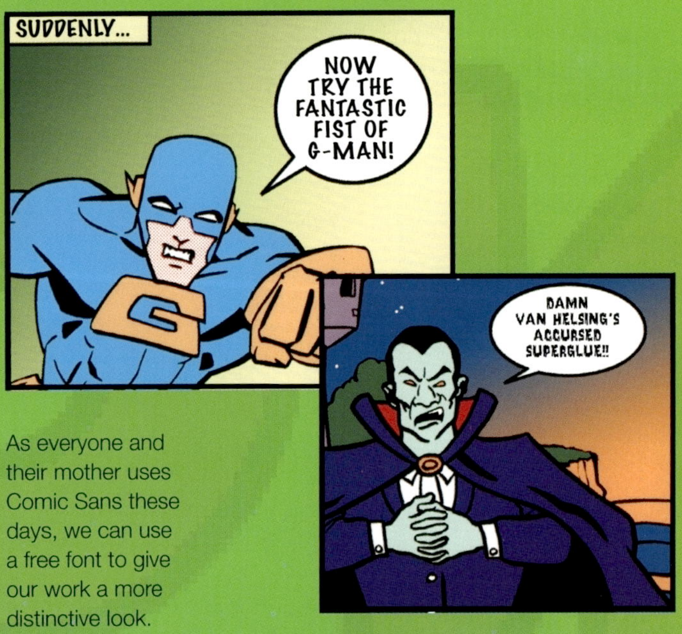

As everyone and their mother uses Comic Sans these days, we can use a free font to give our work a more distinctive look.

We can even try to find fonts to suit specific characters.

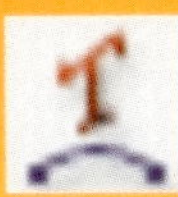

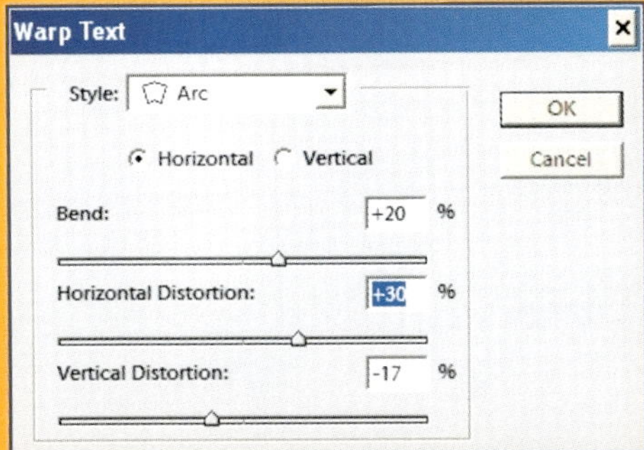

Another important use of fonts is in the creation of sound effects. For a lively look, go to the Create Warped Text button on the Options bar in Photoshop Elements. Here, you can twist the sound effect into a more expressive shape.

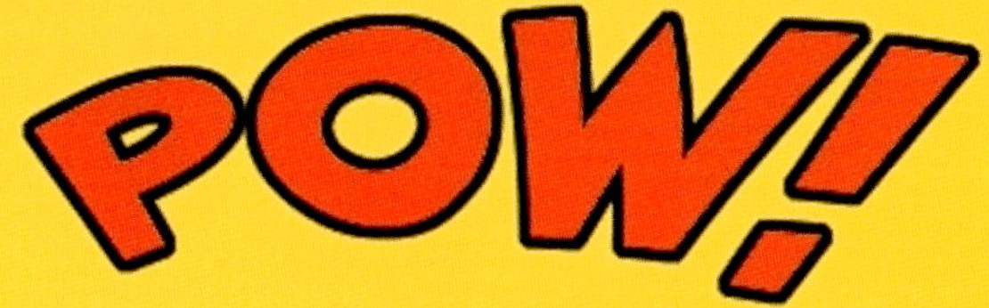

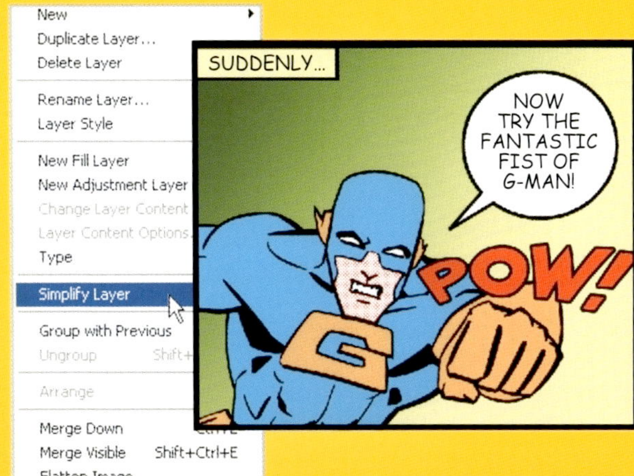

To make the sound effect stand out from the artwork, you can edge it with black—or any other color—by first going to Layer > Simplify Layer on the Menu bar. Then simply go to Edit > Stroke to get a nice outline around the text. You can then drag it across to your picture to give it some extra POW!

comic sans

Right

Times New Roman

Wrong

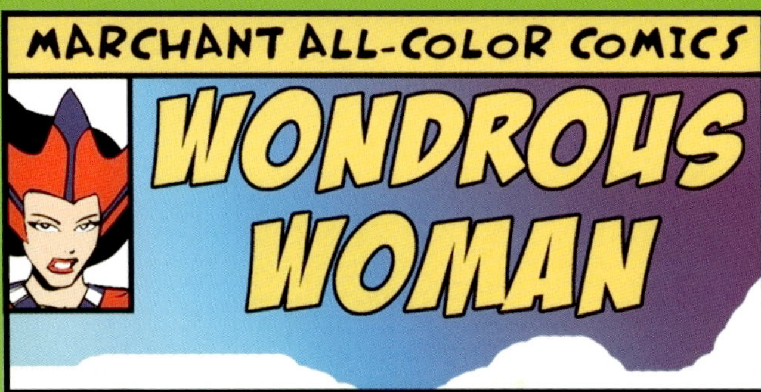

Despite the old saying, people do tend to judge a book by its cover. When you reach the stage where you're ready to unleash your wondrous wares upon the world, remember to use these techniques to create cover lettering and logos that will really catch the eye.

Simple SFX

Photoshop Elements comes with a couple of amazing boxes of tricks: the Filters and Styles & Effects menus. With these, you can alter the whole look of your work, or areas within it. Should you wish, you can make a cartoon appear as though it has been rendered in watercolor or charcoal, add texture to a flat area of color, or even distort the entire thing into a work of neo-Cubist abstract expressionism. Best of all, these effects are all totally reversible via Edit>Undo, so you can be as adventurous as you like.

Filters can be accessed in two ways: from the Styles & Effects menu in the Palette Bin, which will give you a thumbnail photo of each filter in action (also accessible via Filters>Filter Gallery); or directly from the drop-down list under Filters, which contains even more filter options.

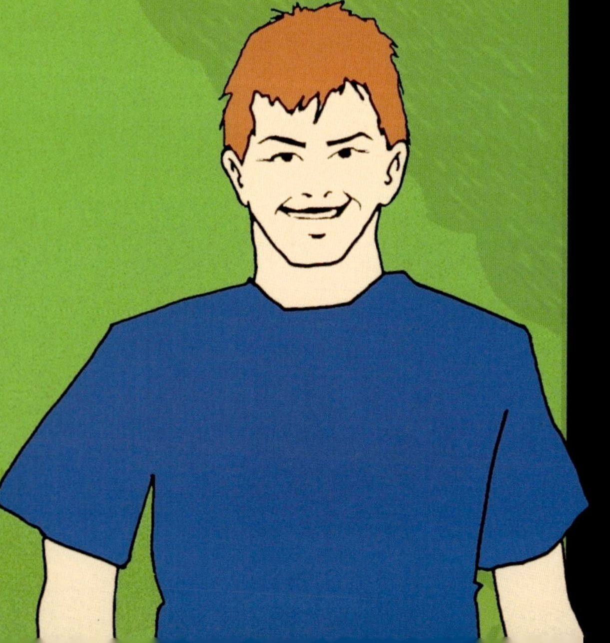

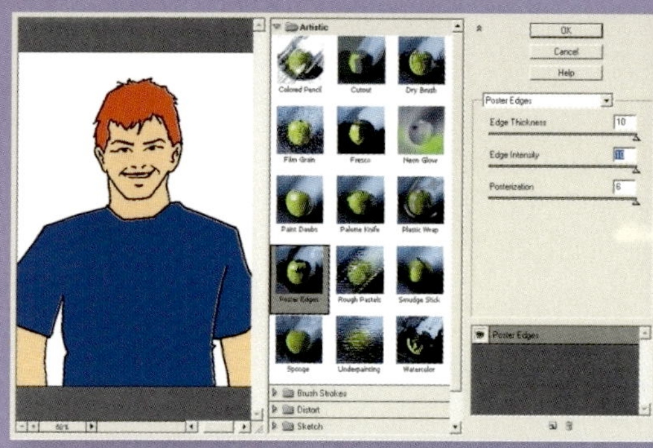

Filters can be used to alter the quality of a picture's lines after coloring. You might wish to simplify or thicken the linework of a drawing if it will subsequently be reduced in size to be placed in the background of an image; or maybe you just like simple, thick guys.

By going to Filters>Artistic>Poster Edges you can adjust the sliders and watch the changes take place in the preview window.

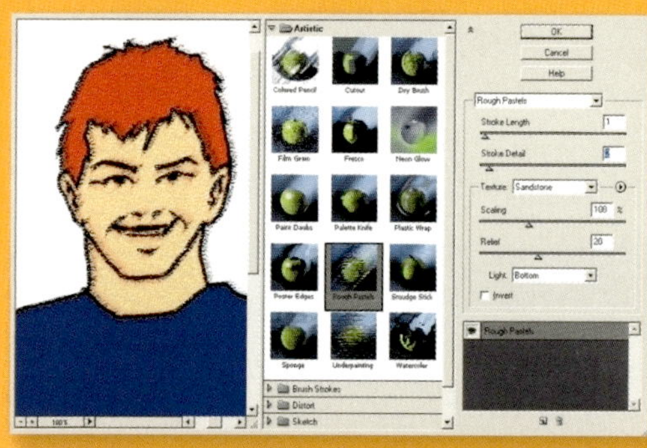

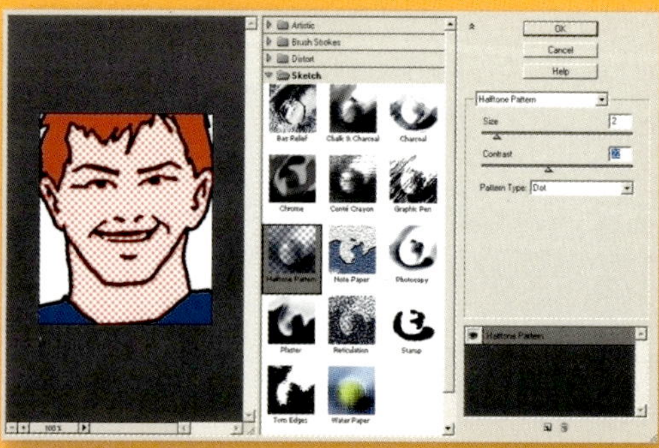

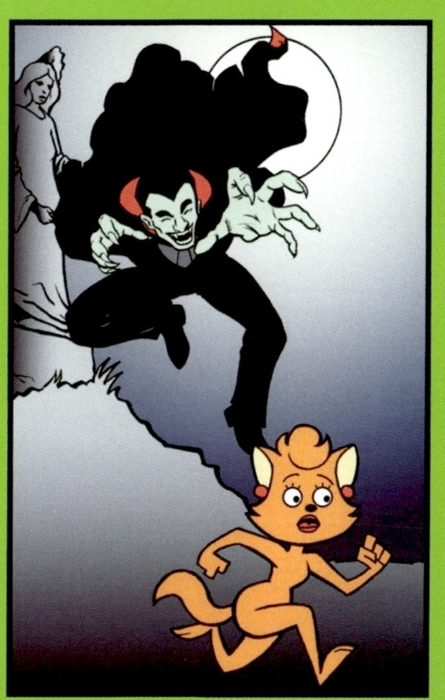

In the example here, the picture was colored as usual, and the results are perfectly acceptable. But with a few filters, the scene can be made more atmospheric. First, the sky was selected and the Blizzard effect applied from the Styles & Effects menu. Next, the statue was selected and Noise was added (Noise>Add Noise); this gives the selected area a grainy appearance, in this case to suggest a light dusting of snowflakes. The ground needed to look snowy, too, but before adding Noise to this area, a couple of shadows were added as the surface would appear lighter once the filter was applied. A decision was made not to apply the Blizzard effect to the figures, so that their details would more easily be seen.

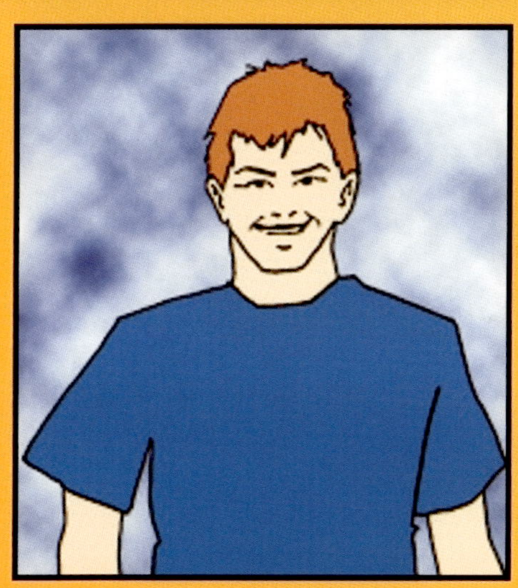

The Artistic>Rough Pastels filter completely transforms the look of the linework. Or, to achieve that old-fashioned printing effect for skin tones and other areas, select the are with the Magic Wand and use Pixelate>Halftone Pattern. Backgrounds can be selected and filled with a texture, or in this case, Render> Clouds (which draws its hues from the currently selected foreground and background colors).

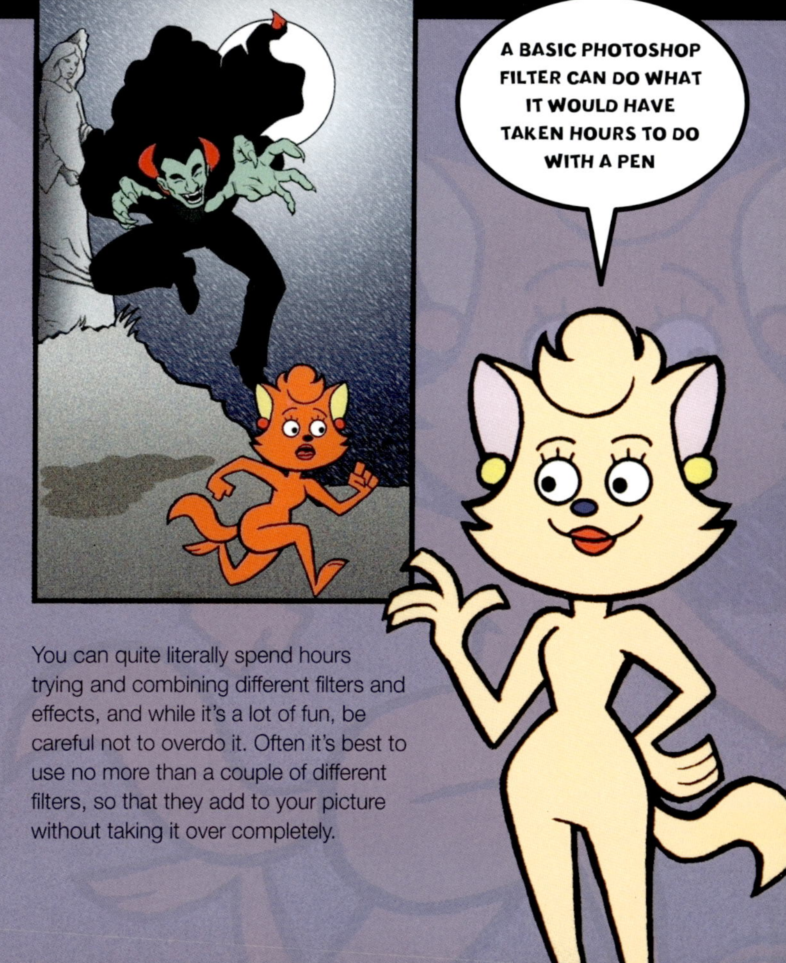

You can quite literally spend hours trying and combining different filters and effects, and while it's a lot of fun, be careful not to overdo it. Often it's best to use no more than a couple of different filters, so that they add to your picture without taking it over completely.

4 A Picture's Worth 999 Words

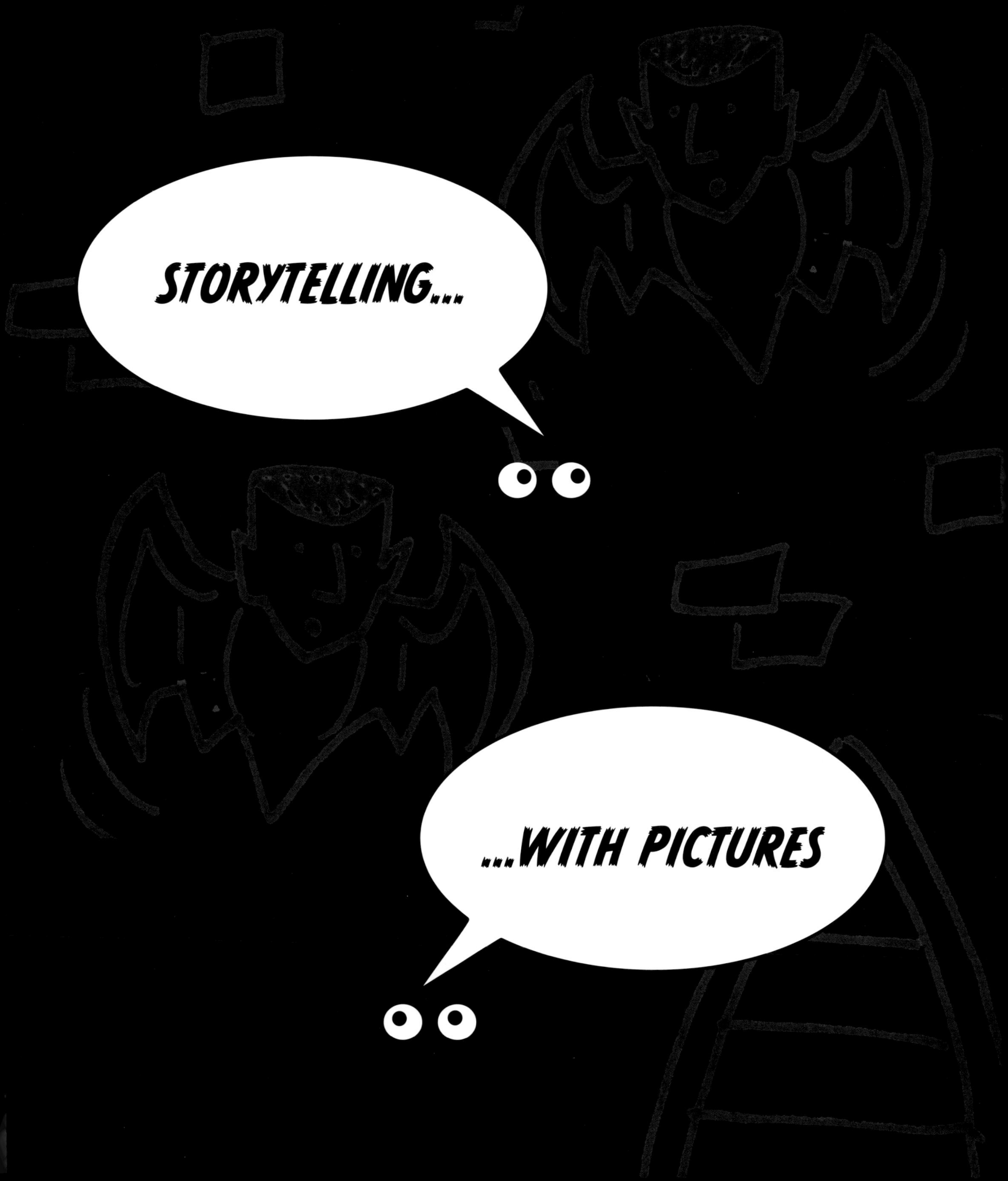

STORYTELLING...
...WITH PICTURES

Basic Storytelling

Where do you get your ideas from? It's a question often asked of writers and storytellers, and there's never an easy answer. Even the humble single-panel gag merchant might have a hard time explaining what inspires his crazy view of the world.

While a turn of phrase, an ironic comment, or a jarring juxtaposition of words and image might provide the basis for a single-panel cartoon, those attempting to write and illustrate a story told through a sequence of pictures might find a basic framework useful on which to peg their initial ideas.

Virtually every story—whether it's comedy, tragedy, or stirring space-opera—involves characters facing some kind of problem. That problem can be large or small, an external event, or an internal dilemma. How the characters deal with the problem provides interest, and how the problem is solved—or not—provides the resolution.

A very basic plot can be laid out in six parts. These parts could be pages or chapters, but here we are going to treat them as six panels comprising a one-page comic strip.

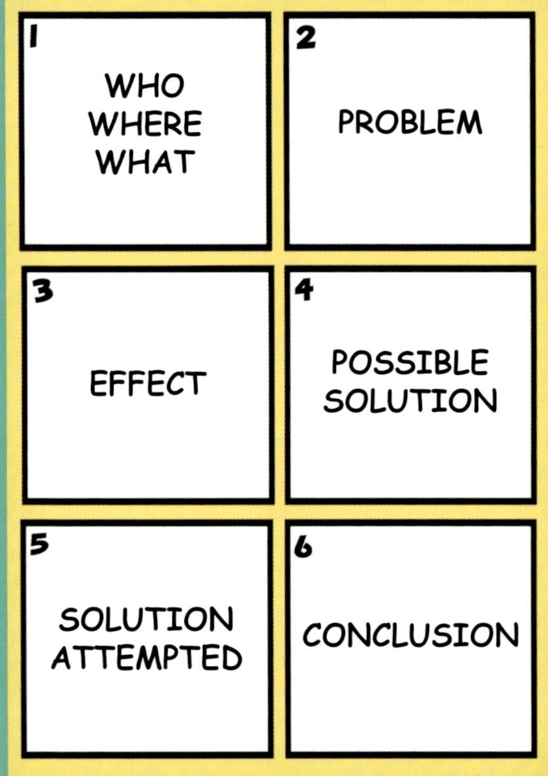

In our first panel, we can set the scene; we need to see who the strip is about, where they are, and what they're doing. Next, some kind of problem presents itself; this may arise as a direct result of actions in the previous panel, or it might have no connection at all. We then see the effect that it has on the protagonist and others in the scene. A solution presents itself in the form of an idea or a new development. The solution is attempted, which brings us to the conclusion. This might be a happy ending, an unhappy ending, an open ending, or even a surprise ending.

Simple, yes; but the above could be used to summarize anything from a Thomas Hardy novel to a *Star Wars* movie.

Similarly, a humor strip can lead the reader through six panels (or less) toward a punchline. With humor strips, there is a tradition of having characters merely sitting around or walking along as they take us through to the joke at the end. Slice of Life strips, too, often feature characters doing everyday things while chatting or musing on life's ups and downs. In this type of strip, the dialogue is all-important, otherwise the reader will be treated to a slice of a very boring life.

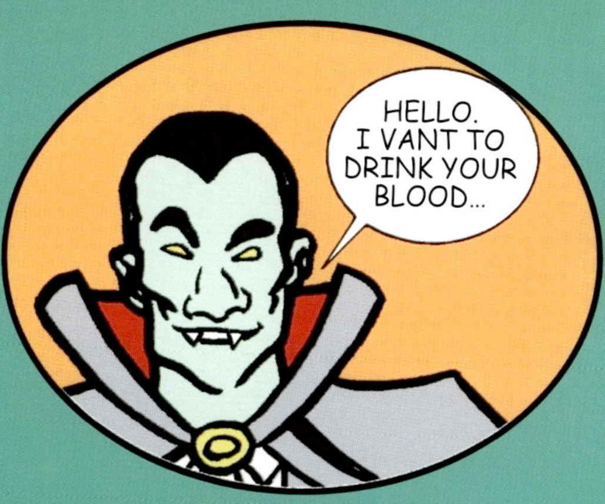

1 **WHO** DRACULA **WHERE** OUTSIDE CASTLE **WHAT** GOING TO BED	**2** **PROBLEM** HE CAN'T FIND HIS KEYS!
3 **EFFECT** IT'S ALMOST SUNRISE AND HE COULD GET FRIED	**4** **POSSIBLE SOLUTION** HE'LL FLY UP TO A WINDOW AND LET HIMSELF IN
5 **SOLUTION ATTEMPTED** BUT HE'S FORGOTTEN HE LOCKED THE WINDOW	**6** **CONCLUSION** ZAPPP!

In Panel 1, we'll set the scene: Dracula has returned from a night of feasting to his castle in Transylvania, and he's looking forward to a nice day of rest.

In Panel 2 there's a problem—he's lost the keys to his castle!

Panel 3 shows him realizing that the sun is about to rise, which always means death to him and his kind unless they're safely stashed away in the dark.

In Panel 4, he gets an idea—he'll simply fly up to the window and climb inside.

Panel 5: shock horror—the window is locked!

And so in Panel 6, we see Drac getting shafted by sunlight for the umpteenth time.

So, let's see how the six-part plan might be applied. To keep it interesting, we're going to use everyone's favorite Lord of the Undead, Count Dracula.

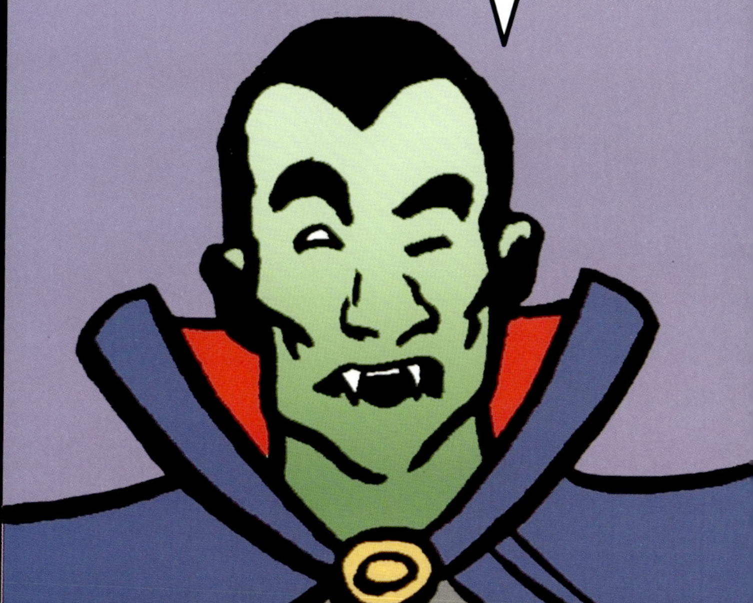

Thumbnails

Thumbnails are so called because some artists literally draw them the same size as their thumbnail. They are small, rough sketches that the artist uses to plan out a strip before committing to a final layout. There is no reason for them to have more detail or imagination put into them beyond merely getting an idea of how the panels will be laid out.

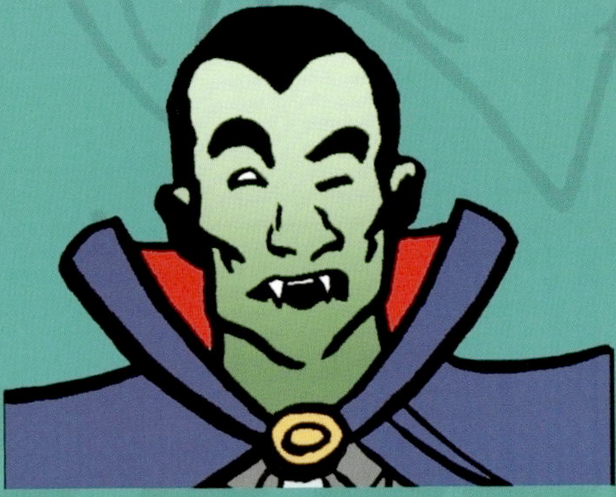

It's at the thumbnail stage that the artist decides how each panel should look in terms of content, viewpoints, and areas of dead space to leave for word balloons. Also, in our particular case, we should at this stage bear in mind the types of images available to us on the CD.

So, in the first picture, it's important that we see Dracula outside his castle; to get a decent view of the castle, he should be some way away, perhaps basking in the rewards of a good night's feeding. It's very important that the reader is aware that sunrise is not too far away, so there should be enough of the background showing to see that there is a glow on the horizon.

The problem arrives in our second panel: Dracula has lost his keys, and so can't get in to the safety of his coffin. It's important that we see the front door with a huge lock to emphasize his despair, and as we only saw Drac from the waist up in the first panel, it might be nice to show him in his entirety here. The picture on the CD of him waving his cape around might be perfect to suggest him rummaging for his keys.

We haven't had a close-up yet, so the third panel might be a nice place to see Drac's concern about the approaching dawn; however, this might mean a small amount of re-drawing to create a worried expression.

Following the six-part plan, in Panel 4, our favorite vampire gets a bright idea: he'll fly up to the window to get inside the castle. It might be possible to distort the background so that the castle seems to loom above him at this point. Also, for the situation to make sense, all other windows should be erased.

In his bat-form, the fifth panel should show Drac at the window as he remembers that he'd locked it earlier. It might be nice to try and stick a Dracula head onto the bat that comes on the CD.

Drac gets zapped by the sun as it rises, a comedy moment, but with plenty of opportunity to have fun showing him in mid-disintegration. For this purpose, he should be shown away from any object in the background.

In this instance, we're not working to a tight script. We have the six-part plan, and a decent Thumbnail rough, so it's going to be fun to save the dialogue until last. This is not without precedent: it's the way that Marvel comics were produced in the 1960s, and how many comics are created to this day.

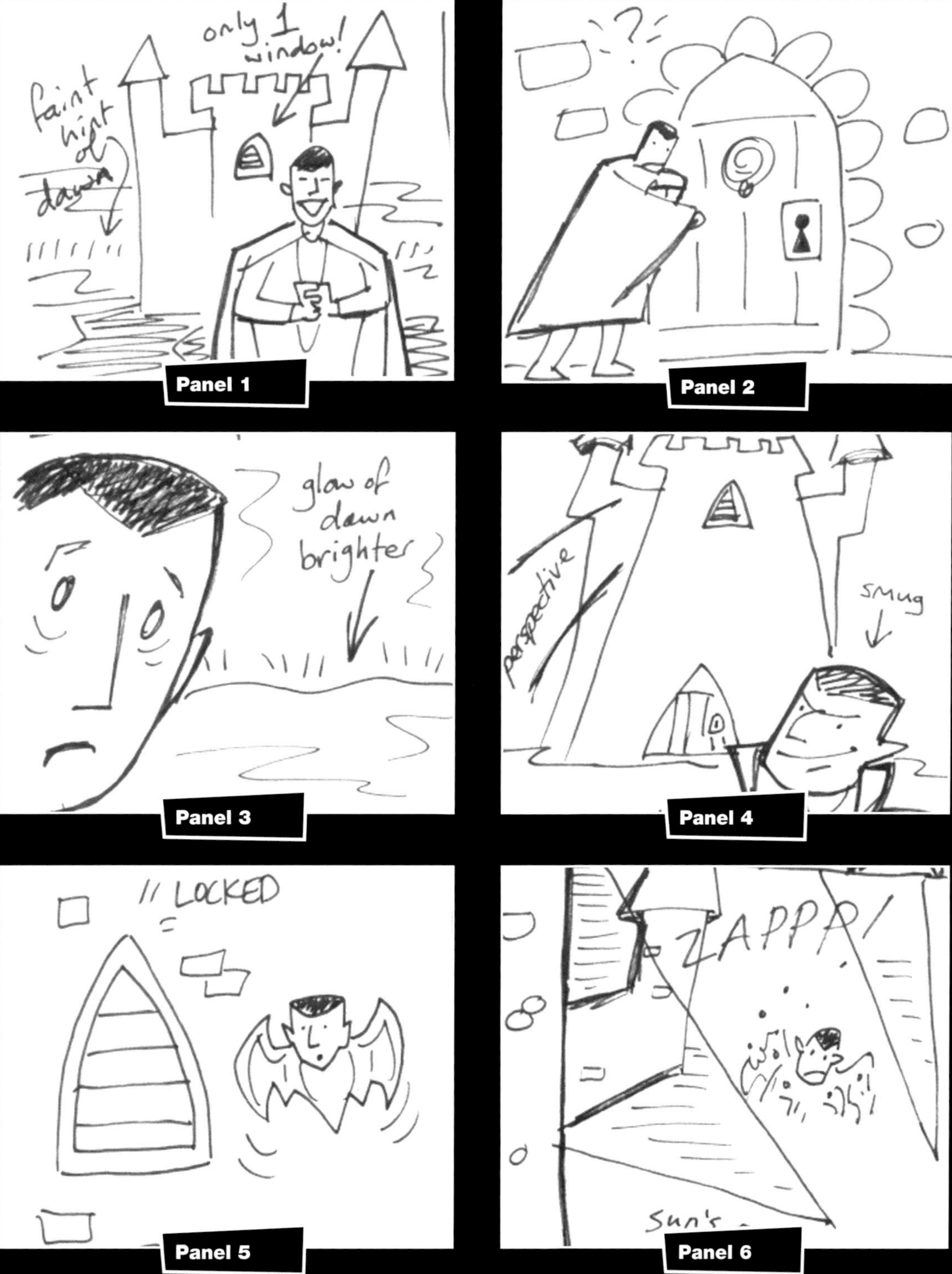

Panel 1
faint hint of dawn
only 1 window!

Panel 2
?

Panel 3
glow of dawn brighter

Panel 4
perspective
smug

Panel 5
LOCKED

Panel 6
ZAPPP!
sun's

The Process

The first step in constructing our Dracula strip should be to locate the pictures we need on the CD. We're going to use the Castle exterior, the full-frontal Dracula picture, and the one where he seems to be swirling his cloak about in a menacing way; bear in mind, though, that all our pictures are adaptable, and that their meaning can be shaped by context.

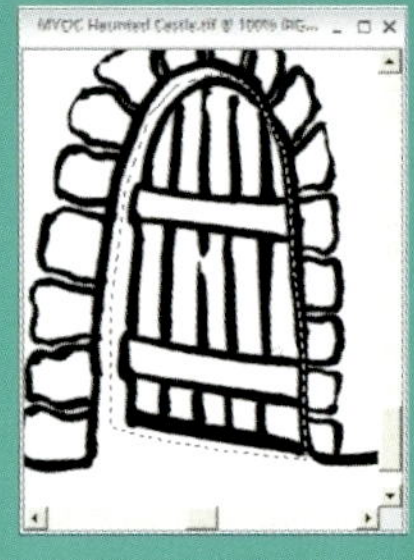

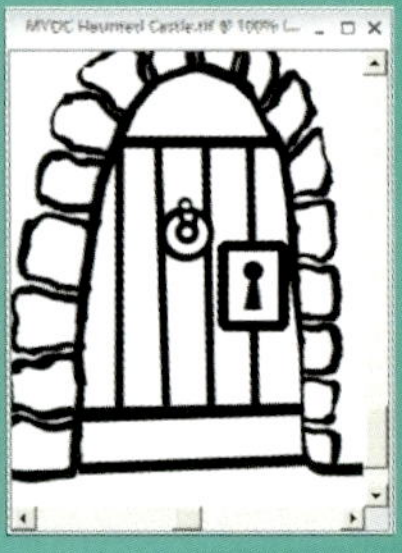

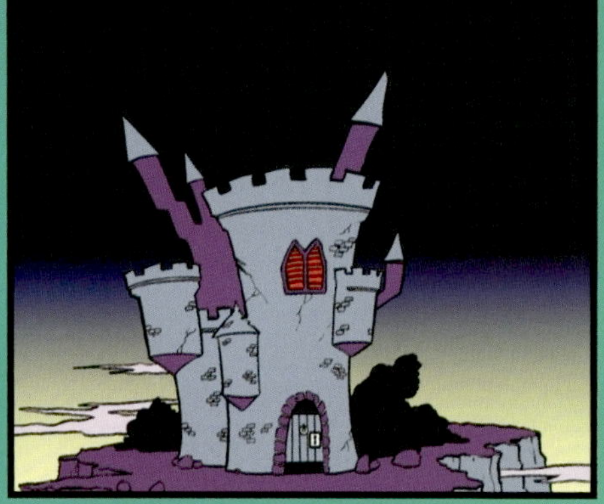

We may need to redraw certain elements to suit our purposes, such as the castle door, which needs to be closed, rather than open. This is easily accomplished by using the Lasso tool to select the doorway, fill with white, and then redraw with black.

Next, we need to color them—it's easier to move and resize pre-colored images. As you color each picture, it's worth saving it onto your hard drive or another CD.

On the Background picture, it's important to see that dawn is fast approaching, so a Gradient fill between dark blue and light yellow is used on the sky; the wispy clouds and mist are colored pink to reinforce the idea of an imminent sunrise. The castle walls and the lighter side of the cliffs are colored gray with a hint of purple, and a solid purple is used elsewhere along with the blue of the sky to harmonize the colors in the picture, giving the look of twilight.

Certain areas are made to stand out since they are important to our narrative, namely the lock on the door and the window. The other windows are painted out, giving Dracula only one to choose.

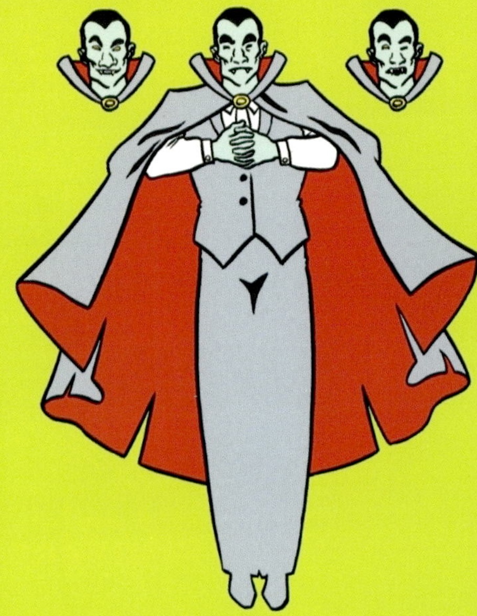

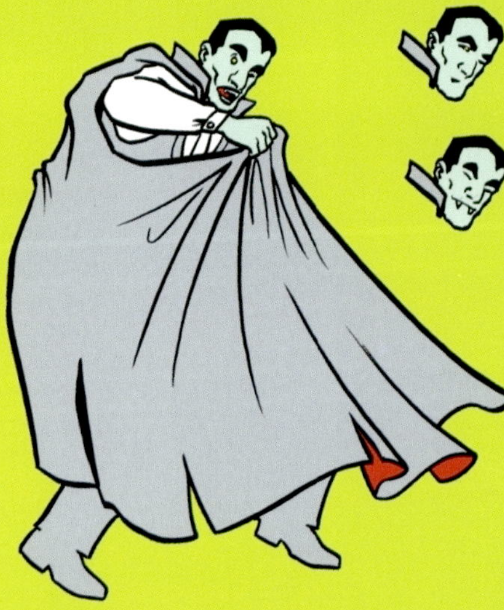

Dracula's clothing is usually colored black, but as the background is quite dark, he's been colored a lighter gray— call it "artistic license."

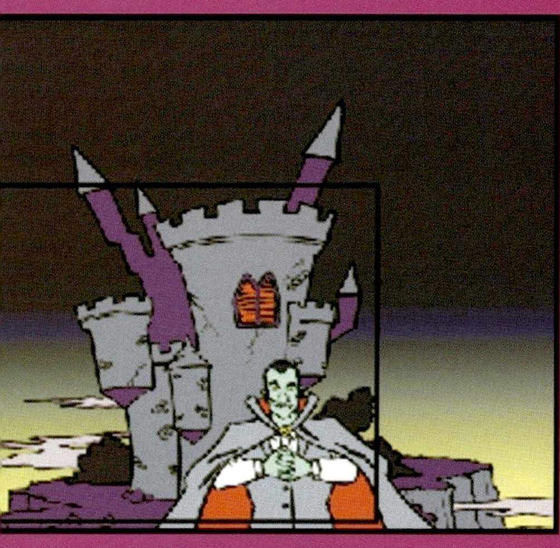

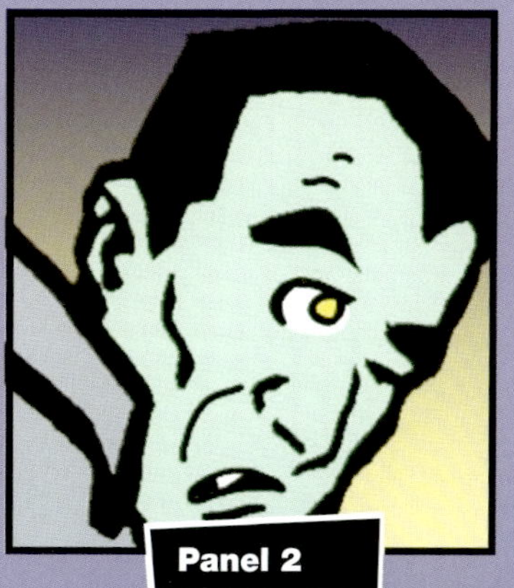

Panel 2

We then re-open the Castle background, and follow the same procedure to construct Panel 2 so that it matches our thumbnail; don't forget that you can easily shrink Dracula to fit by using the handles on the Move tool's bounding box. These are also useful for resizing the panel when you drag it onto the blank page.

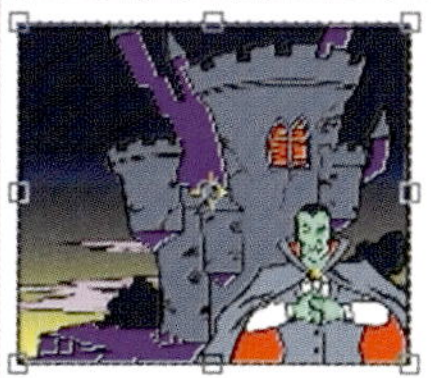

Panel 1

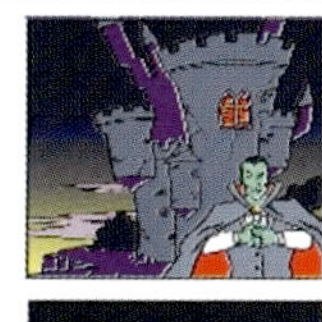
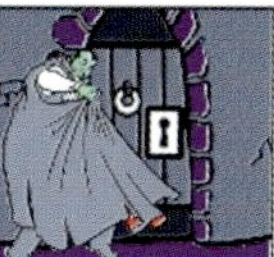
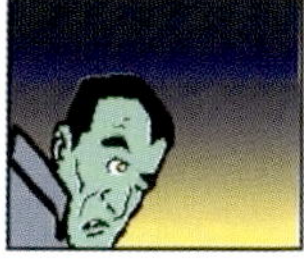

Panel 3

For our third panel, we've chosen a close-up as Dracula outlines his dilemma. For this, we can go to one of the alternate Dracula faces and do a bit of redrawing. This can then be moved onto a patch of sky on the background, framed, cropped and flattened. Filling the empty area beneath his collar with gray creates the rest of his cloak, and it can be dragged across to the blank document.

To construct our first panel, we first replace Dracula's face with the smiling one, as he's pleased to be home. Then we move him over to the background picture and place him in front of the castle. Next, we open the rectangular panel border, move it across and resize until it matches our original thumbnail idea. We can then crop the image at the panel borders to create our first frame. Either save it to use later, or, if you can't stand the excitement, open a new blank document (in this case, Letter size); then flatten the layers of your panel and drag it with the Move tool into place on the empty page.

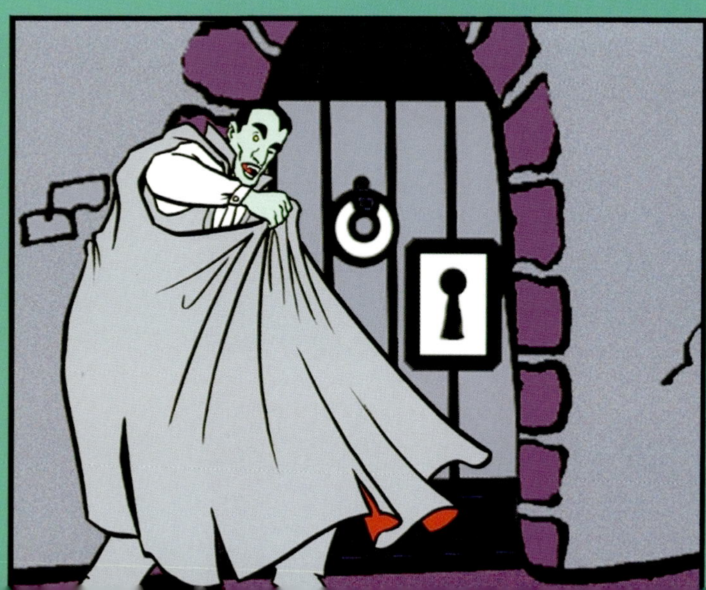

The Finish

The first three panels of our Dracula strip were fairly straightforward to accomplish. However, two of the final three might be a little more tricky.

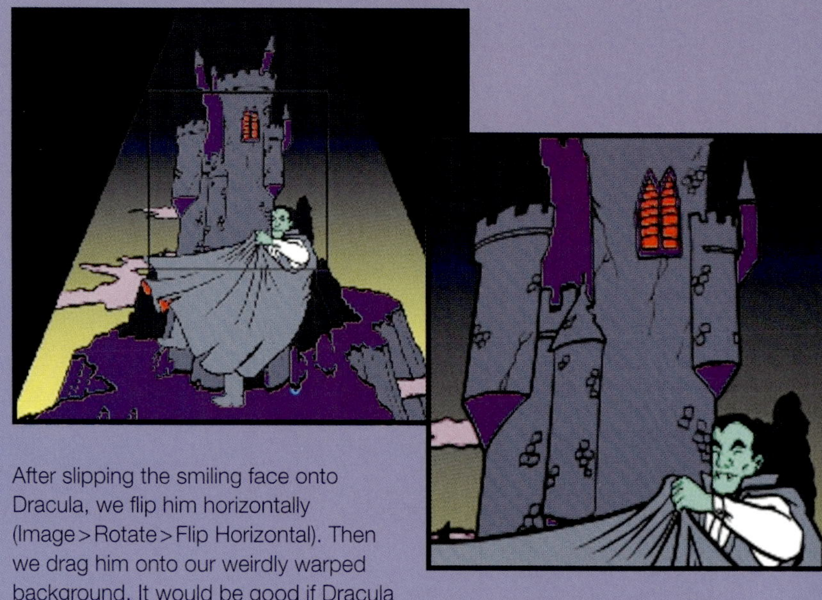

After slipping the smiling face onto Dracula, we flip him horizontally (Image > Rotate > Flip Horizontal). Then we drag him onto our weirdly warped background. It would be good if Dracula appeared to be looking up slightly, so using the bounding box-handles, we can rotate him. Placing the panel border over him in the right place will prevent him appearing to stand on one leg. Crop, flatten, and save it or move it onto our emerging comic strip page. Close and reopen the background.

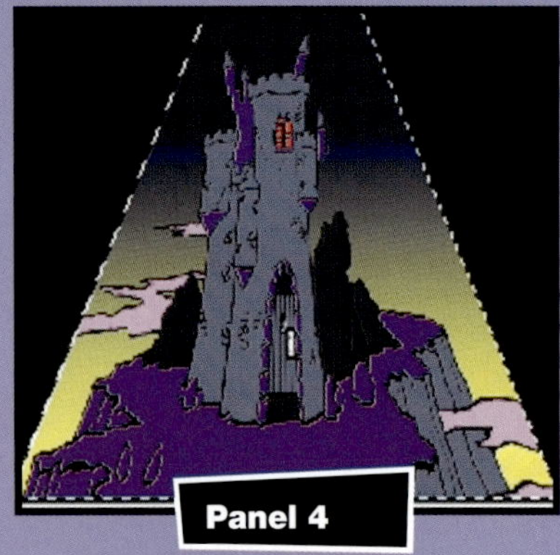

Panel 4

On our thumbnail rough for Panel 4, since this is where Dracula gets his bright idea to turn into a bat and fly up to the window, we thought it would be good to emphasize the castle's height by using a bit of perspective. To do this, we can select the whole of the Castle background picture and then go to Image > Transform > Perspective from the main Menu bar. By dragging the top handles, we can distort the whole image. The bottom of the castle looks a little odd, but we'll be cropping the picture further up.

Panel 5

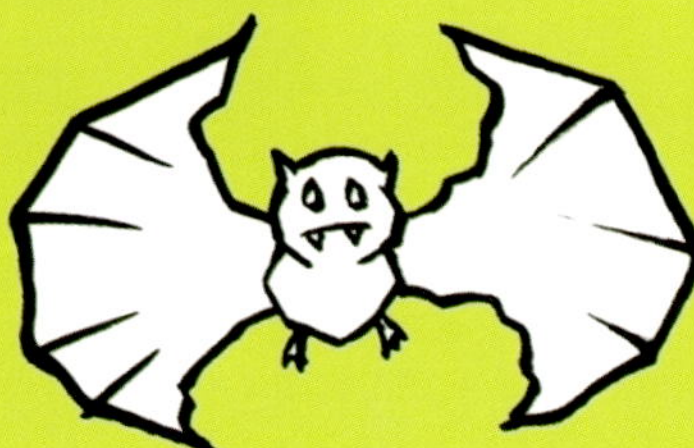

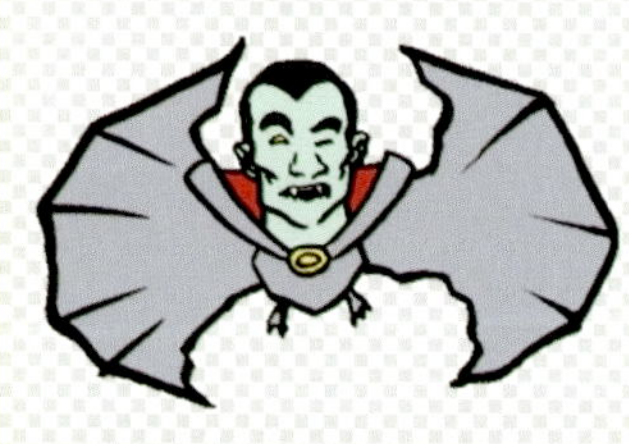

In Panel 5, Dracula needs to be seen in his bat-form. We could have just used the bat image on the CD, but it'll look funnier if the bat has Dracula's head. Open the Objects from the Horror section, and crop the bat. Drag a Dracula head over and resize until it fits neatly on the bat's shoulders.

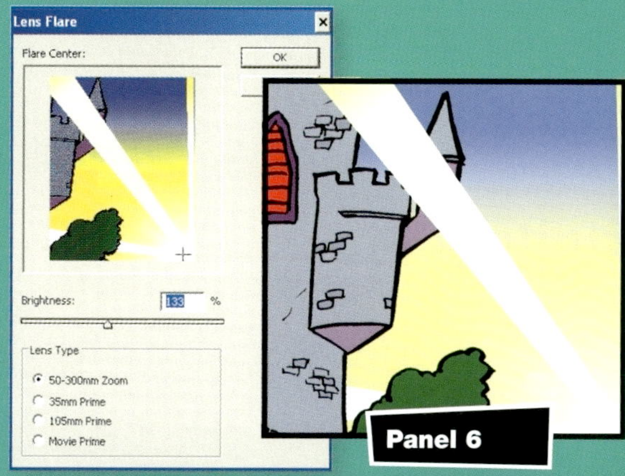

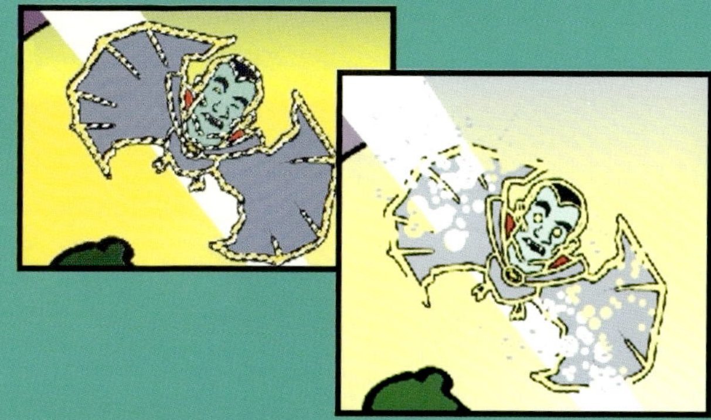

Panel 6: Sunrise! Selecting the sky on the Castle background, we can change the Gradient fill again, taking it from a nice sky-blue down to a light yellow. Next, we can add some sunbeams using the Polygonal Lasso tool to do a series of gradient fills. For extra brightness on the horizon, we select the sky and go to Filter > Render > Lens Flare, adding a flash of light where our sunbeams meet in the corner. Then we can frame and crop the image before we add the star of the show.

If we place Dracula directly in the path of the sunbeam, we should be able to go for a nice "disintegration" effect. By clicking the Magic Wand on the bat's black outline, and then going to Select > Modify and Contracting by one pixel, we can then fill with yellow. Now Dracula looks as though he's beginning to burn in the rays of the sun, but to really make him look as though he's done for (for the umpteenth time, he's sure to be back!) we can pepper him with the Eraser tool and use a tiny brush to add tiny bat-bits. A slightly more surprised look to the eyes completes his gruesome and hilarious demise.

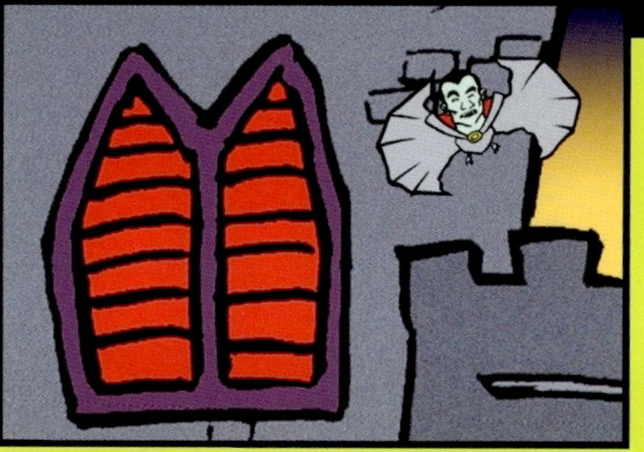

Over at the Layers palette, ensure that the head layer is above the bat layer, and then turn off the "eyeball" for every layer except those two. Then go to Layer > Merge Visible, and our batty vampire is ready to be moved onto the panel, which needs to be a close-up of the windows.

We've added a Noise filter to the castle walls to make them look grainy, and to help the bat stand out. Also, notice that the sky's Gradient fill has been altered to show a stronger glow from the encroaching sun.

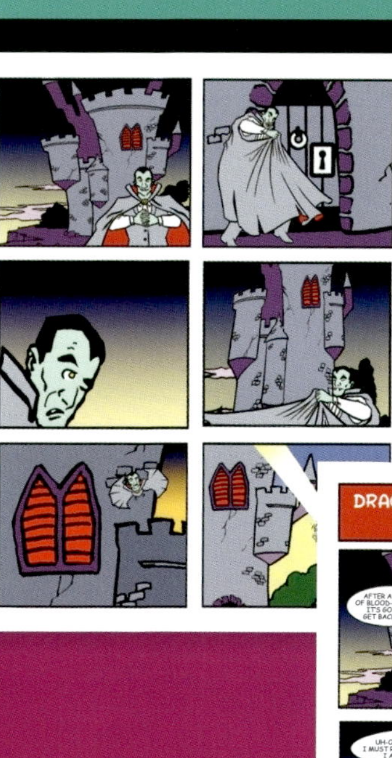

With all of our panels now in place on the page, all we need to do is enjoy writing the dialogue, add a sound effect, and furnish the strip with a title at the top of the page.

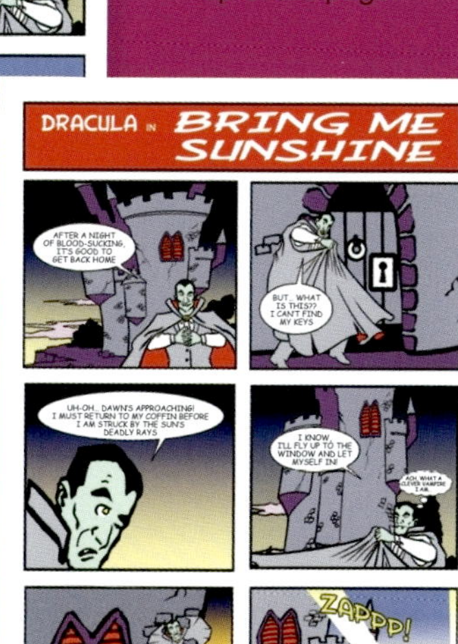

5 "If This Be My Density"

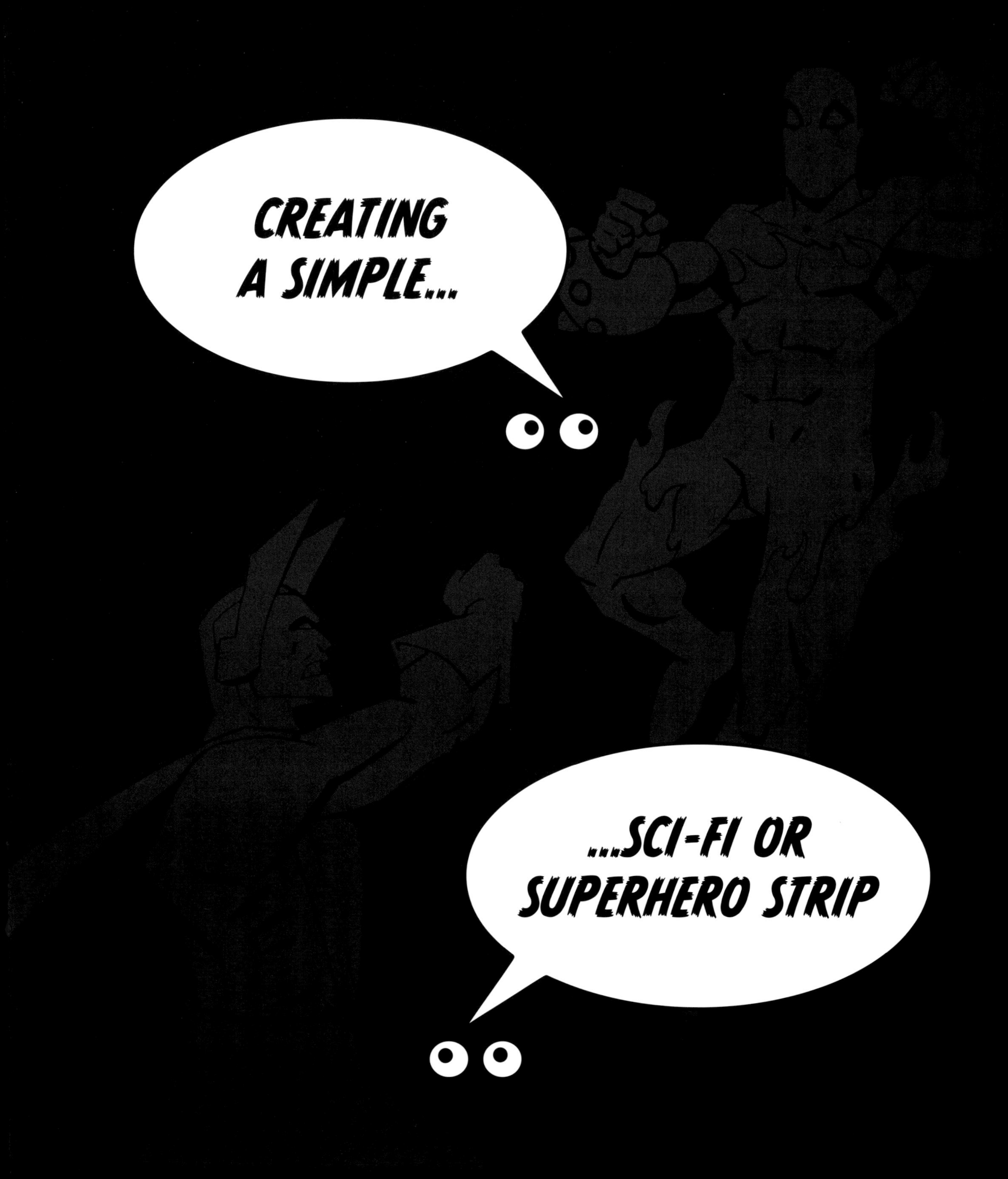

CREATING A SIMPLE...
...SCI-FI OR SUPERHERO STRIP

Sample Script

For each of these projects, we're going to use our six-panel plan to come up with the ideas, and to pace the story out across the page.

So, let's meet our heroes: a chap with an outfit displaying a fiery motif might be named after anything to do with light and heat. "The Human Torch" has, sadly, been used already; and "Fire Man" brings to mind a guy in a yellow helmet and waterproof clothes. So, let's go with "Solarman." Our female character has no particularly defining costume details, so let's make her a fairly generic "Wonder Woman"-type of character. We'll call her "Ultra-Girl." As for our villain, he is again fairly neutral; but as we all have an instinctive distrust of the medical profession, he can be "Dr. Devious."

In Panel One, we need to set the scene: our heroes arrive at the city to see what's going on; perhaps they were alerted by a signal, or a phone call to a "hotline," or maybe they were just tuned into CNN. Whatever, they are here to help. The problem is that Dr. Devious has grown to colossal size and is jeopardizing the city. As a result, Solarman flies in to try to bring the big guy down. Our fourth panel should show the arrival of a solution to the dilemma, but let's up the stakes a little: Solarman is grabbed by the villain, who proceeds to squeeze the life out of him. In the same panel, though, we can also show that help is at hand, as Ultra-Girl flies into view. Ultra-Girl uses her zappy powers to clobber Dr. Devious, our "Solution Attempted." Does it work? Well, yes… but it might be fun to show that Solarman has suffered a nasty side-effect from being grabbed so tightly. He's actually been squeezed in the middle as though he were made of modeling clay; our heroes win the day, but we have a fun, memorable image to leave the reader.

Okay, this script isn't going to win any awards for Best Graphic Novel, but what it does is allow us to have a bit of fun with the characters. By completely changing the scale of the villain, we have more possibilities for a couple of interesting panels than if it were just a typical superhero slug-fest. Also, it can be fun to subvert the clichés of the genre, by here having the female character come to the rescue of the male, and for him to end up in a comedy predicament. It's a bit of a nod to the wonderful old *Plastic Man* comics by Jack Cole.

The opportunity immediately presents itself to combine the first and second panels into one big establishing shot, having the heroes arrive to see the problem. As this would leave us with only four remaining panels, it might be possible to make one or two of them larger than the rest, to provide a bit of variety in the layout. We'll decide this at the Thumbnail stage.

So, let's give ourselves some directions and dialogue, and perhaps a little thought to the pictures available on the CD.

Panel 1

Background: A cityscape at sunset. Dr. Devious towers above the buildings like a 2,000-foot giant. Close up to us in the foreground, Solarman and Ultra-Girl have just arrived on the scene.
SM: **Holy Cow!**
UG: **In his giant size, Dr. Devious could destroy the city! He must be stopped!!**

Panel 2

Solarman swoops through the sky to take on Dr. Devious, who reaches out for him as he flies past.
SM: **Okay, Devious...**
DD: **Bah! I'll crush you like the gnat you are!**

Panel 3

Dr. Devious has grabbed Solarman and is squeezing the life from him. Ultra-Girl is flying to the rescue.
SM: **Agh! He's got me... Squeezing... uuugh...**
UG: **Hang on, Solarman!**

Panel 4

Ultra-Girl zaps Dr. Devious on the jaw with the ultra-rays that emanate from her hands. Dr. Devious is stunned by this unexpected attack.
UG: **Pick on someone your own size!**

Panel 5

In the background, we can see Dr. Devious' foot, showing that he's lying on the ground, defeated. Ultra-Girl is descending from the sky. In front of them, Solarman is standing, dazed and confused – his torso has been squashed in the middle like an old toothpaste tube from the grip of Dr. Devious.
UG: **Are you okay?**
SM: **Uh... No! Did we win??**

All of the above should be achievable with our images, except for the cityscape. However, a basic "city" shape should suffice, which we can use our uncanny artistic abilities—and Photoshop's Line tool—to construct from scratch.

Thumbnails

Our first panel is going to be a "double," taking up the whole top tier of the page. A gigantic Dr. Devious (or, to his patients, "It's pronounced Dev-eye-ous!") towers above the city in the background. As the probability is that, to emphasize his size, our heroes might well appear a little small in many panels, it might be nice to give them a close-up here. In the second panel, Solarman swoops into action, and we can clearly see that Devious is way larger than his antagonist, who really does seem like a firefly in comparison. The third panel is a close-up of Solarman caught in Dr. Devious' fist; Ultra-Girl is on her way, but it might be nice if she appears in silhouette against the sky, so that the focus is on our hero's predicament. In the fourth panel, she should come into her own, bravely zapping the villain right in the face; his face should appear huge in comparison, again emphasizing the size of his threat. Our last panel has Solarman against the backdrop of their downed foe, whose darker colors should help Solarman's now-distorted form to show clearly. Ultra-Girl, who has really saved the day, is framed by an empty background.

Examining the Thumbnail, the opportunities for a bit of panel variation presents itself. Panels three and four could be made a little larger without altering the essential layout of the other panels. This would give a bit more "oomph" to Solarman getting crushed, and to Ultra-Girl's revenge. Part of the point and purpose of doing thumbnails is so that you can sit back and make these decisions before any of the hard work has been done.

It doesn't hurt to get ideas for layouts from the genius of artists that have gone before. While single-page superhero strips are rarely seen in mainstream comics these days, back in the mid-20th Century, American Sunday newspapers often ran a one-page color strip of Flash Gordon, Superman, The Phantom, and their ilk. These days, you'll find these online or in book collections, and the work of those old craftsmen still displays a lot that can be learned in our digital age.

Older readers might remember the single-page comic-strip advertisements in '70s comics for fruit pies, in which famous superheroes would immediately find themselves in a jam, and sort the situation out by enticing the villain with flaky pastry and a fruit filling. Similar novelties survive on bus stop posters and ads on trains for airconditioning units, or whatever.

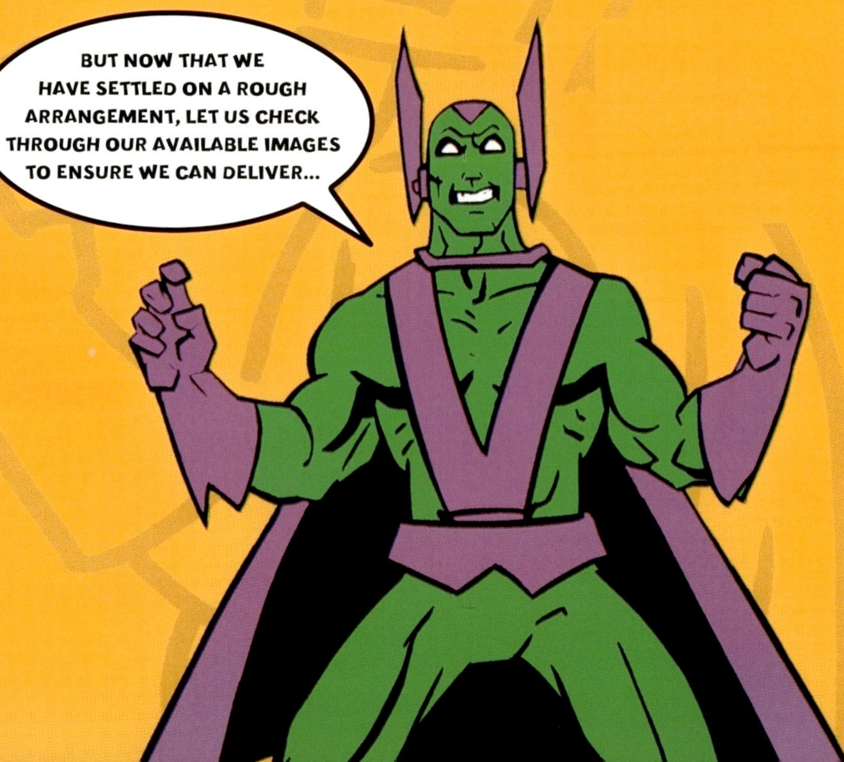

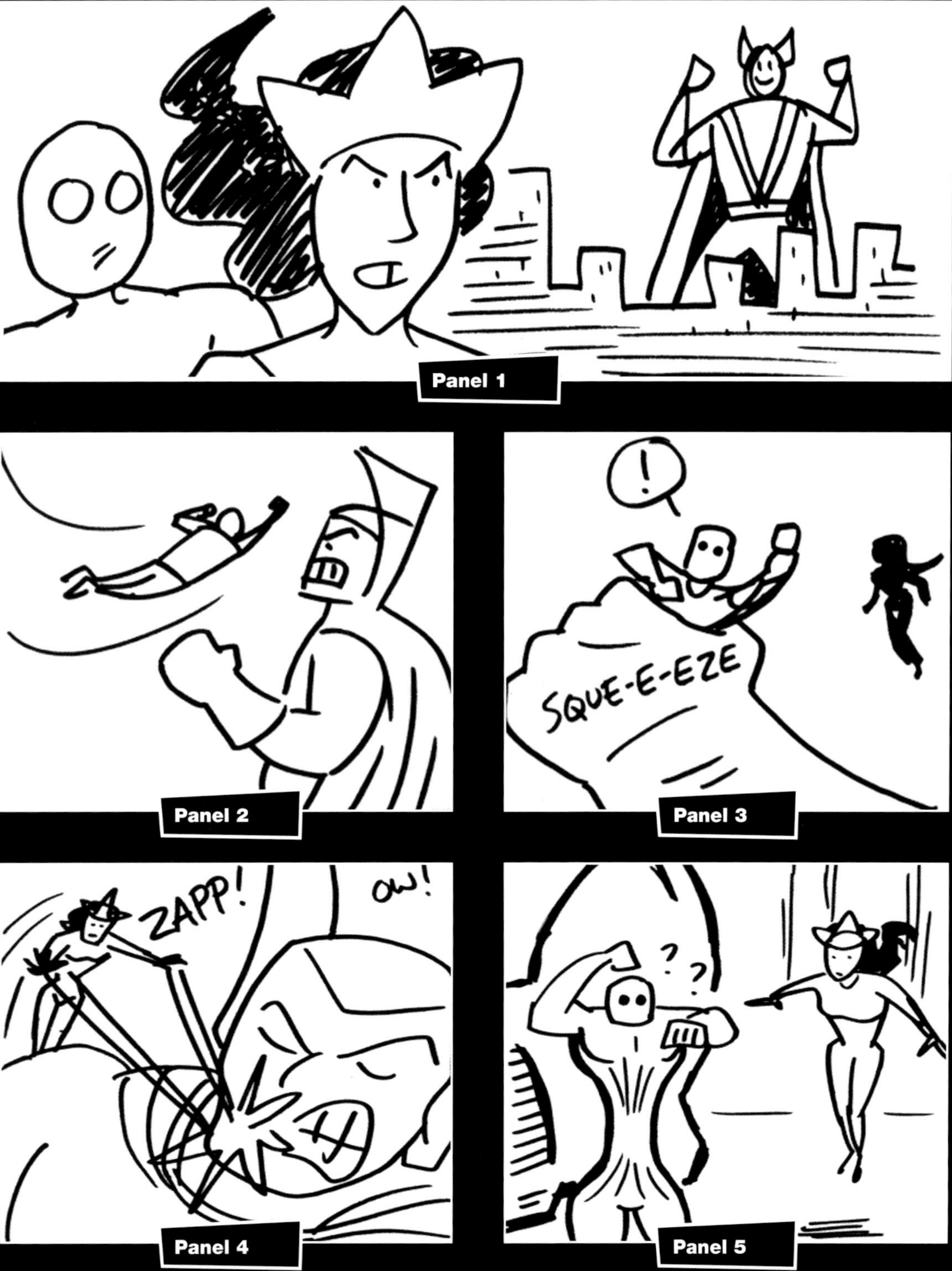

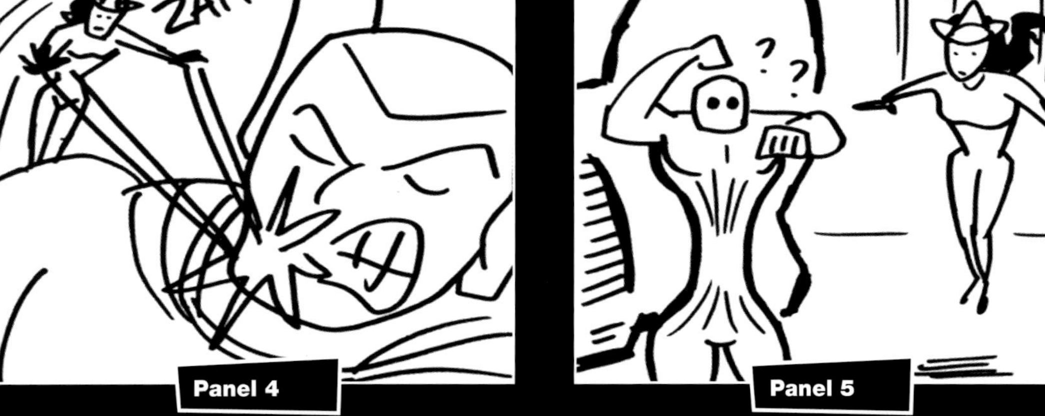

Panel 1

Panel 2

Panel 3

Choosing Pictures from CD

For our first panel, we'll be creating a cityscape background from scratch, and for the rest we'll probably just have a plain-colored sky so that the heroes, and the action, stand out visually. Therefore, this time we won't be using any of the pre-drawn backgrounds—let's live dangerously!

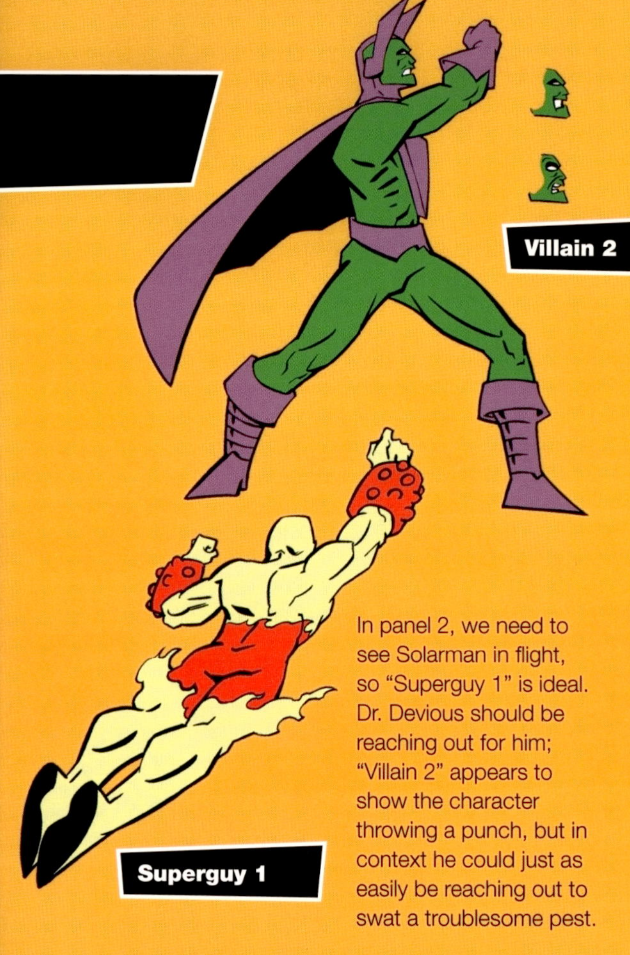

Villain 2

Superguy 1

Dr. Devious needs to be towering triumphantly above the city, and so "Villain 1" seems to fit the bill. We want full-frontal pictures of Solarman and Ultra-Girl, and they don't need to be doing anything specific—taking a head and shoulders portion of "Superguy 2" and "Superwoman 3" should give us what we need. These pictures should also be useful for panels 4 and 5.

In panel 2, we need to see Solarman in flight, so "Superguy 1" is ideal. Dr. Devious should be reaching out for him; "Villain 2" appears to show the character throwing a punch, but in context he could just as easily be reaching out to swat a troublesome pest.

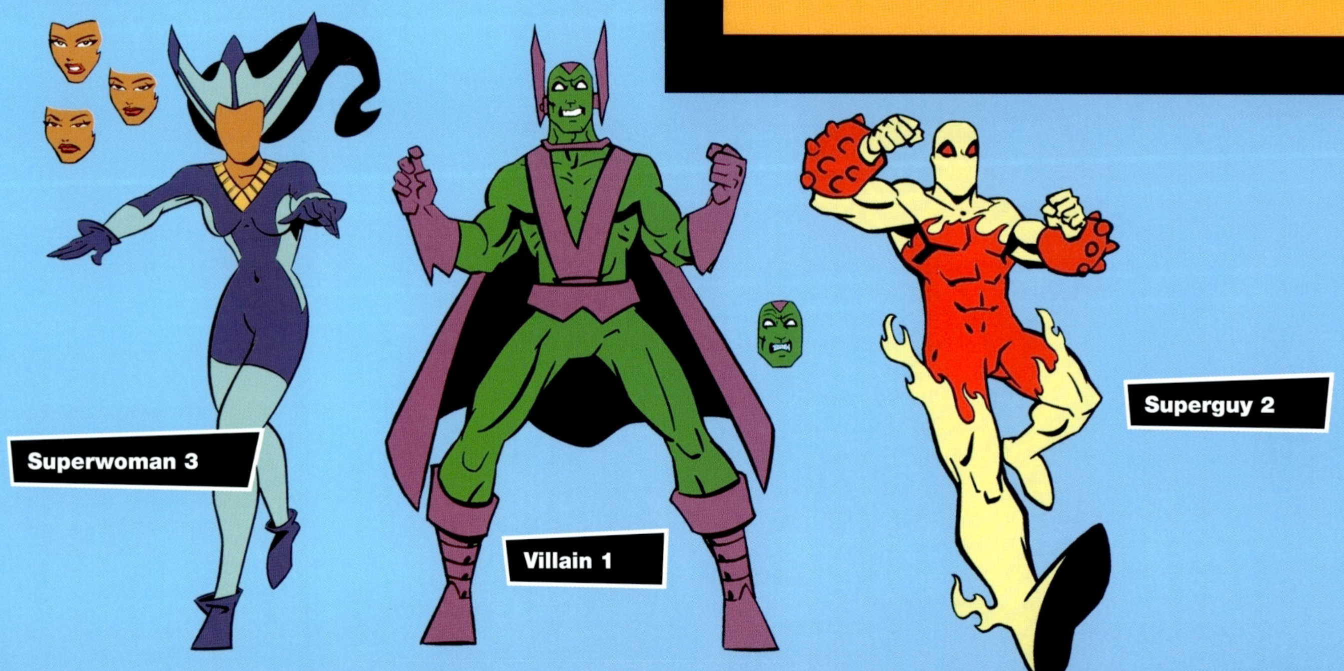

Superwoman 3

Villain 1

Superguy 2

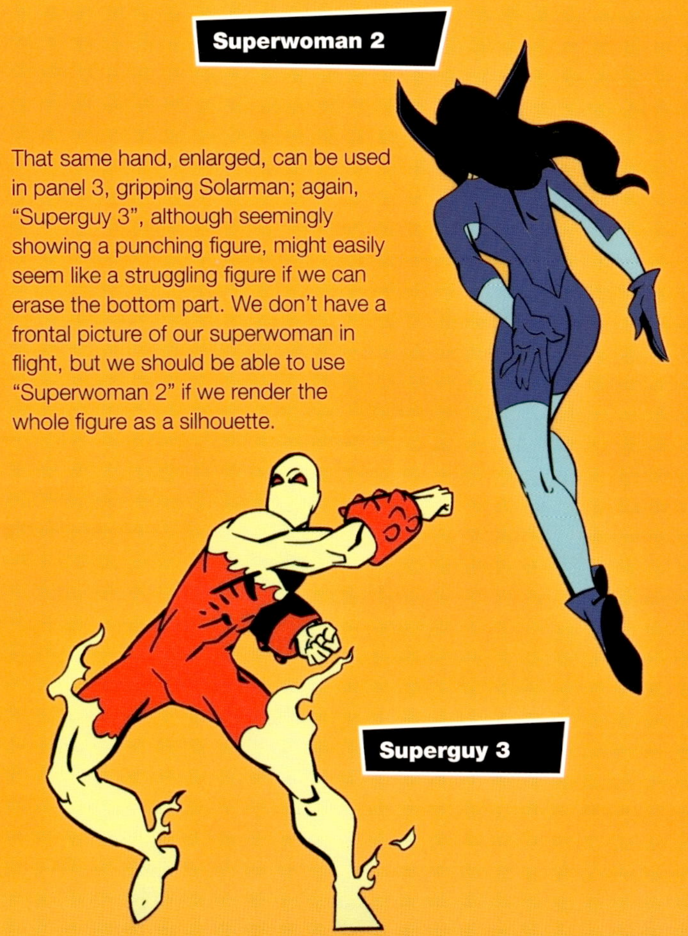

That same hand, enlarged, can be used in panel 3, gripping Solarman; again, "Superguy 3", although seemingly showing a punching figure, might easily seem like a struggling figure if we can erase the bottom part. We don't have a frontal picture of our superwoman in flight, but we should be able to use "Superwoman 2" if we render the whole figure as a silhouette.

The head and shoulders of "Villain 3" will be perfect for our view of Devious getting blasted in panel 4, and the boot of the same figure, cropped and enlarged, will be suitable for the prostrate villain in panel 5 (as opposed to the prostrate villain, who can't be with us because he's in the bathroom).

The squeezed-out Solarman in panel 5 could feasibly be achieved from any of the pictures, but since it was "Superguy 2" we had in mind at the Thumbnail stage—giving the best overall frontal view of the character—let's stick with that one.

So, having decided to use these pictures for our strip, we need to color them. This is going to need a little forethought—we don't want the colors to blend in with those of other characters, or of the background.

Back at the scripting stage, we decided that the scene should be lit as though it was approaching sunset. This wasn't an arbitrary decision—a fiery sky might appear to be more dramatic than the clear blue sky of a lovely summer day. However, the pattern of Superguy's costume dictates that he should be decked out in fiery colors—how can we ensure that he will stand out from the background? Perhaps by giving him contrasting tones, a very light yellow and a deep, rich red; that way, if the sky and the city are rendered in orange and brown, he should appear at once lighter and darker than the background, and not get lost within the picture.

Blue is the contrasting color to orange, so it makes sense to give Ultra-Girl a two-tone blue outfit. While Superguy's outfit completely obscures his features, we can see Superwoman's face, giving us a choice of skin tone when she becomes Ultra-Girl. Making her a black woman might cause problems with her dark skin being too close in tone to the orange sky, but framing her face with black hair will act as a color barrier.

We need Dr. Devious to be as distinct from the heroes as from the background. The only primary color we've yet to use is green, and a dark green will have enough of a blue cast to it for him to stand out from all other elements of our pictures. Purple accessories are the "in thing" at all of the Super-villain catwalk shows this summer.

Having chosen our characters' colors with care, we can now attempt to assemble our page, using the Thumbnails as a guide.

Assembling Page

Before assembling the panels for our page of artwork, it can be very useful to work out a set of measurements for each horizontal row, or "tier" of panels. This is dependent on the size of the finished page; we are using Letter paper, which measures 8½ × 11 in (similar to the European A4). Allowing for a ½ in (13 mm) border between the panels and the edge of the page, a width of 7 in (180 mm) for each tier should suffice: this means that, no matter how many panels we choose to use, their total size including the empty spaces between them should not amount to more than 7 in (180 mm).

The height of each panel depends on how many tiers we will place on the page, and whether we wish to add a title block at the top. Since this is our intention, complicated mathematics tells us that 3 in (77 mm) will work well, allowing for a ½ in (15 mm) border along the bottom of the page, the spaces between tiers, and a fair amount for a title block. So, our panels will always be 3 in (77 mm) high, and anything up to 7 in (180 mm) wide. Since our first panel takes up the whole first tier, these are the first measurements we'll use.

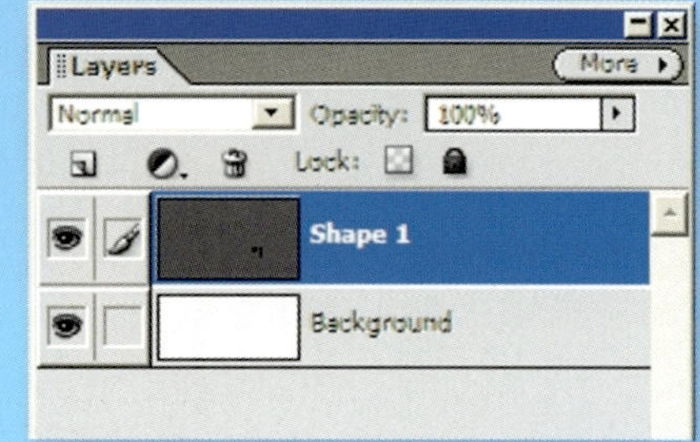

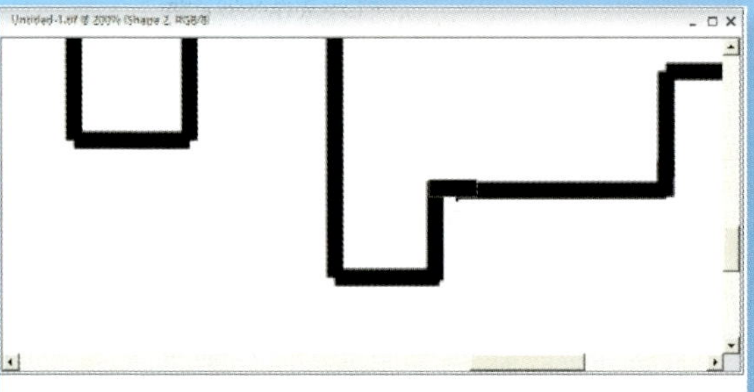

Open a new blank document 3 × 7 in (180 × 77 mm), and ensure the pixels/inch matches the pictures we're going to use. Then, choose the Line tool and draw the outline of buildings right across the panel. Each time you use the Line tool, it will appear in a new layer above the Background in the Layers palette, so when you've finished, go to Layer > Flatten Image at the top Menu bar.

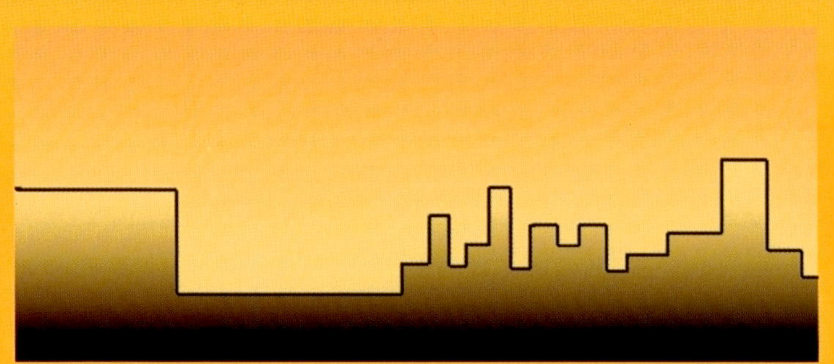

Select the sky with the Magic Wand, and then use the Gradient tool to fill it with a blend from orange to golden yellow; this gives us a nice "sunset" effect. Next, fill the lower part of the panel with a gradient from golden yellow to black. Almost instantly, we have a hazy cityscape to use as our background. Now for something we're going to save until a little later: select the sky with the Magic Wand, and go to Select > Save Selection at the top. You can name the selection "Sky." Next, deselect it—we'll come back to it in a moment.

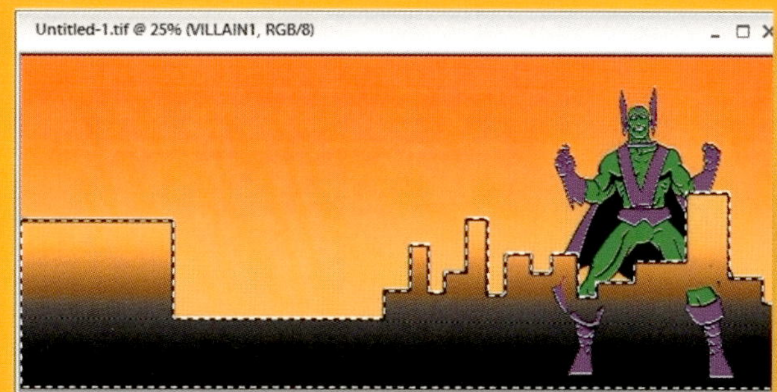

We need to see Dr. Devious towering above the city. Simply dragging the figure we've chosen across to the panel with the Move tool won't work, because the image will be huge and too unwieldy to resize with the bounding box. Instead, go to Image > Resize at the Menu bar and reduce the size of Devious until you can drag him neatly into the picture. Making sure that his layer is highlighted in the Layers palette, go back to Select at the top, and choose Load Selection. This will enable us to reselect the sky, but we need to then choose Inverse from the Select menu. Now the area of the buildings and their linework are selected, but on Dr. Devious' layer. This means we can now erase all the parts of his figure that should be obscured by the city's tower blocks.

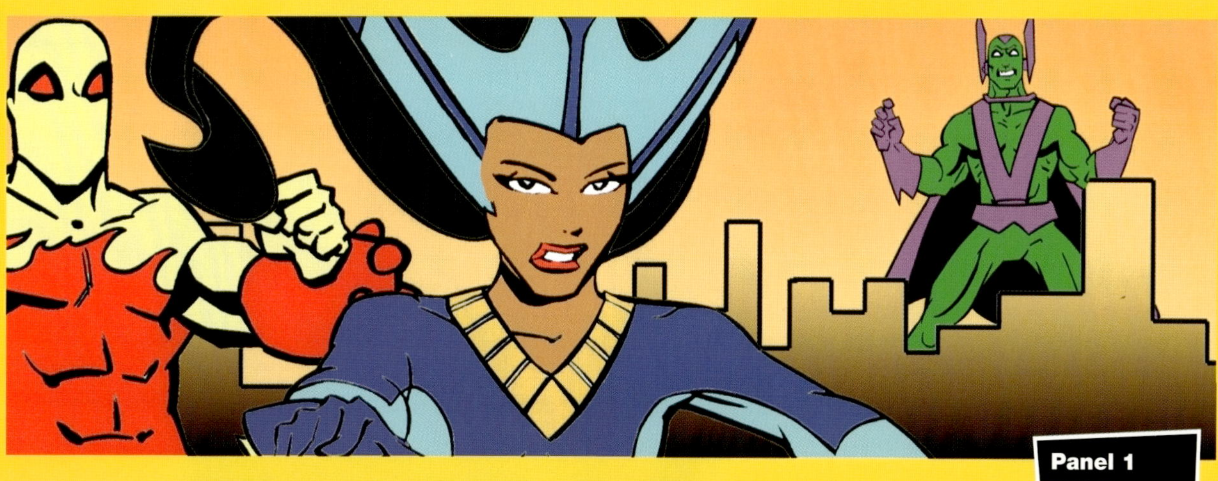

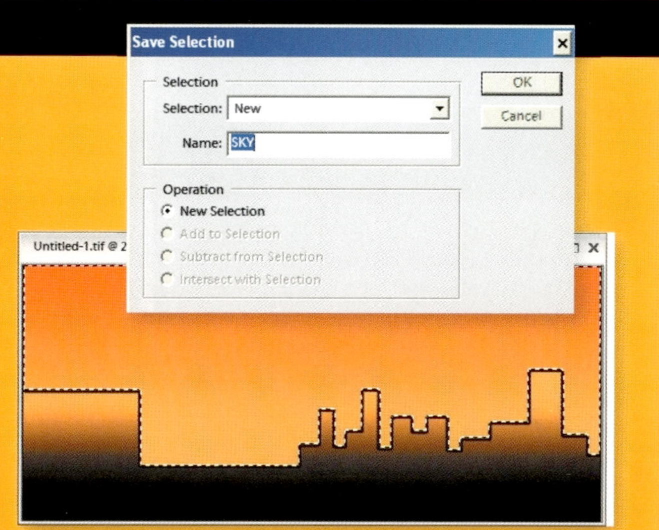

To finish the panel, we drag across our heroes and flatten the image. A black border can be added by going to Select > All, Edit > Stroke, and choose the "Inside" location. Save as "Panel 1."

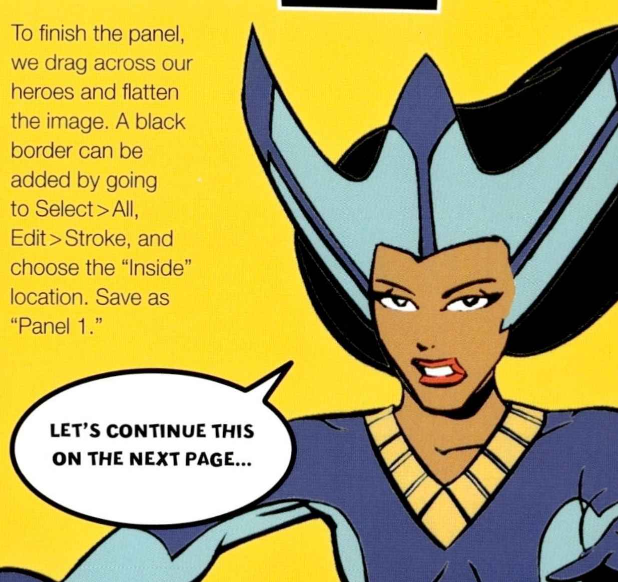

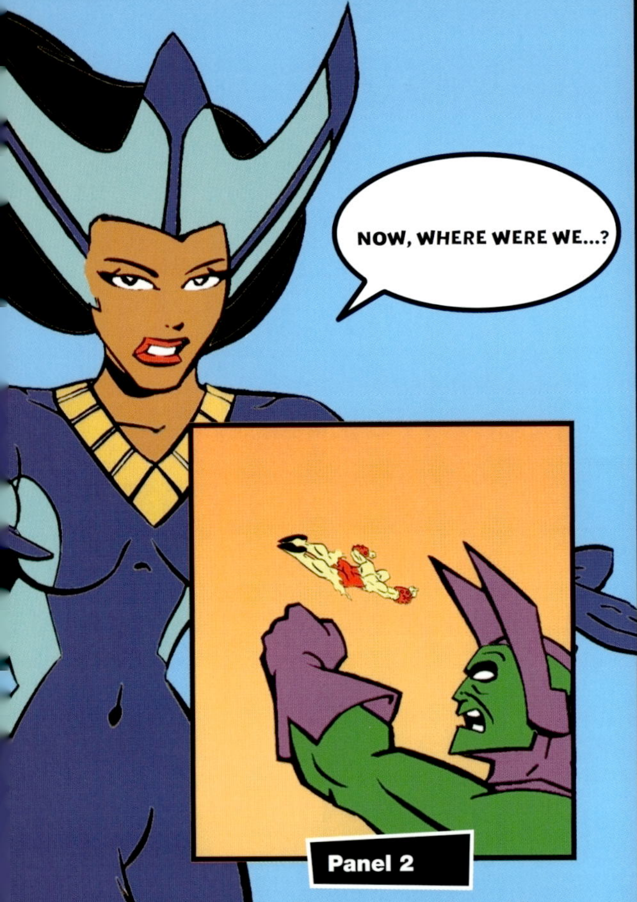

Panel 2

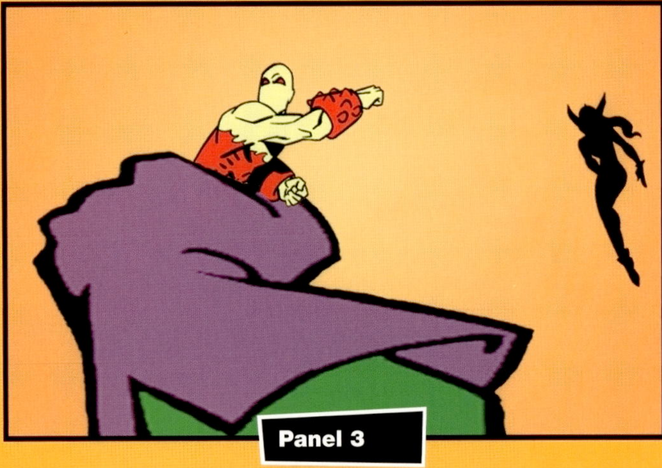

Panel 3

For panel three, we resize Devious and drag him across so that just his hand reaches into the panel. We then use the same "select-save-invert-erase" trick that we used in panel 1 to make it look as though Solarman is gripped by a giant hand. To create a silhouette, Ultra-Girl is filled with black, resized, and dragged into position.

Bearing in mind that, at the Thumbnail stage, we decided to try to make a couple of the "action" panels larger than the rest, we're going to allow more space on our second tier for panel 3 than for panel 2. If we create a new blank document for panel 2 at 2¾ × 3 in (70 × 77 mm), then panel 3 can be a healthy 4 in (105 mm) wide, allowing for a ¼ in (5 mm) gap between panels.

Compared to panel 1, our second panel is a lot easier to construct. Fill the background with a gradient from orange to a slightly lighter tone, and then drag Dr. Devious across and into position. Resize Solarman and drag him into place, using the bounding-box handles to rotate him into the correct position.

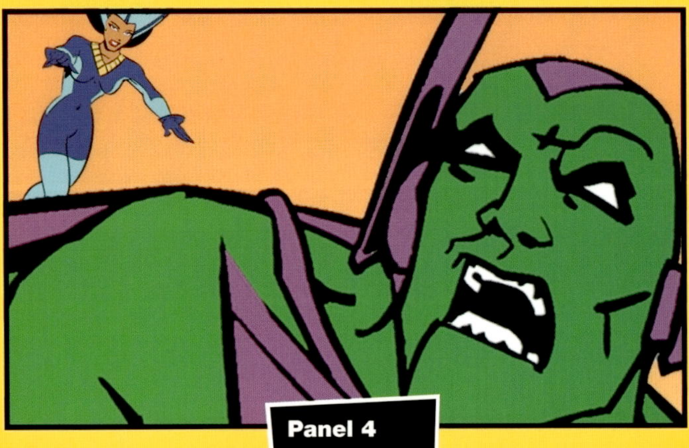

Panel 4

In panel 4, we again want to use a little more space for this explosive image: a close-up of Dr. Devious' face as he gets zapped by Ultra-Girl. She should be positioned first, so we can then enlarge Devious and drag him into place till he slightly overlaps Ultra-Girl, as though she's flying over his shoulder. At the moment, she just appears to be waving at him, but we're going to add some zappy rays later.

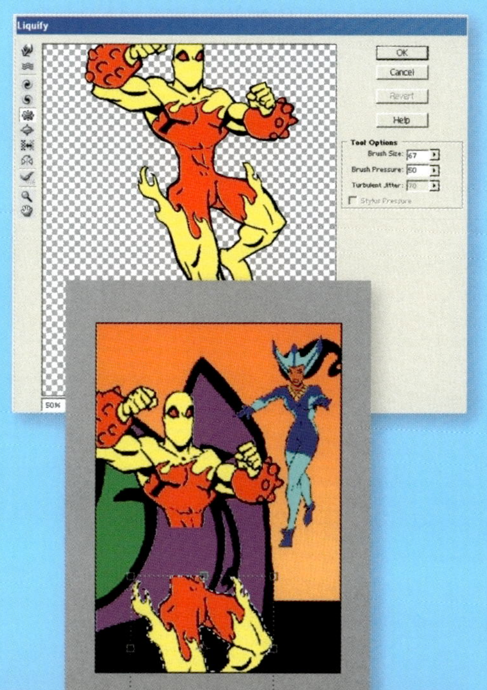

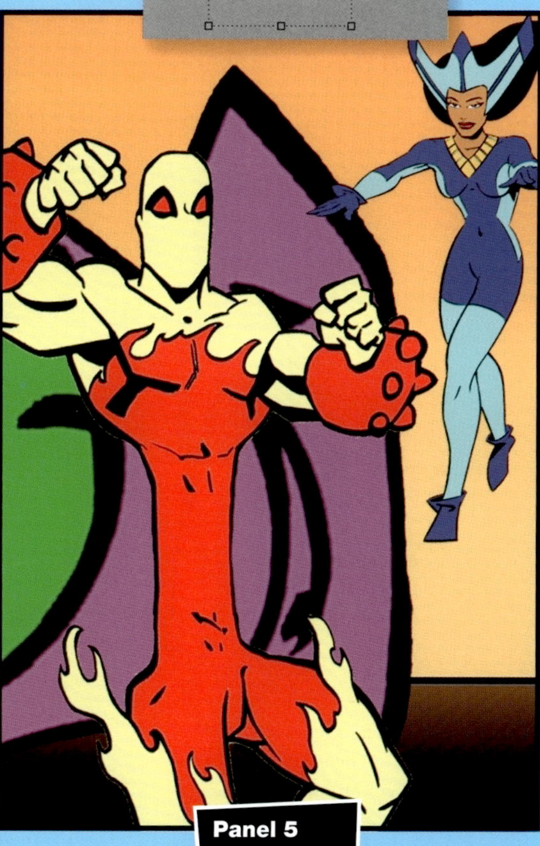

Panel 5

The background of panel 5 needs a division between the ground and the sky, easily achieved with the Line and Gradient tools. We should also see the leg of the defeated villain, which we can attempt by cropping off his foot in the original image, resizing, dragging across, and rotating. The "money-shot" here is Solarman's distorted torso, for which we are going to need Liquify in the Filters menu (Filter > Distort > Liquify). Liquify comes with its own set of tools, from which we select "Pucker."

Choosing a large-ish brush size, clicking on Solarman's outline in the preview window, and you'll see that it squeezes inwards. Working at either side of his midriff, he ends up looking as though he's wearing a tight corset. Click OK, and drag him into position on the panel. To get him really looking squeezed out, we can use the Rectangular Marquee tool to select the area around the lower part of his torso, and use the Move tool to drag it down, creating a gap that we can fill with the Paintbrush. Now he really does look as though he's been squeezed by a giant hand.

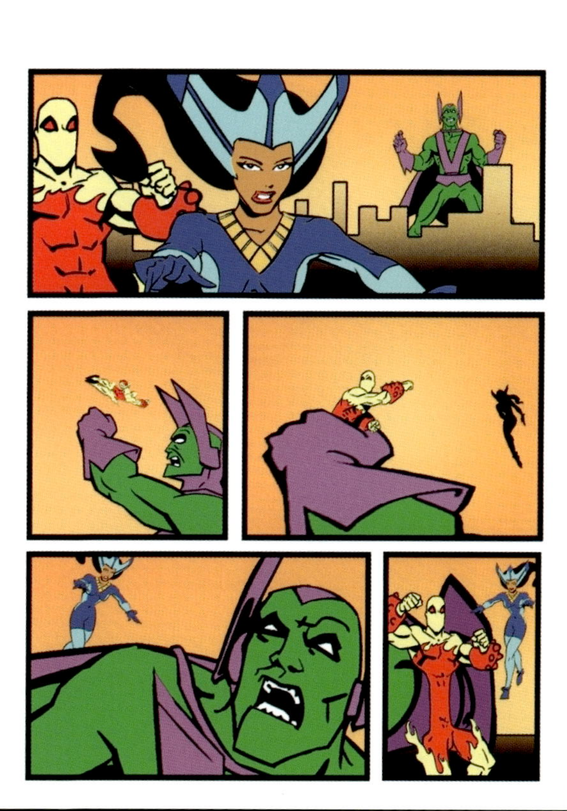

With all panels completed and their layers flattened, open a new, blank, letter-size document and use the Move tool to position them all neatly on the page.

Adding Text & Balloons

Some people prefer to add their text before the panels are assembled as a page, and there's no reason why you can't do it this way. However, adding the text once the page is completed allows you to more readily gauge whether it will be legible should the finished page need to be reduced in size for publication or display.

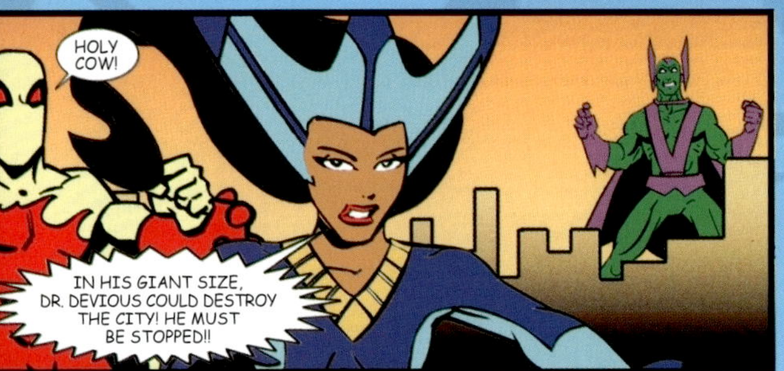

As we have already covered the rudiments of word balloon construction, let's examine some other important points to keep in mind. Also, for those readers who always wanted to make contact with Ultra-Girl, here's your chance.

The placement of balloons within each panel can be an area where novice creators consistently fall down, so we will be paying considerable attention to this aspect.

In panel 1, we certainly don't want to obscure the view of Dr. Devious standing astride the city, so the temptation might be to keep the word balloons over to the left. However, this makes the left-hand side of the panel incredibly "busy," a confusing amalgam of shapes. At the same time, the lower right of the panel looks bare and empty, as though we were too lazy to draw in any more city details—which is a fair point(!).

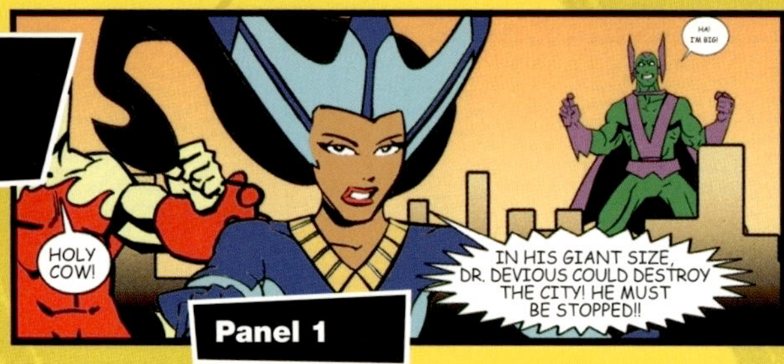

A better solution is to have Ultra-Girl's balloon in the lower right-hand side, and to bring down Solarman's. Now their side of the picture has a clearer arrangement, and Ultra-Girl's balloon covers the dead space on the right, leaving the reader's imagination to conjure what might lie behind.

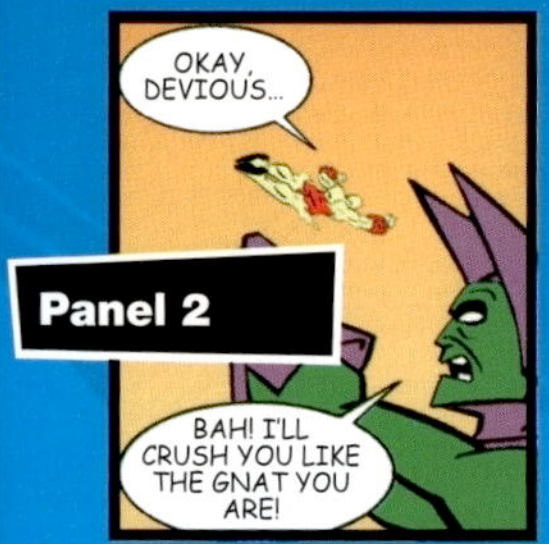

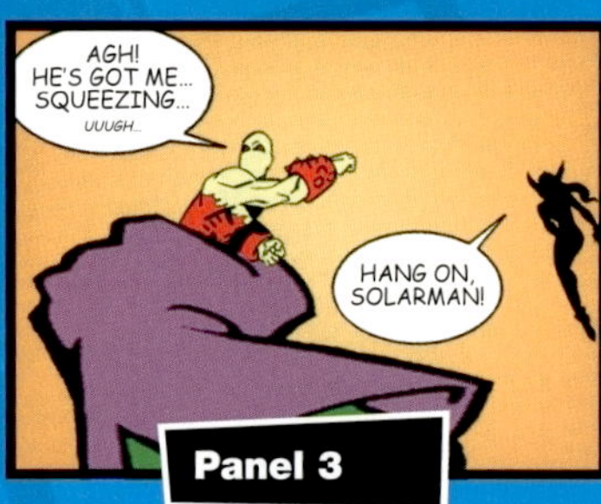

Panels 2 and 3 are no-brainers, really; there is plenty of empty space in which to place the text and balloons out of the way of the action.

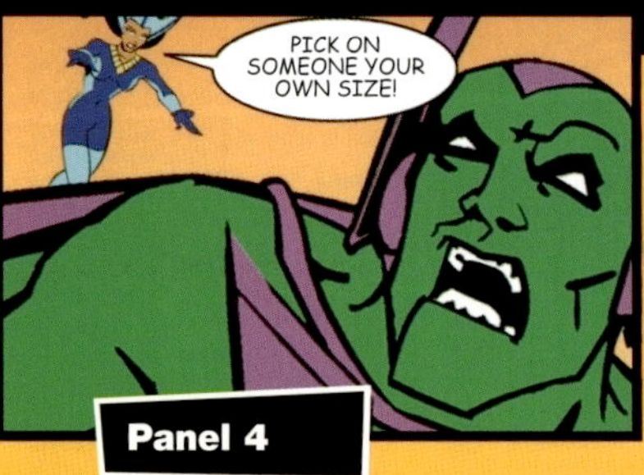

Panel 4 needs a little more thought. As well as Ultra-Girl's balloon, we're going to have a sound effect for her blast of Ultra-power, and a large, sound-effect-style "Arrgh!" from Dr. Devious might emphasize his size more than an ordinary word balloon.

By placing Ultra-Girl's balloon between her and Devious' head, we keep it out of the way of the space where we will create her zappy rays.

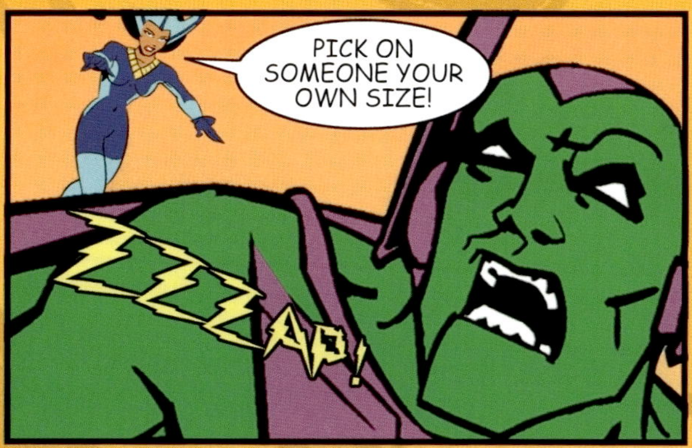

Zappy rays will need a zappy sound effect, so we should try to choose a font that suggests that kind of sound, and type it in using a brighter color than those around it so that it will really stand out. We can use the Warp text button on the Options bar to give it a little extra pizazz, and then simplify the layer and outline the sound effect with black. Placing it over Dr. Devious' shoulder should keep it out of the way of the blast—but we can always move it afterward if needs be.

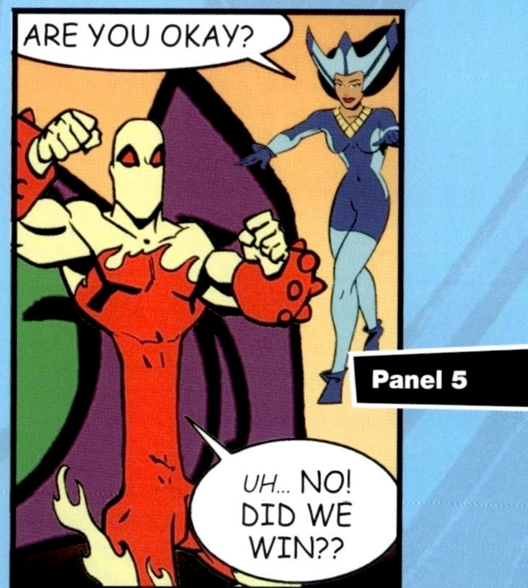

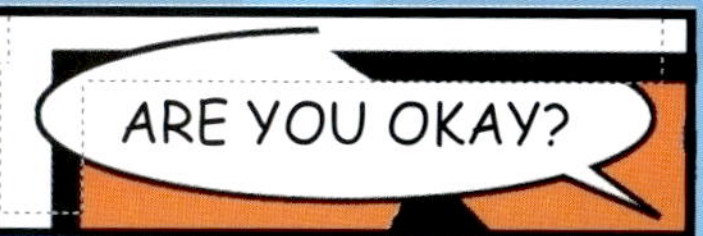

In panel 5, we're going for a top and bottom arrangement for the balloons. As we don't want to obscure Dr. Devious' giant foot any more than it is already, we can push the first word balloon right to the top corner of the panel. To make it fit snugly, we just need to select around the inside and outside edges of the panel border using the Rectangular Marquee tool (hold down Shift to add the second rectangular selection to the first). Ensuring that the balloon's layer is highlighted in the Layers palette, we simply use the Eraser to wipe away the part of the balloon that we don't want.

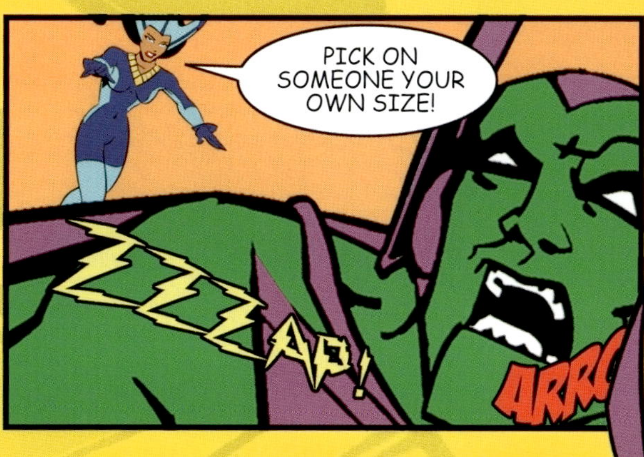

Dr. Devious' cry of pain and surprise is rendered in exactly the same way, using a different font.

Polishing

The hard work is over, and now we can enjoy adding the final finishing touches to our strip. With "If This Be My Density," we have one major outstanding task: creating Ultra-Girl's ultra beams in panel 4.

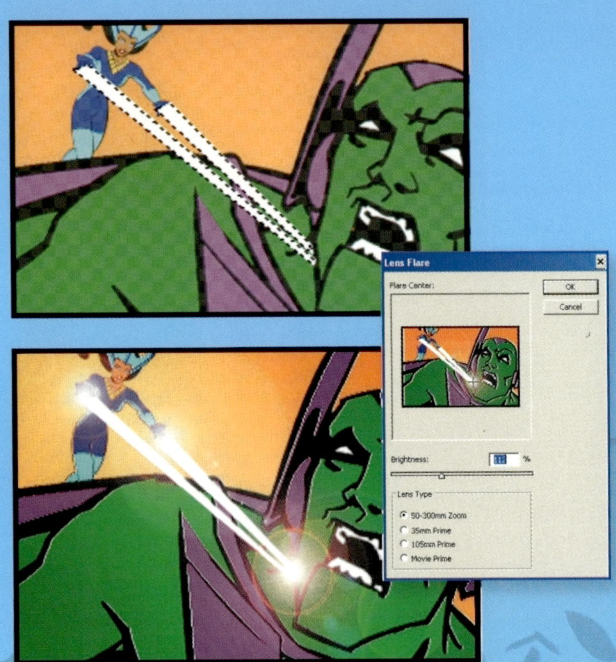

What we can do to really convey a sense of power unleashed is to use the Lens Flare filter.Use the Rectangular Marquee tool to select the panel's boundaries (otherwise, the filter will affect the other panels). Then go to Filter > Render > Lens Flare and place a flare on Devious' chin. Repeat this on each of Ultra-Girl's hands and see that power light up the sky. Deselect the panel and turn the text layers back on to see a much-improved panel.

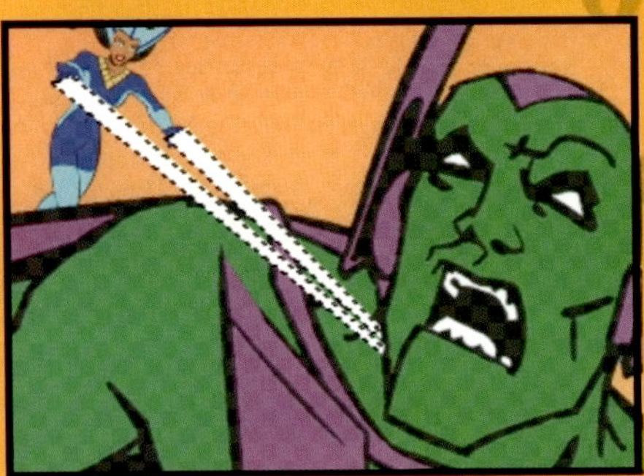

First, we need to turn off the text layers so that we can see the image more clearly. Next, ensuring we are working on the panel layer, we can use the Marquee selection tool to select a tapering area from one of Ultra-Girl's hands to Dr. Devious' jaw. Holding down the Shift key, we select a similar area tapering from the other hand. Next, we choose white in the front color box on the Toolbar and use Edit>Fill to create beams of Ultra-Force. Not too spectacular, though…

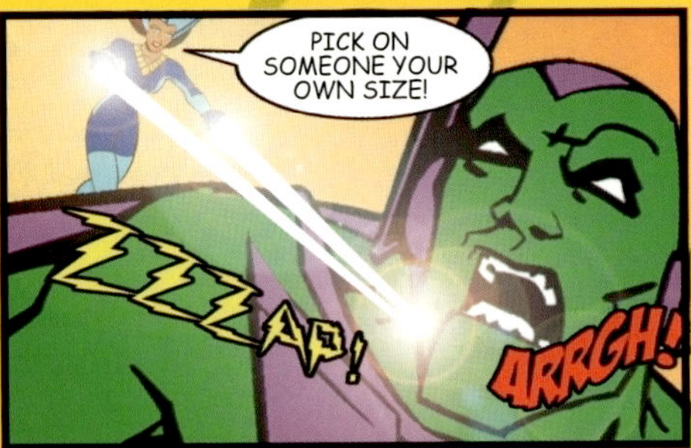

To complete the effect of Ultra-girl's laser dentistry, sound effects reveal the exact goings-on.

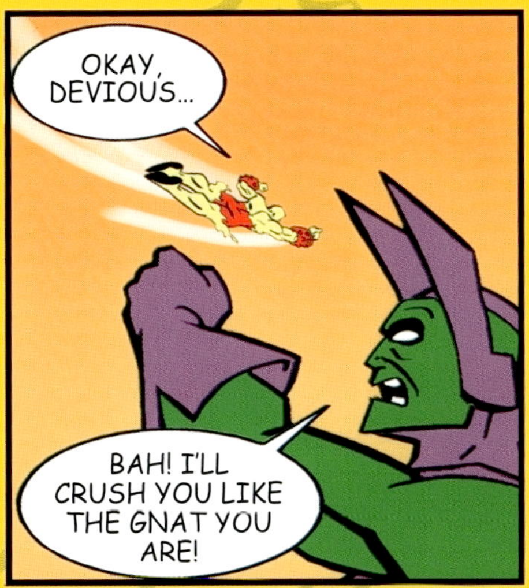

In panel 2, Solarman might benefit from a visual "whoosh" effect as he streaks through the sky. Select the background and use the Brush tool on its Airbrush setting.

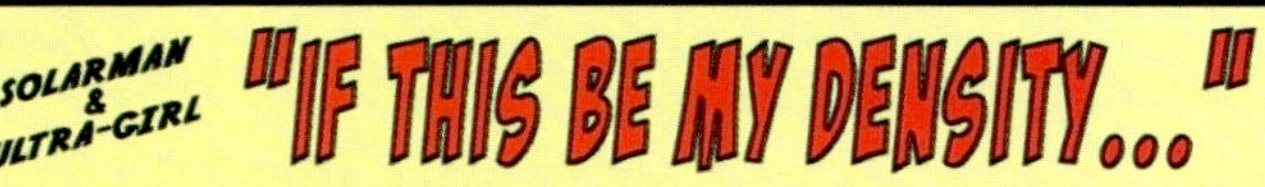

The job is almost done. All that remains is to create a title block across the top: simply fill a rectangular selection with yellow and outline with black. Then use the Text tools to create your lettering. Don't forget to Simplify text layers before you attempt to Stroke letter outlines with black.

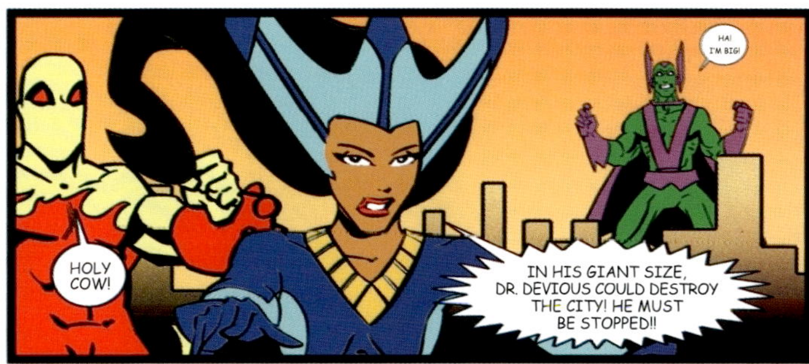

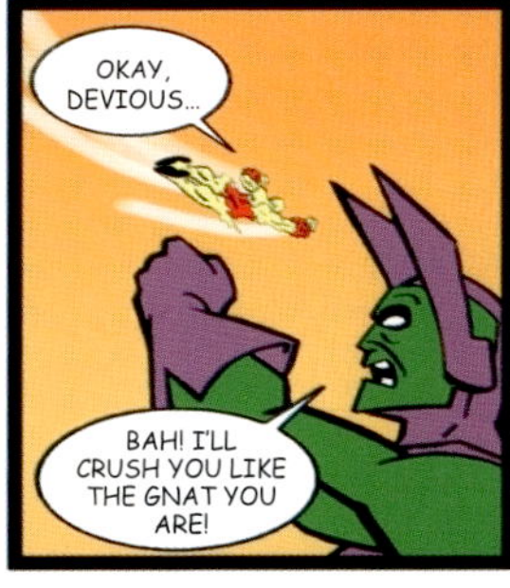

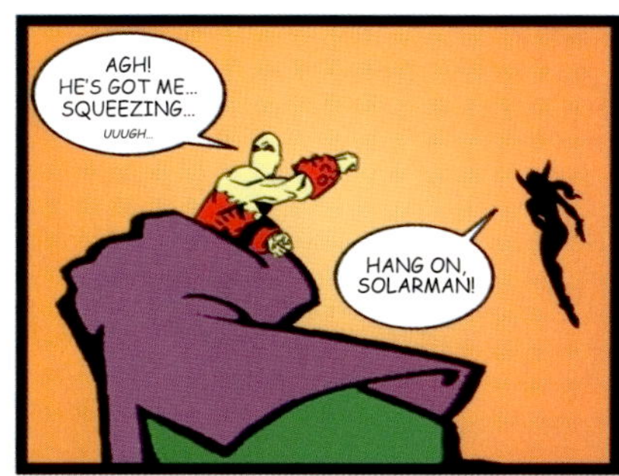

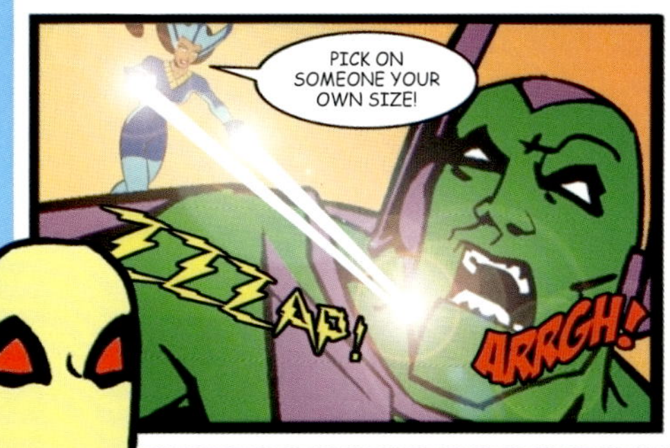

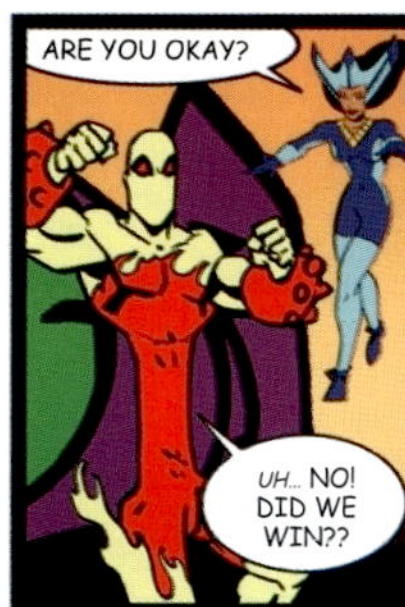

6 "Mourning Has Broken"

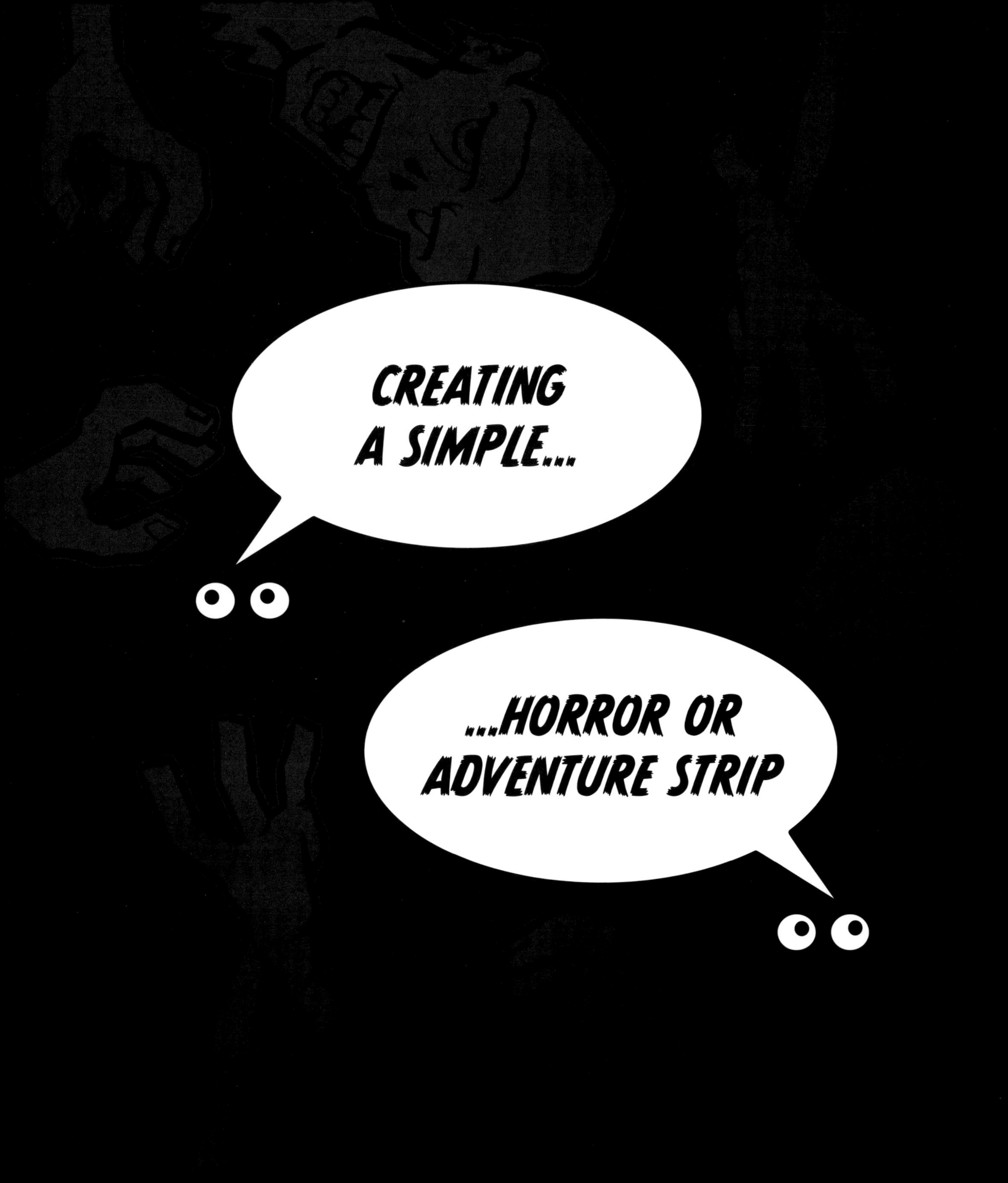

CREATING A SIMPLE...
...HORROR OR ADVENTURE STRIP

Sample Script

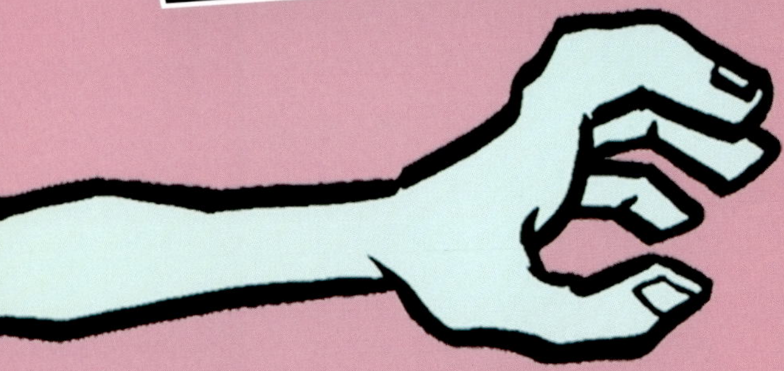

Back in the days when Mary Shelley wrote *Frankenstein*, horror stories were generally referred to as "gothic romance," so it might be fun to attempt a little romance of our own. We'll save the regular romantic stuff for our Slice of Life strip; here we can have a little more fun.

Our horror strip is going to center around Colin, a recently deceased zombie, and his erstwhile girlfriend, Dolores. Let's use the six-panel plan to construct a storyline reflecting one of life's enduring mysteries: why do pretty girls go out with ugly guys?

In panel 1, our story begins with Dolores mourning Colin at his graveside. The problem arrives in panel 2, in the shape of Colin, bursting out of his grave as a card-carrying zombie.

As all horror fans know, zombies maintain their existence by devouring human flesh, so in panel 3 we might see Colin looking a little hungry. In panel 4, Colin lunges for Dolores shouting that he's hungry; Dolores, oblivious to her potential plight, offers to cook him dinner. In the penultimate panel, Colin makes his intentions known, but in the final panel, Dolores is still seemingly oblivious to her impending fate. We leave what happens next to the reader's grisly imagination.

It's a sketchy start, but at least we have something to go on. Let's script the strip and see if the dialogue can make the whole thing work.

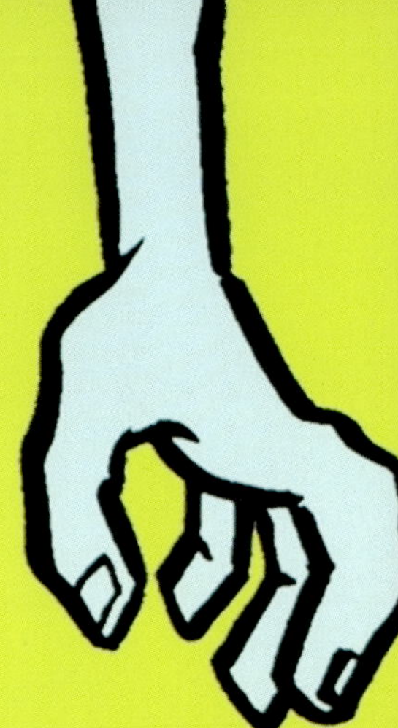

Panel 1

Background: a graveyard at night. Dolores is standing next to what appears to be a recently filled-in grave.
D: Oh, Colin! If only you hadn't made that ill-fated trip to the convenience store!

Panel 2

Same background, but slightly closer in. Colin is rising from the grave as Dolores recoils in horror.
C: Don't worry, baby! I live again!
D: Colin! You're a zombie!!

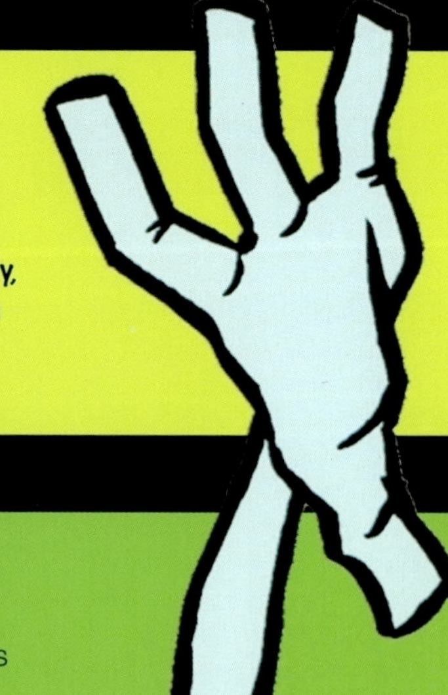

Panel 3

Colin is delighted to realize he is not as other men.
C: A zombie? Oh... Yeah! (Actually, I do have a hankering for human flesh...)

Panel 4

As they walk away, Colin grabs Dolores by the arm.
C: Hey, Dolores! I could kill for a bite to eat!
D: Oh, you poor soul! Of course... you must be starving!

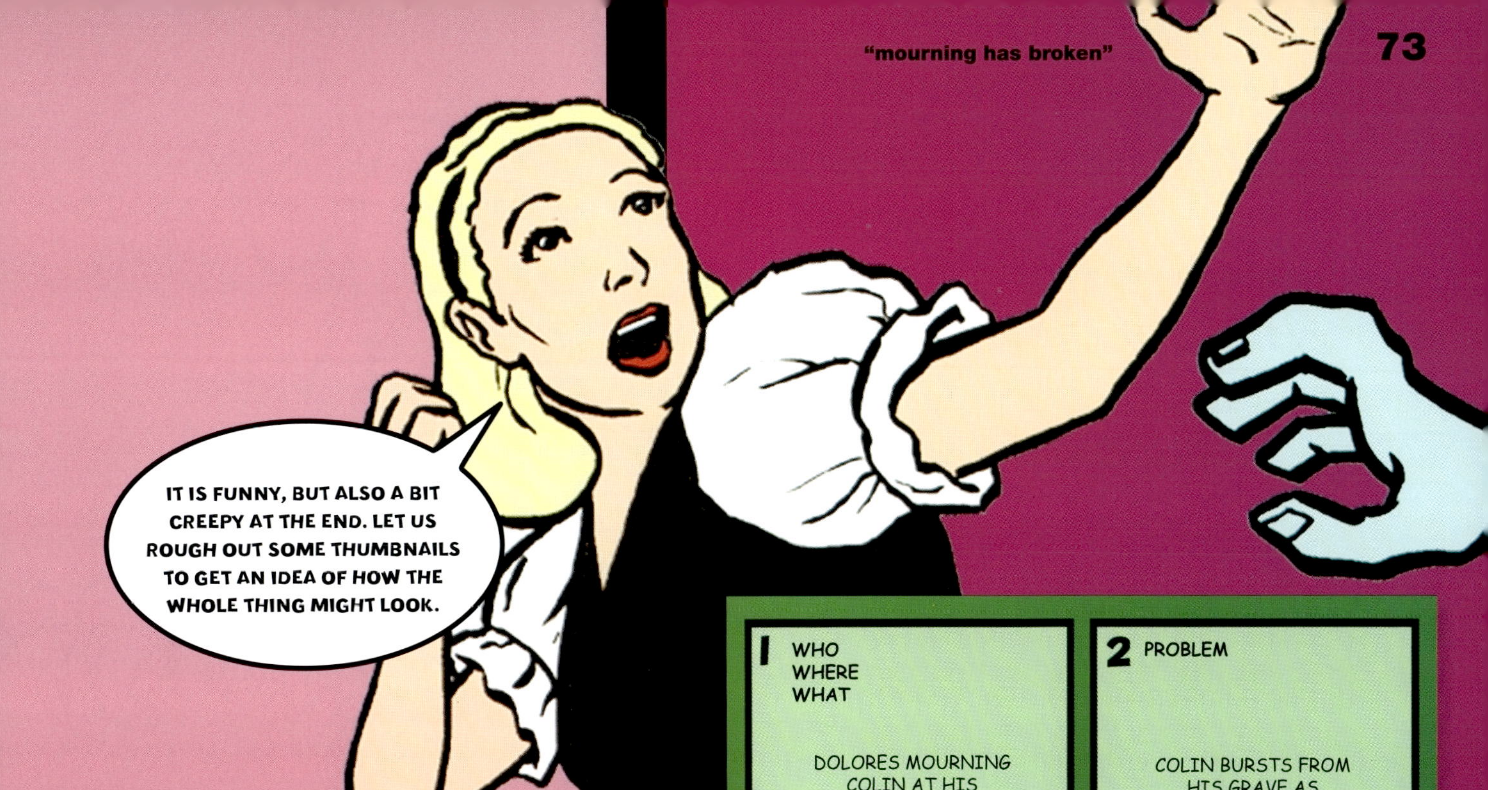

Panel 5

Inside Dolores' house. Colin is bounding around and licking his lips.

D: I've put some turnips in the oven... Is there anything else I can do?

C: I'd like to see you naked, drenched in ketchup!

Panel 6

Dolores turns away, as Colin turns toward us, the readers.

D: You only want me for my body!!

C: In a manner of speaking...

1 WHO WHERE WHAT	2 PROBLEM
DOLORES MOURNING COLIN AT HIS GRAVESIDE	COLIN BURSTS FROM HIS GRAVE AS A ZOMBIE
3 EFFECT	**4 POSSIBLE SOLUTION**
COLIN REALIZES THAT HE HUNGERS FOR HUMAN FLESH	DOLORES, MISUNDERSTANDING COLIN'S APPETITE, OFFERS TO COOK HIM DINNER
5 SOLUTION ATTEMPTED	**6 CONCLUSION**
INSIDE DOLORES' PLACE COLIN REVEALS HIS TRUE TASTES	DOLORES STILL DOESN'T GET IT AND WE FINISH FULLY AWARE OF COLIN'S MURDEROUS INTENT

Thumbnails

For the first panel, we need a regular establishing shot showing Dolores at the graveside, with other graves in the background. A tree or hill in the distance might help to frame the situation and give a slightly closed-in feeling, even though this takes place in the open air. The second panel could use the same background, or be slightly closer in, as Colin erupts from his earthly tomb and Dolores recoils in surprise. A close-up is good for panel 3, giving us a clear view of the new Colin (then again, we don't know what he looked like before—maybe he always looked like that!). In panel 4, they are moving on, so we should use a different part of the background. Dolores must show no adverse reaction to Colin's declaration of hunger; she's a sweet girl, she wants to help. Panel 5 needs a completely different background for the inside of Dolores' house, perhaps a section of the Castle Interior from the CD. Colin will be jumping around, unable to control himself much longer. In the final panel, Dolores still doesn't get it and turns away, but we can see an expression of pure evil on a close-up of Colin's face, a nice counterpoint to the lightheartedness of the previous panels.

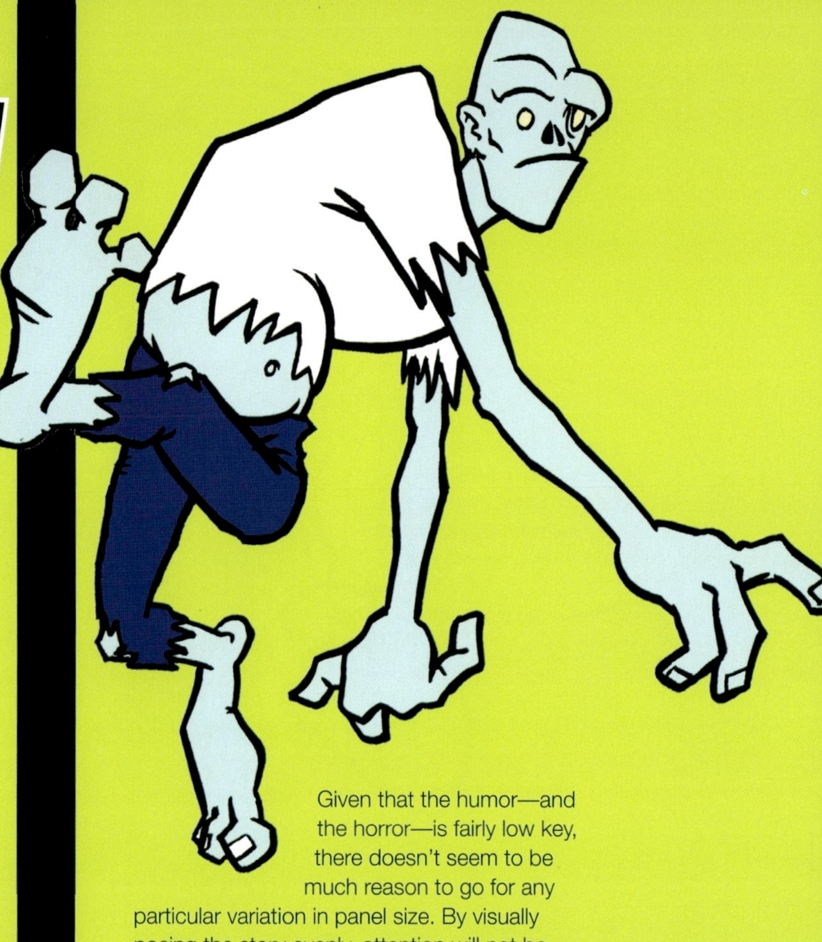

Given that the humor—and the horror—is fairly low key, there doesn't seem to be much reason to go for any particular variation in panel size. By visually pacing the story evenly, attention will not be drawn to the final panel before the reader gets there in the natural flow of reading the strip— and then they get the scary face.

Comedy horror strips have a long history in comics. As well as the grimly humorous endings to many of the old EC comics of the 1950s, British comics stalwarts Frankie Stein and Faceache, both originally drawn by Ken Reid, brought chills and chortles to schoolboys in the 1960s and '70s; in fact, for a time, there was a British weekly called *Monster Fun* that capitalized on children's need to laugh at scary topics. You also see this reaction to Scooby Doo cartoons in the very young. As for the truly spine-chilling, the early issues of Alan Moore's *Swamp Thing* and Jamie Delano's *Hellblazer* for DC Comics have rarely been equalled.

Most likely, no one's going to leave the light on after reading "Mourning Has Broken," but it should be a lot of fun to put together. So, let's sort out the best pictures to make it happen.

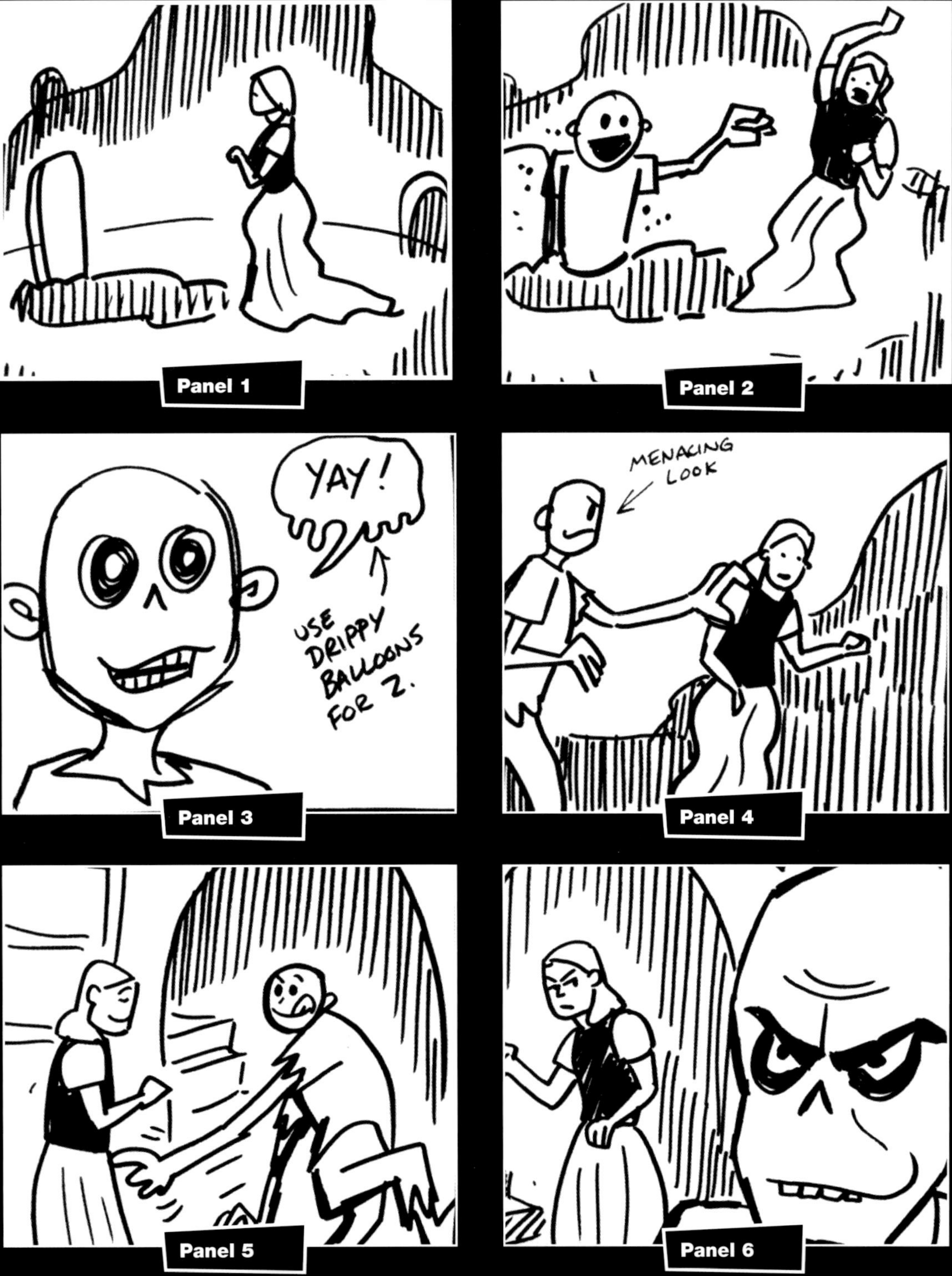
Panel 1
Panel 2
YAY!
USE DRIPPY BALLOONS FOR 2.
Panel 3
MENACING LOOK
Panel 4
Panel 5
Panel 6

Choosing Pictures

Our first four panels all take place in the graveyard, and we have a wonderful graveyard scene right there on the CD. Although we will only be using small sections of it, it's best to color the whole thing so that we have the maximum number of choices when we come to assemble our panels. While it might be disarming to set the strip in the middle of a sunny day, folks expect gloom with their horror, so let's not disappoint. Choosing varying shades of one color—in this case, ghoulish green— gives a harmonious look to the whole scene. Just because Photoshop has ten million colors, you don't have to use them all. The same is true of our section of the Castle Interior. We only have one woman and one zombie to choose from in this section, but we can make the best possible use of the choice of faces available, as well as flipping characters horizontally when necessary.

We want our characters to be distinct from the background, but not so much that they're jumping out from it. So by making Dolores' skirt dark red, we'll be using the complementary color to green, but not in a brazen way. Her blonde hair and white sleeves contrast nicely with her black bodice. Colin is the star of our show, so he needs to stand out slightly more. We've colored him light blue, as though permanently tinted by moonlight. This is matched by his dark blue trousers and contrasted by the white of his shirt. Yellow eyes complete his unearthly, spectral appearance.

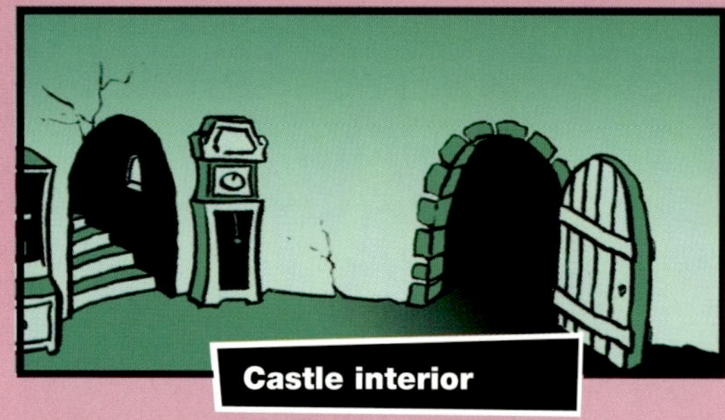

Castle interior

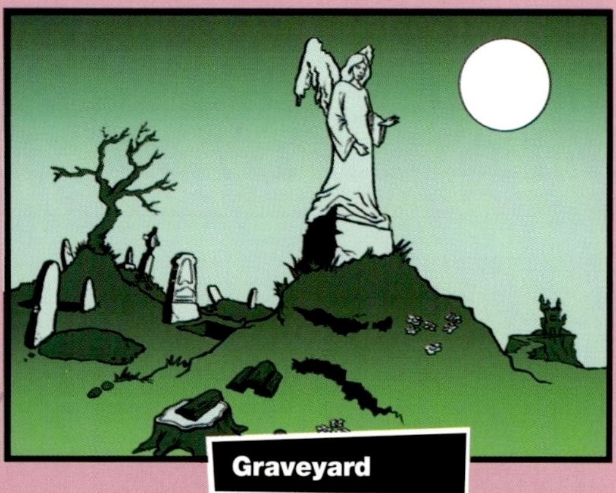

Graveyard

In panel 1, we'll use Woman 1 as is; she has a mournful expression right off the bat. In panel 2, Woman 3's look of alarm needs no alteration. As Colin is delighted to be alive once more, we'll be able to swap the head on Zombie 1 for the cheerier-looking Head 1 in this panel.

Zombie 1's original head might be best for panel 3—it has more of a look of vacant curiosity.

Since they are both on the move in panel 4, Zombie 2 and Woman 3 will work well, as long as they are both facing in the same direction. There's a mean, contemplative face that we can stick onto Zombie 2 here, and since Dolores feels sorry for him in this panel, there's a sorrowful face we can slide onto Woman 3.

A happier face on Woman 1 will suit panel 5, as Dolores tries to do her best for her lover. For Colin, Zombie 3 is perfect, with the face showing his tongue hanging out. Is it lust or hunger?

For the final panel, we can use Woman 3 for Dolores—its inbuilt expression has a hint of disdain. Face 2 on Zombie 1's shoulders, in close-up, should provide a suitably creepy finale—the laughter has gone....

It's worth making notes such as these as you plan your work; you'll find it easier to build your panels with a bit of advance planning.

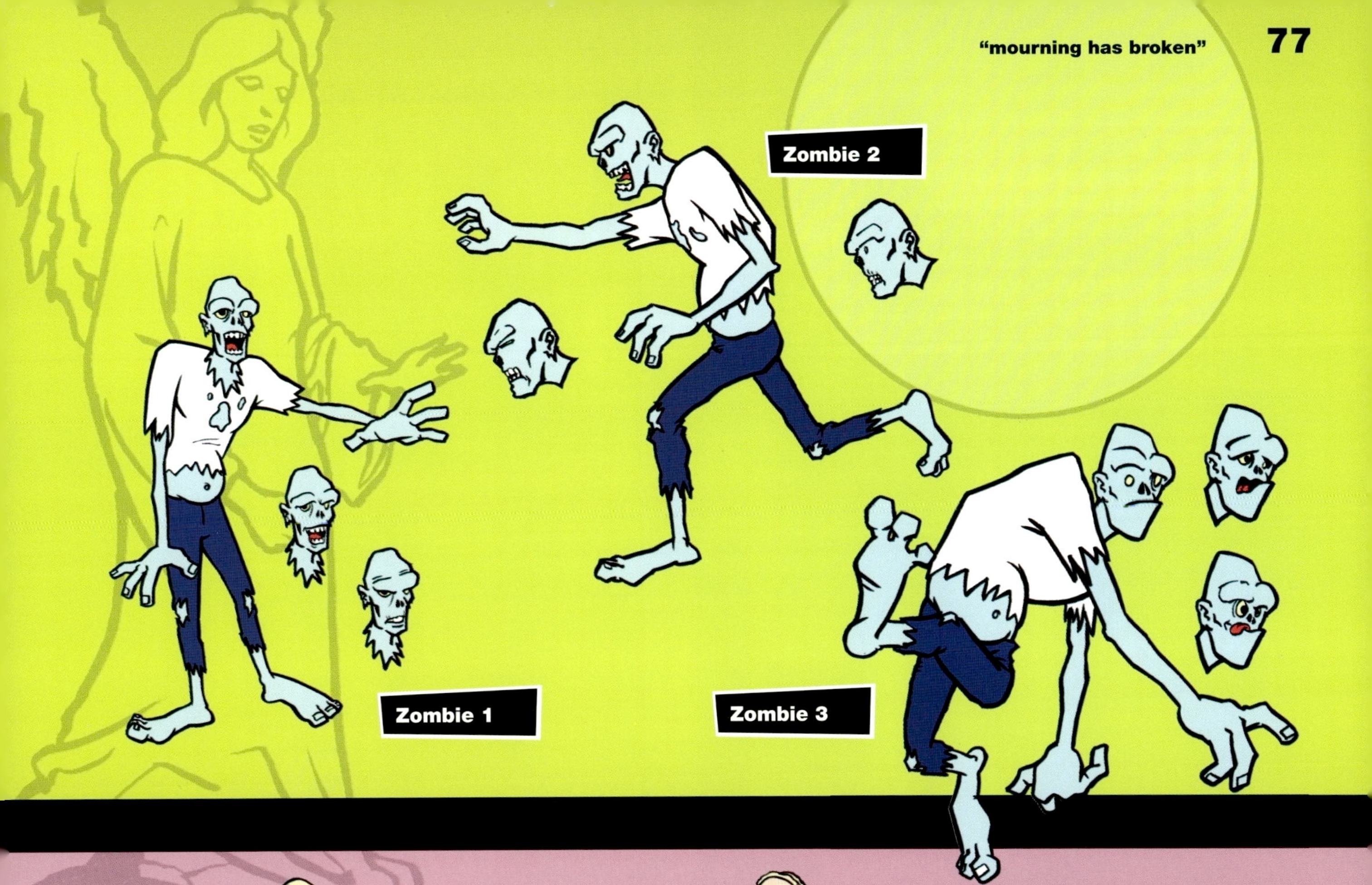

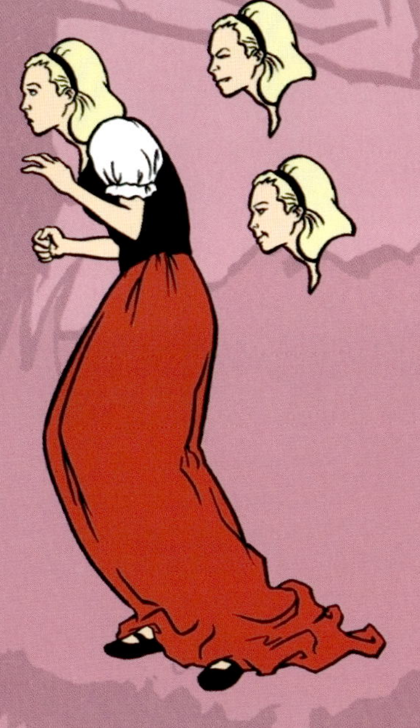
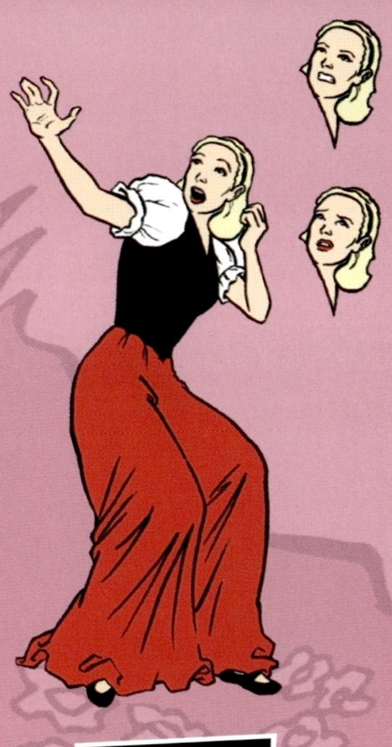
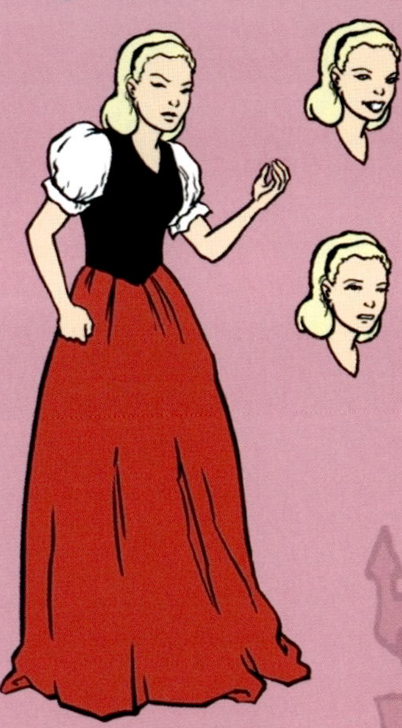

Zombie 2
Zombie 1
Zombie 3
Woman 1
Woman 2
Woman 3

Assembling Page

In the previous section, we found that a panel height of three inches was useful for fitting three tiers of panels on a letter-size page, and that a maximum width per tier of seven inches will give us a decent border between our artwork and the edge of the page. So why break the habits of a lifetime?

Unlike our Sci-fi/Superhero strip, however, we're going to use equally sized panels throughout. This means that each panel should be 3½ inches wide, allowing for a ¼-in gap between the two panels per tier. This is why all artists should have paid closer attention in their math classes at school.

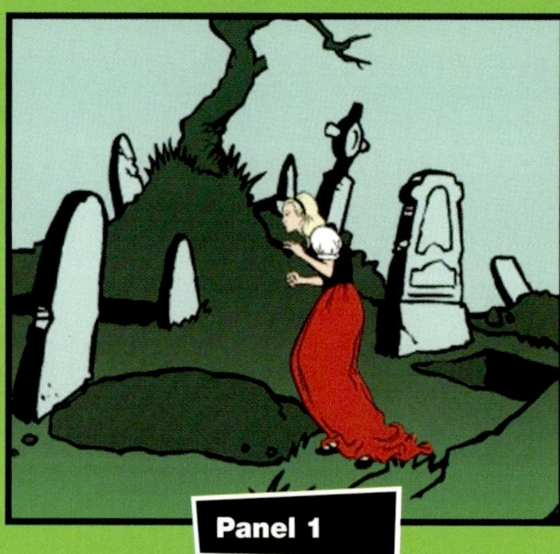

So, for panel 1, we need a section of the graveyard background that is 3 × 3½ in. This is easily achieved by opening the Rectangular panel border and resizing it to those measurements. We can then place it over the background and choose the area we want to use. If necessary, the graveyard pic can be enlarged so that just the right bit falls within the frame—this may take some tweaking back and forth to get just right. When you are satisfied, crop to the edge of the panel border, slide Dolores into place and save.

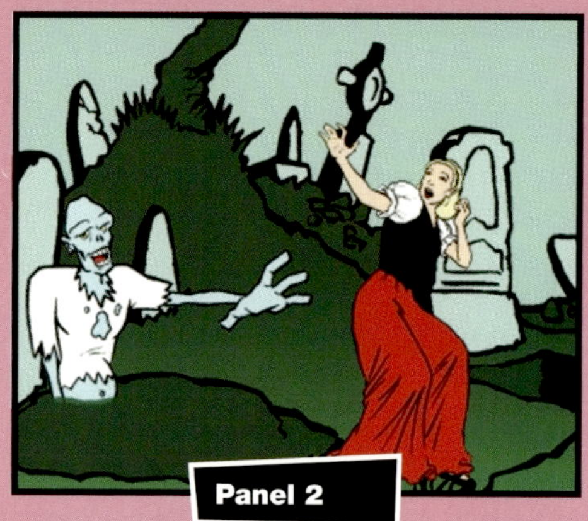

Zooming in slightly for panel 2 is actually fairly simple. Go back to panel 1 and delete all layers except for the background. Then reduce the size of the Rectangular panel border by half an inch and place it back over the background again. Crop to the edges and resize to 3 × 3½ in. Then, with Dolores in place, slide Colin across and erase him from the waist down—now he looks as though he's rising from the grave.

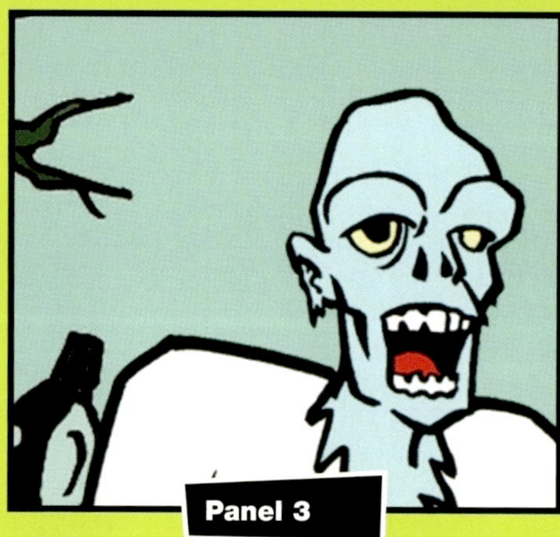

The background of panel 3 could be plain, but it might be good to show a little context. Reopen the graveyard scene, slide Zombie 1 where we can see a gravestone or two over his shoulder, and then do the Rectangular panel thing. Make sure you leave enough dead space, such as a patch of sky, for his word balloon later.

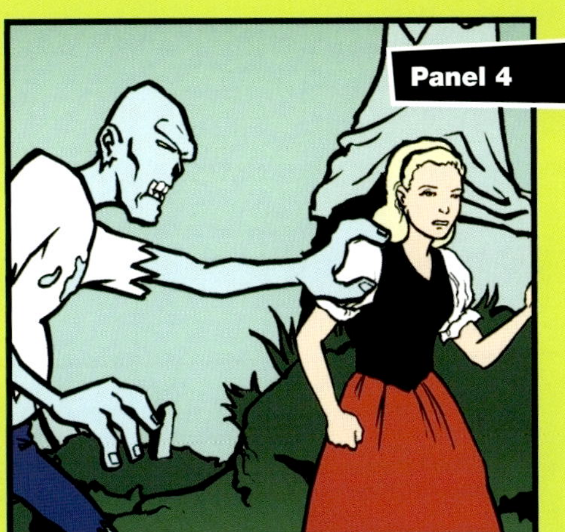

You know the drill for grabbing part of a larger background now, so for panel 4, we'll just move along a bit and choose an area in front of the statue. Add Dolores and Colin, and if you erase Colin's rear two fingers, it'll look as though he's grabbing Dolores by the arm.

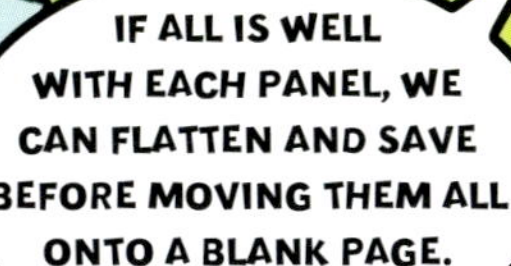

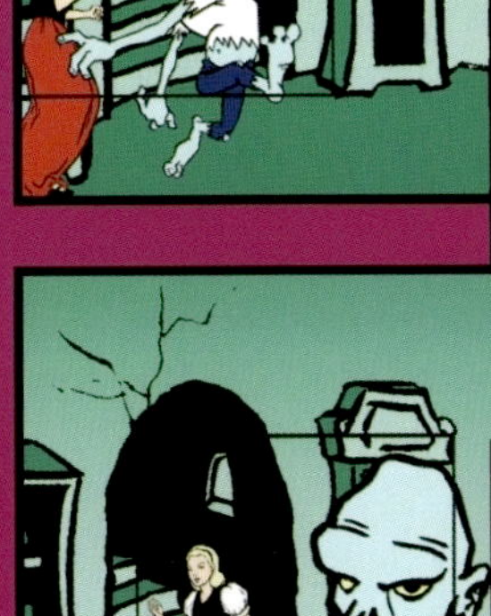

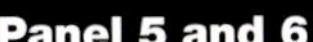

For panels 5 and 6, we're using part of the Castle Interior background, and actually only using a part of that. If we don't want it to appear that Dolores lives by herself in a huge castle, we can make the background appear cozier by using the Rectangular panel border again to select a few background details. Now all we can see is a cabinet and a stairwell; it could be anywhere. The figures have been resized before they were moved into place. Moving the panel border to the top of the Layers palette for each picture keeps it visible.

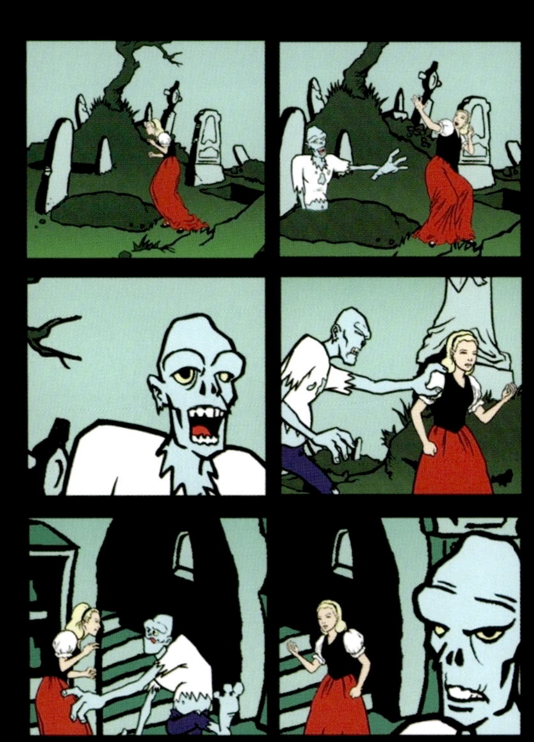

Adding Text & Balloons

As our Horror strip contains more dialogue than the Sci-Fi strip we examined in the previous section, we are going to think carefully about where to place the balloons so that they do not obscure important elements of each panel.

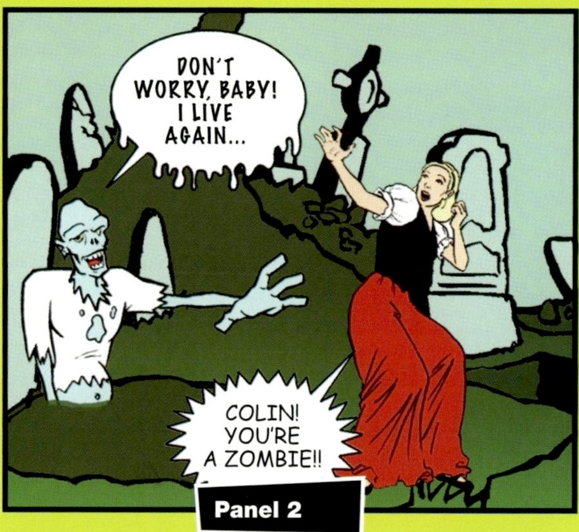

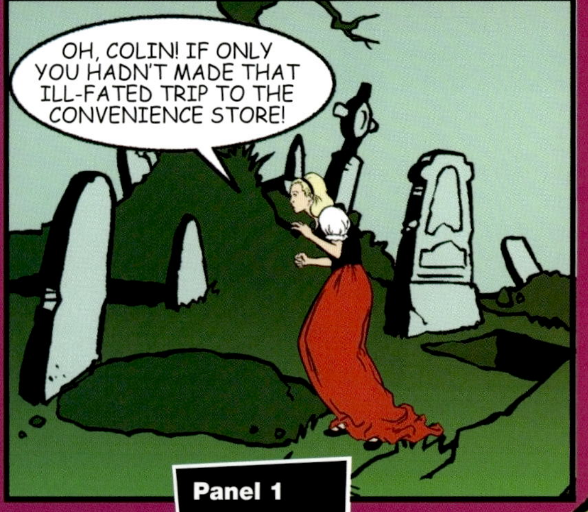

Panel 2 has two balloons to place. Colin's is in pretty much the same place as the balloon in panel 1, since it needs to be read first. Dolores' balloon could have been placed at the very right of the panel, but placing it where she was originally standing emphasizes that she has stepped backward, and the visual arrangement of balloons and Dolores' outstretched arm serves to frame the rising Colin within the panel.

Also, we get to experiment with balloon shapes: spiky alarm for Dolores, and our dripping balloon suggesting a gurgling, throaty rasp for Colin. Adding to the effect, a looser font style will be used for all of Colin's dialogue.

In panel 1, the main things we need to see are Colin's grave, Dolores, and enough of the background to set the scene for the reader. Obviously, it's a graveyard, but the open grave to the right and the leaning gravestones suggest that this is a place where spooky things happen.

So, placing the balloon to the top left of the panel is probably the best solution.

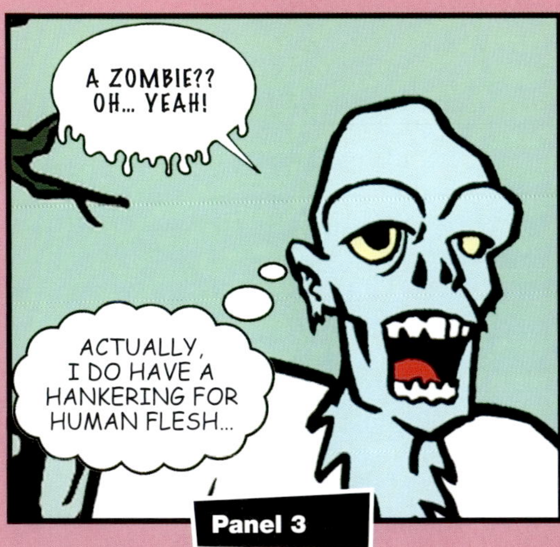

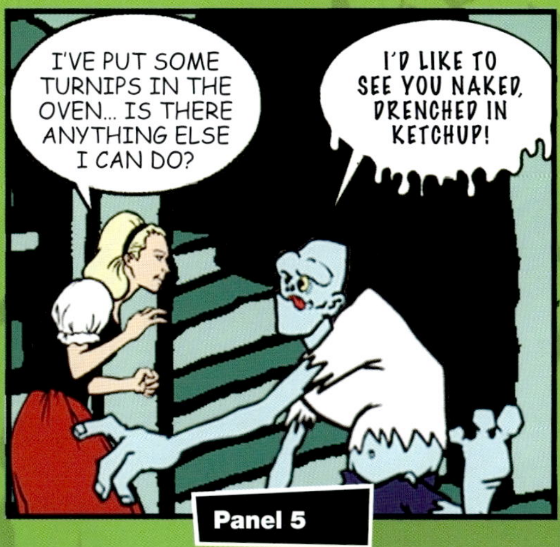

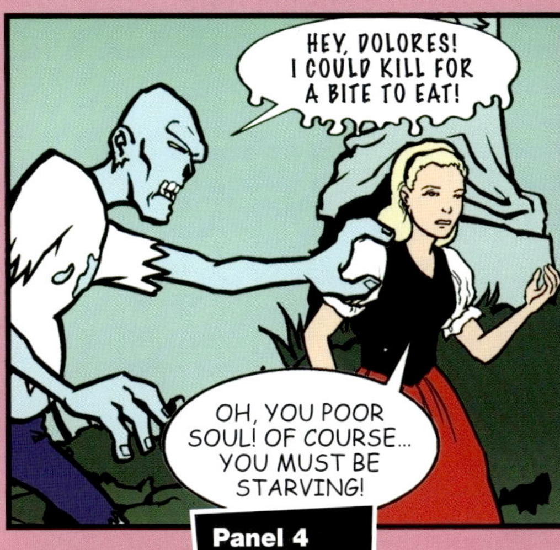

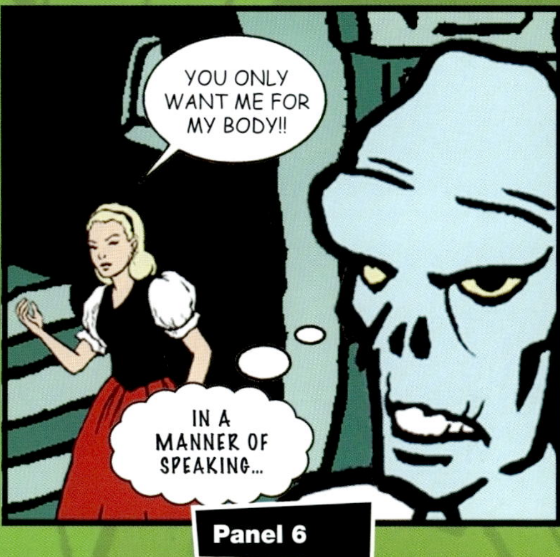

There is plenty of empty space in panel 3 for Colin's word balloon and thought balloon, but things are a little tight in panel 4. Using the bounding box around Colin's word balloon as we drag it across from its source, we can squash it flat and place it above the heads of the characters. This also mimics the horizontal thrust of the picture, Colin's arm reaching out to Dolores, whose arm is similarly gesturing away from her. The reader's eye will move from top, to Colin at left, across to Dolores and instinctively move down, which is where we place her balloon, taking care not to completely obscure the lower part of her body.

Space is not a problem in panel 5, and the balloons are easily placed. Panel 6 has adequate space up top for Dolores' balloon, but we need to be careful placing Colin's final thoughts; we don't want to cover any part of that sinister face.

With practice, you'll start to consider the amount of space needed for balloons when you rough out your thumbnails.

Polishing

"Mourning Has Broken" is looking pretty good, but using the dark arts of Photoshop Elements, we can make it look a little more moody.

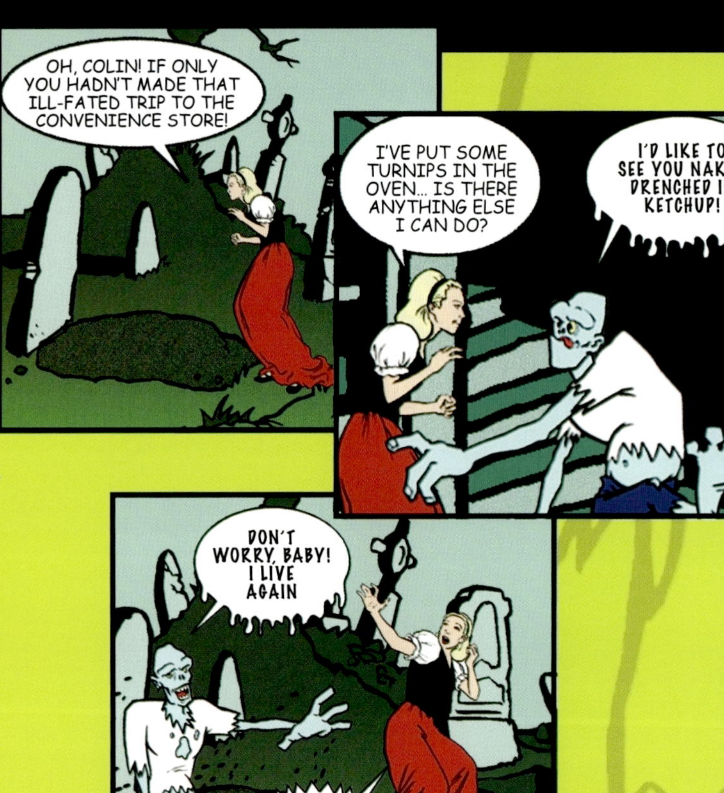

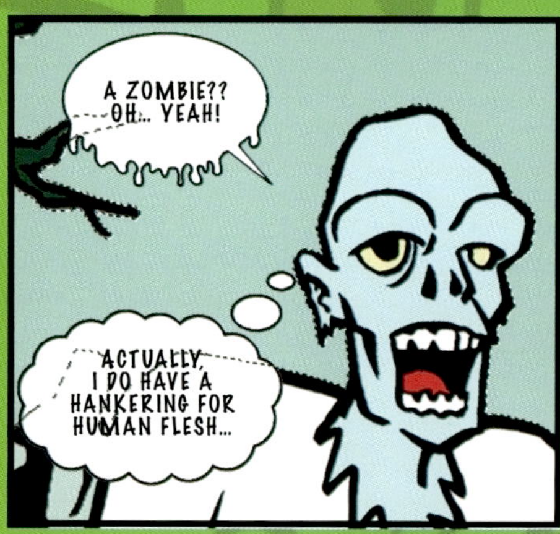

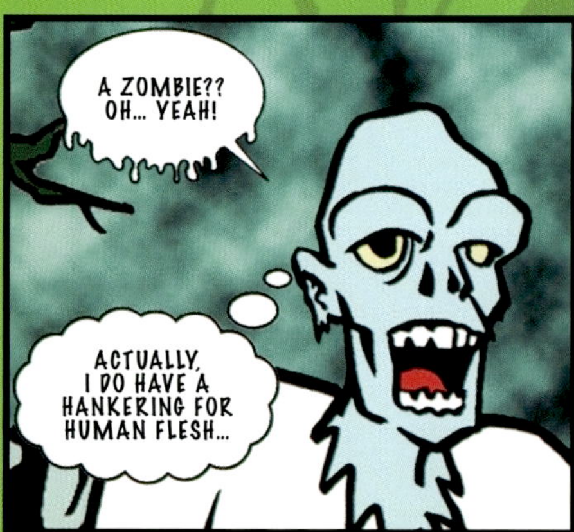

First of all, we can select areas of the background to fill with the Noise filter, such as the ground outside, and the walls and stairs of Dolores' home. This will add a subtle grainy quality to each panel. Next, we can use the paintbrush to add a little falling soil as Colin rises from the grave in panel 2.

Right now, the sky is a little bland. We can spook it up considerably by using the Clouds filter (Filter > Render > Clouds). Select every part of sky in panels 1 – 4 with the Magic Wand by holding down Shift as you click around. You'll notice that the selected area slips beneath your word balloons on the layers above. Choose black in the Toolbar's Color box, then use the tiny arrows to switch this to the rear box. Use the Eyedropper to select the existing green of the sky for the front Color box. Then we simply click on the Clouds filter, and end up with a stormy, forbidding sky.

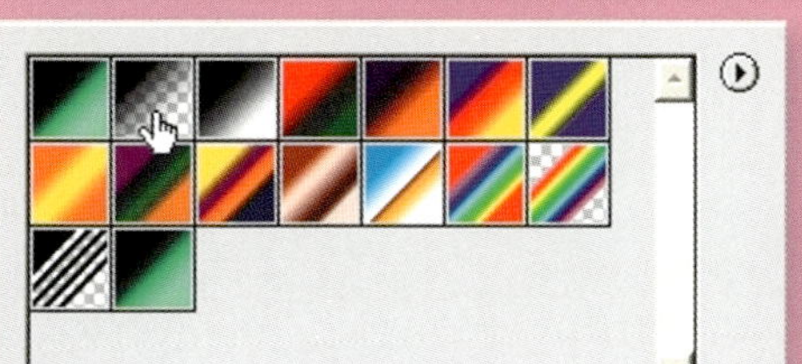

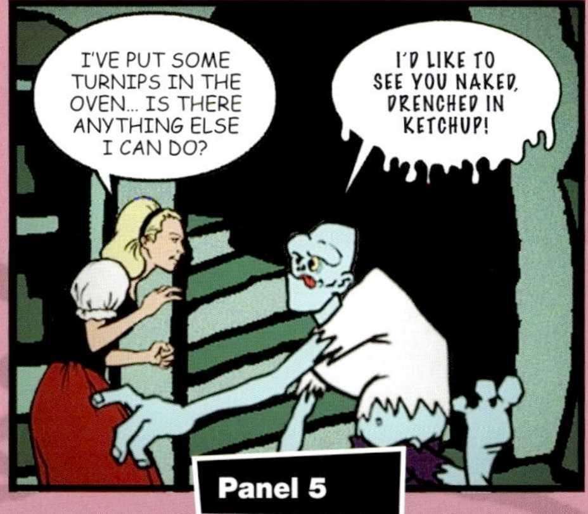

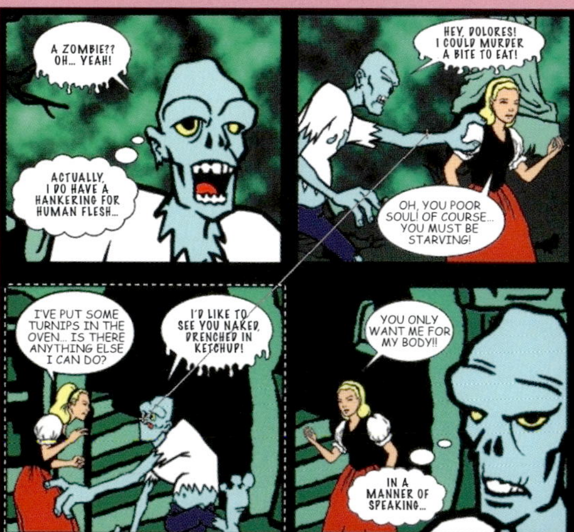

To lend a bit more atmosphere to panels 5 and 6, we can use the Gradient tool, choosing the Radial option. Switch back to the front of the Color box, and then click on the tiny arrow next to the Gradient window on the Options bar to reveal a multitude of variations. Choose the second one, which will create a gradient going from black to transparent. However, we need it to fade in the opposite direction, so we tick Reverse on the Options bar. Use the Rectangular Marquee tool to select around the edges of panel 5. Then drag the Gradient tool's line from the center of the panel out beyond the selected area, into the center of the panel diagonally opposite (the gradient will still only affect the selected area). This will create a slightly shadowed edge to the inside of the panel—good and gloomy. Repeat this process with panel 6, and our page is almost finished.

MOURNING HAS BROKEN

Finally we add some suitably horrifying lettering at the top to create our title, and our spine-tingling strip is complete.

Finished page

MOURNING HAS BROKEN

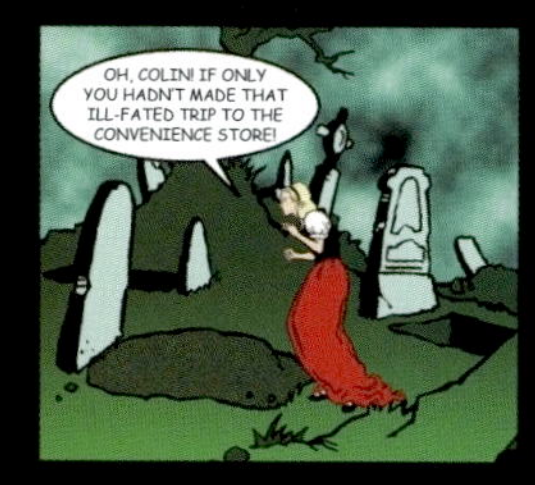

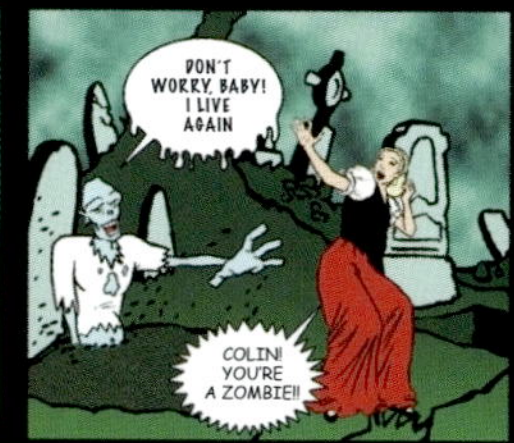

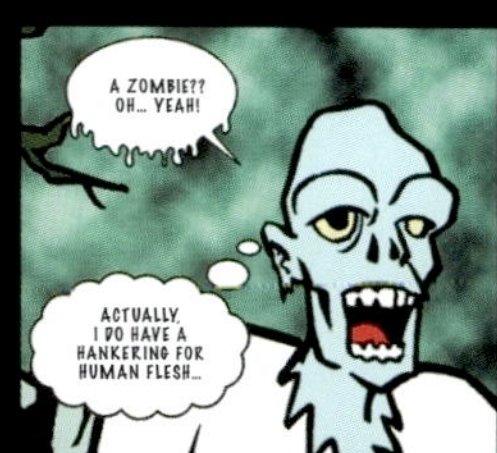

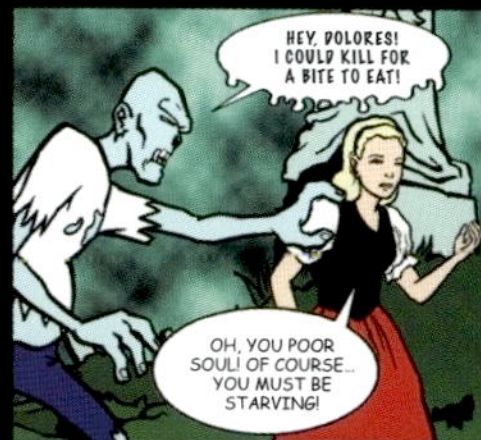

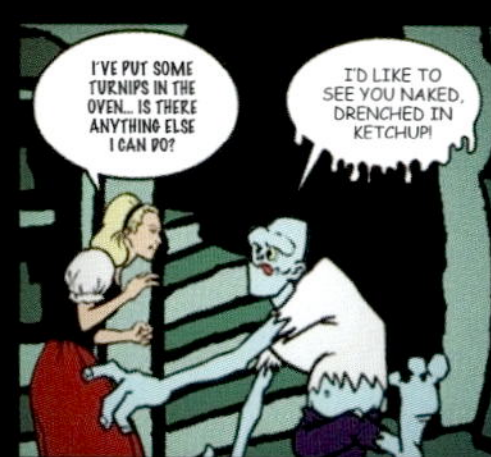

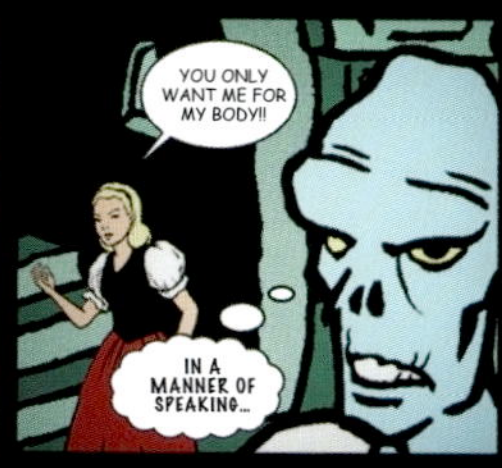

7 "My Heart Belongs to Paddy"

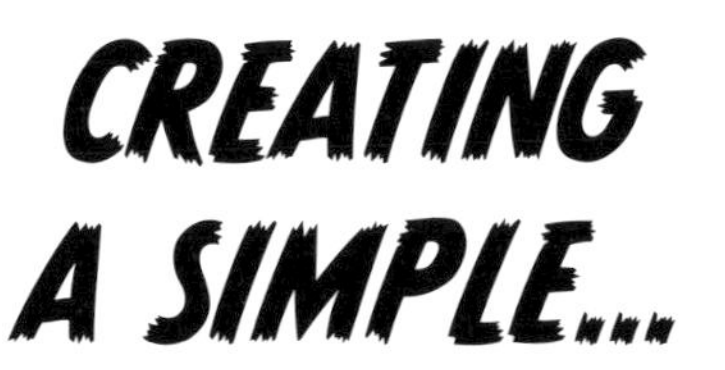

CREATING
A SIMPLE...
...SLICE-OF-LIFE
OR ROMANCE STRIP

Sample Script

Romance comics have come a long way since the idealized fairytale fantasies of the mid-20th century, when the genre was in its heyday. These days, they are more likely to chronicle the times when things go wrong than when things go right, and have spawned an allied genre akin to "general fiction," reflecting many different aspects of everyday life. Cartoonists such as Chris Ware, Seth, Daniel Clowes, and the Hernandez Brothers have brought mature readers into the bookstores to devour volumes of their work. Often, cartoonists take the trappings and conventions of older styles and genres and bring them up to date with an ironic spin.

The romance comics of Britain in the 1950s and 60s were usually printed in black and white, with a single "spot color" used to fill in background areas. We're going to emulate this style, while at the same time feature characters that are a little more up-to-date.

But before all that, we're going to need a storyline, so let's use that six-panel plan.

We'll begin our strip in a café. Paddy has just noticed Dinah waiting for him at a table. He's worrying about telling her a big secret. In the second panel, he thinks about how wonderful his time with Dinah has been, and he's concerned that it's all about to come to an end. But he has no choice but to nervously bring up the subject. In the fourth panel, Paddy's trying to tell Dinah what's on his mind, but he can't get the words out. Dinah interrupts and forces Paddy to spit it out. In the final panel, Paddy reveals his dark secret, and Dinah appears disgusted.

So what is Paddy's secret? Perhaps he's having an affair, or worse, he could be a wanted criminal. Or, it could be something that is actually incredibly banal….

Panel 1

Background: a café or coffee shop setting. Dinah is sitting at a table as Paddy arrives to meet her.
P: There's Dinah, waiting for me... How am I going to break the news?

Panel 2

A flashback: Dinah and Paddy are having fun in the park.
Paddy's voiceover: Things have been great all summer...
D: (within the flashback): I love you, Paddy!

Panel 3

Paddy sits opposite Dinah in the café.
Paddy's voiceover: But now I'm gonna spoil it all forever...
P: Dinah... I've got something important to tell you...
D: Paddy? What's wrong?

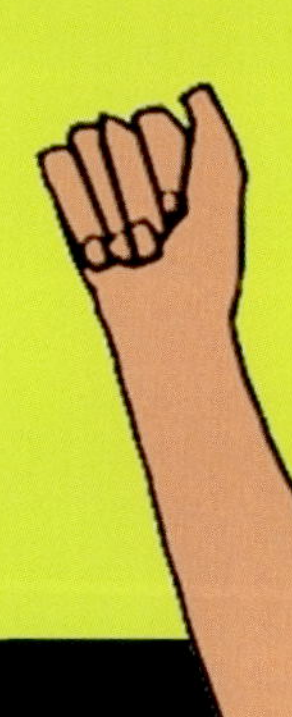

Panel 4

P: I don't know how to put this... It's... Well... You see, I... um... er... I...

Panel 5

Dinah urges Paddy on.

D: What? You're married? You're gay? You only have six months to live? What?? Tell me!!

Panel 6

P: (whispering) I collect comic books.
D: Oh, Paddy! NO!!

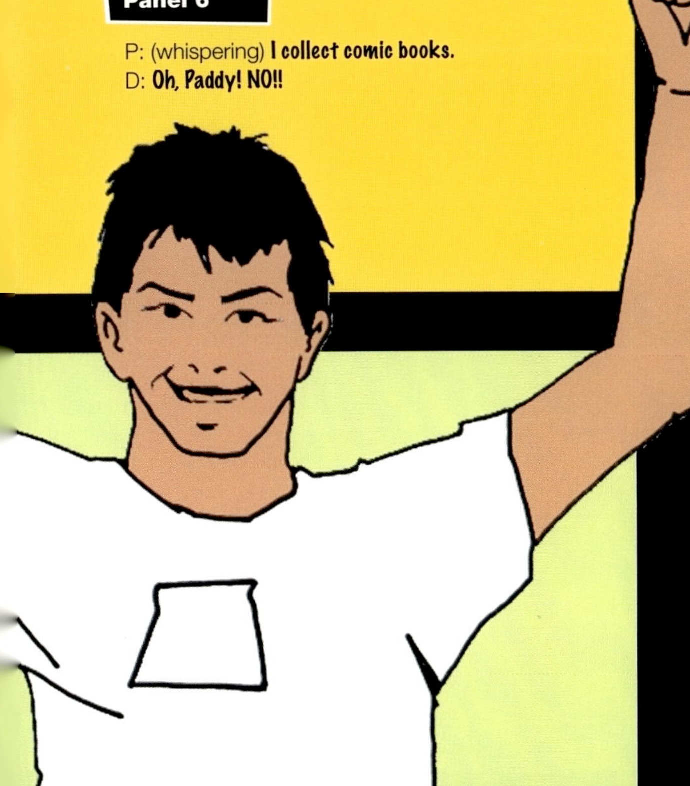

1 WHO WHERE WHAT PADDY AND DINAH IN A CAFE, ABOUT TO HAVE AN IMPORTANT CONVERSATION	**2** PROBLEM PADDY IS WORRIED THAT THIS COULD SPOIL THEIR RELATIONSHIP
3 EFFECT PADDY BROACHES THE SUBJECT	**4** POSSIBLE SOLUTION HE TRIES TO STAMMER THE WORDS OUT
5 SOLUTION ATTEMPTED DINAH TAKES THE SITUATION IN HAND	**6** CONCLUSION PADDY TELLS HER HIS DARK SECRET AND WE SEE HER REACTION

Thumbnails

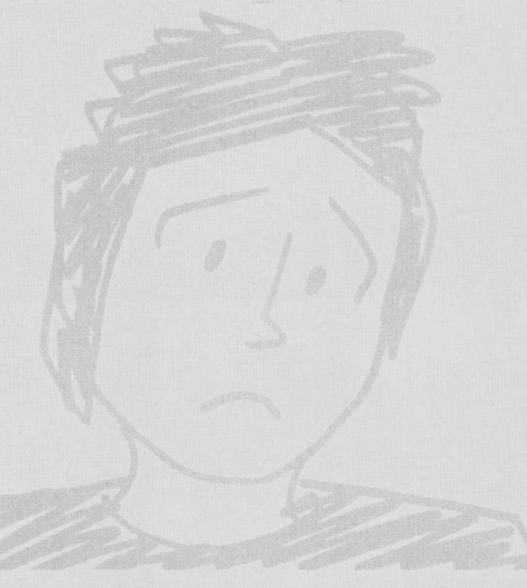

Let's plan out how we might visualize this vignette. We can base aspects of the thumbnail rough on what we know is available on the CD.

In the first panel, we'll set the scene with a fairly wide panel showing enough in the background for the reader to be aware that this is a café. The focus should be on Paddy, with Dinah sitting at a table some distance behind. She'll be beaming expectantly as she spots her boyfriend. Bearing in mind our plans for a monochromatic approach, it'll be good for Paddy to be dressed in black to make him stand out; Dinah's striped top should do the same for her. The second panel is a flashback to summertime in the park, so we'll need to use a different background. By shading Dinah's trousers and adding stripes to Paddy's shirt, we should hopefully suggest that this scene takes place at a different time. Failing that, the cloud-shaped frame should do it.

For the third panel, we should be able to find a way of showing the two of them facing, perhaps by using a bit of trickery to simulate the back of Paddy's head. Having established the scene in panel 1, we don't need to clutter

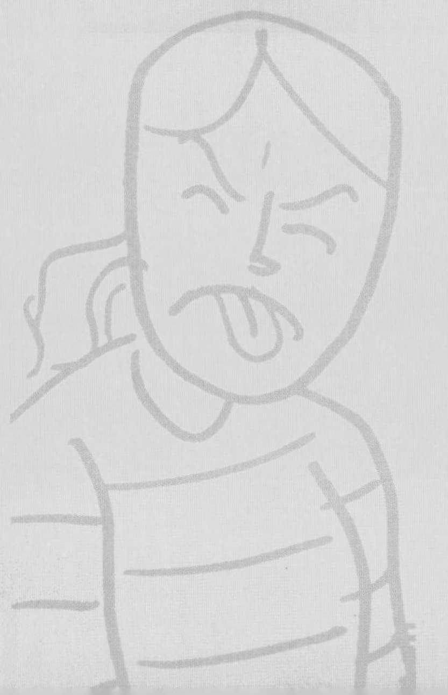

the background with details; we want the attention to be on Paddy and Dinah. With this in mind, we'll keep the background clear in panel 4 as we close in on Paddy's face. In panel 5, we zoom out to see Dinah's consternation and Paddy looking awkward, which will mean that the coffee shop background is used again—not a bad idea, as we've only seen it once so far, and we won't see much of it in the final panel. This needs a close-up of the two of them, as Paddy shuts his eyes and reveals his secret, while Dinah makes a disgusted face.

As it's roughed out, the page looks as though it will have fairly evenly-sized panels except for in the top tier. This is not a bad thing, as it should serve to direct the eye away from the final panel's punchline until the reader gets there. This is a commonly used technique with single-page strips, perhaps most famously seen in the *Peanuts* half-page Sunday strips by Charles Schulz.

Schulz would often use a completely surreal image in the first panel—a smiling tree, for instance—in order to draw the reader to the top of the page. The *Peanuts* strip itself, with its ongoing themes of everyday slights, thwarted romance, and alienation, is a likely contender for being the first major comic strip to reflect the underlying concerns of our daily lives. Well, except for all those strips featuring Snoopy playing tennis.

Let's check through the images on the CD to see which we'll need to use, and how we're going to add a single color to each for that "old-school" comic effect.

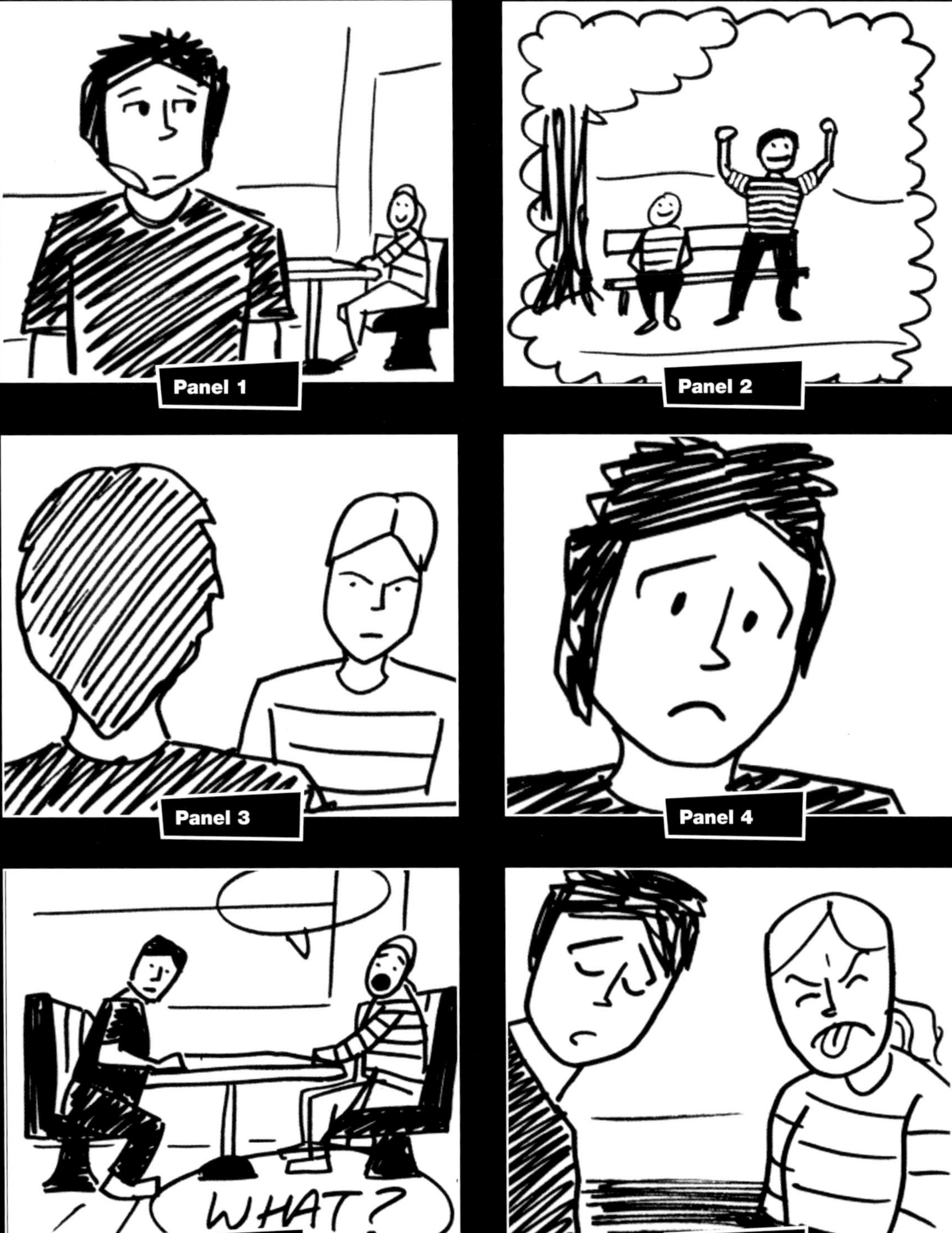

Panel 1
Panel 2
Panel 3
Panel 4
WHAT?
Panel 5
Panel 6

Choosing Pictures from CD

Our strip takes place in a café, the kind of place you'll find in any fairly upscale section of town; alternatively, we might consider it to be a coffee shop—basically, it's the kind of place in which two young lovers might arrange to meet in the daytime.

The Diner background picture is perfect for our purposes, but with one small flaw. In our first panel, we need to see Paddy first as he begins to worry about telling Dinah his big secret. Logic dictates that he should be at the left-hand side of the panel, but the chairs and table of the background—where Dinah should be seated— are to the left of this background. Placing Paddy over the same space won't work too well. The solution is to just flip the background horizontally, as we have done so many times before with other images. Now the seating area is to the right of the picture, with a nice big empty floor space in which we'll be able to slot Paddy.

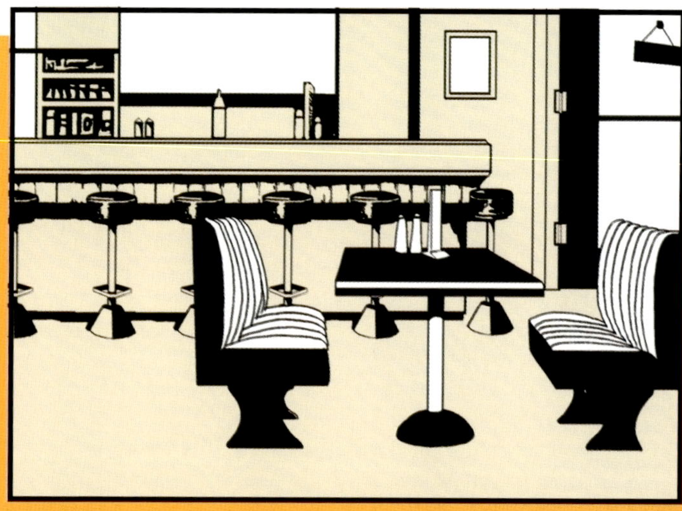

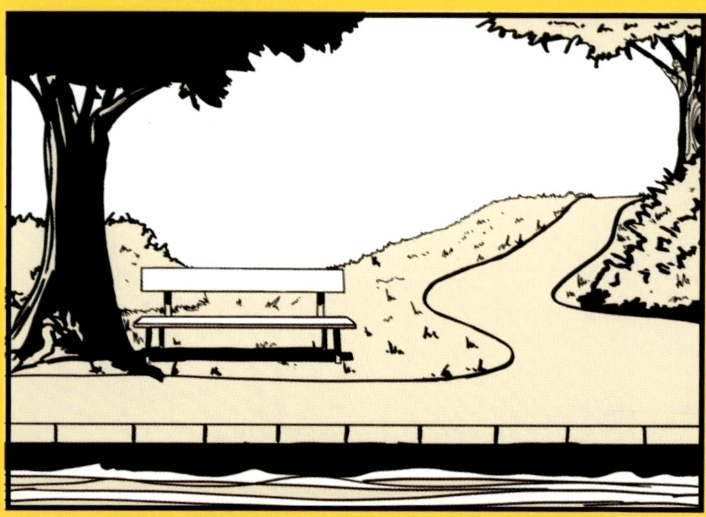

The other background we need is for the flashback to halcyon days in the park, and, lo and behold, we have our Park background. This is what was in mind at the thumbnail stage, using the section of the image around the park bench, and it will be perfect.

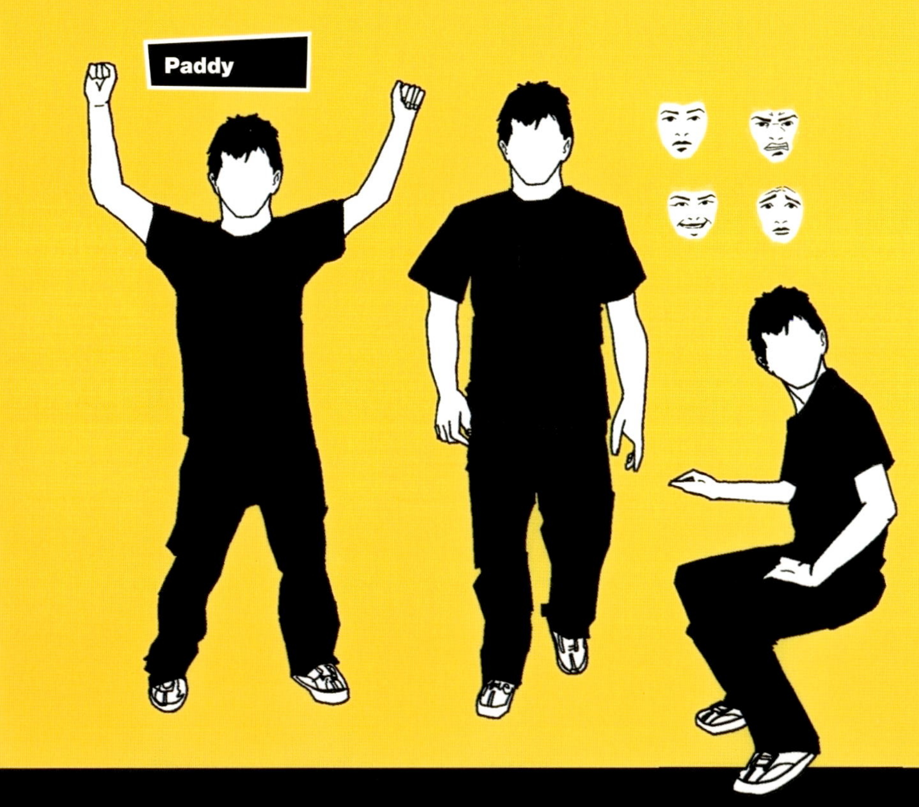

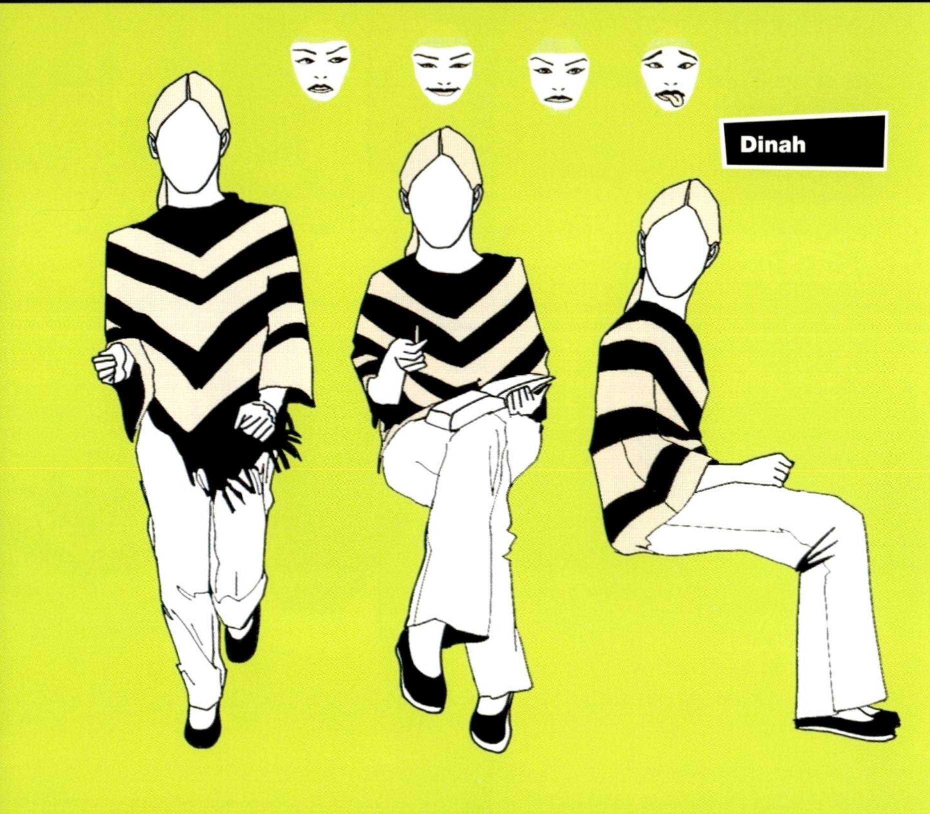

Choosing which set of male bodies to use for Paddy essentially comes down to which gives us the more useful and adaptable poses for this particular strip. Since there will be at least one panel where we see Paddy and Dinah sitting opposite each other from the side, we'll need a character that will easily match this purpose. In many other respects, Character 3 would be fine, but we only have a front-facing seated figure in that set. It was Character 1 we thought of at the thumbnail stage, and he wins through —still, it never hurts to explore your other options. Similar logic dictates the use of Character 4 for Dinah. We will be making much use of the various facial expressions available.

Now to consider the coloring; right from the beginning, the opportunity to give this strip a bit of a "retro" spin presented itself, if for no other reason than providing a change of pace. A light tone of any color could be used to fill in areas of the background, and of parts of the figures. The important thing is to leave the faces of the characters white so that their expressions do not blend in with the background. Obviously, this means that all other areas where skin is showing should also be kept white. This is not to imply that they are both Caucasian; color here is just being used to tone the pictures, in the way that gray is used in black and white photography. Significant sections of the background, such as the seating, should either be left white or filled with black, so that our attention is drawn to these areas.

With these pictures toned and saved, it's time to get really creative….

Assembling Page

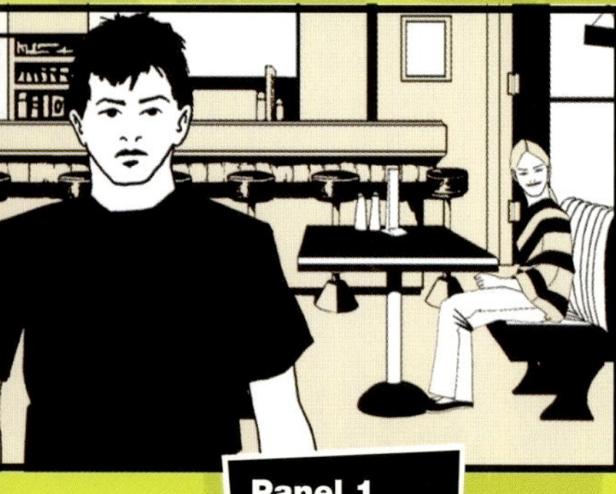

Panel 1

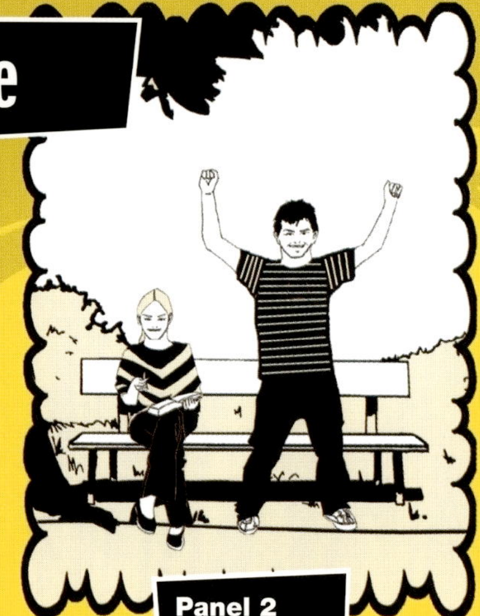

Panel 2

Panel 3

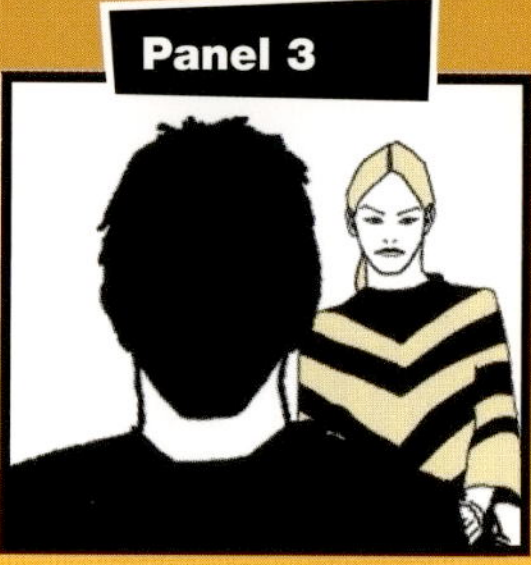

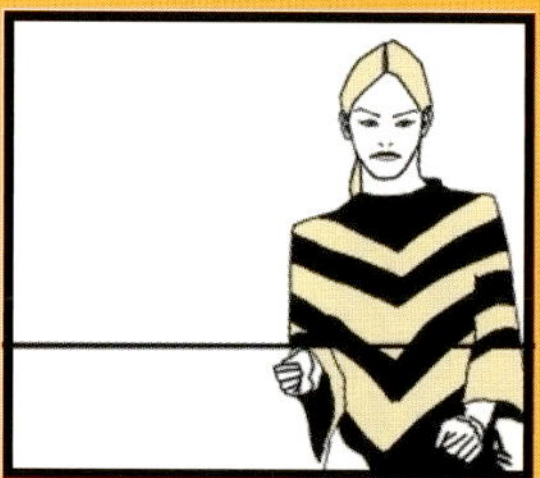

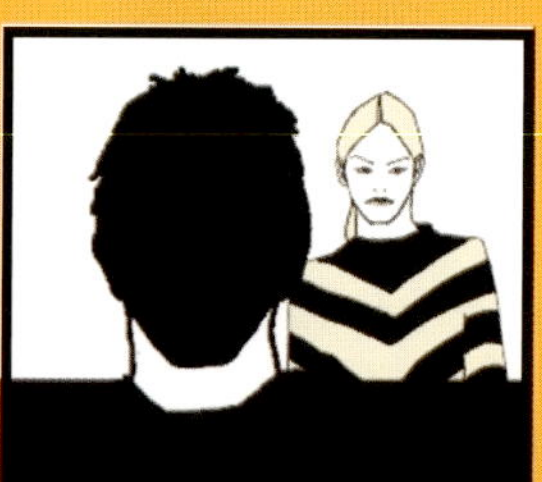

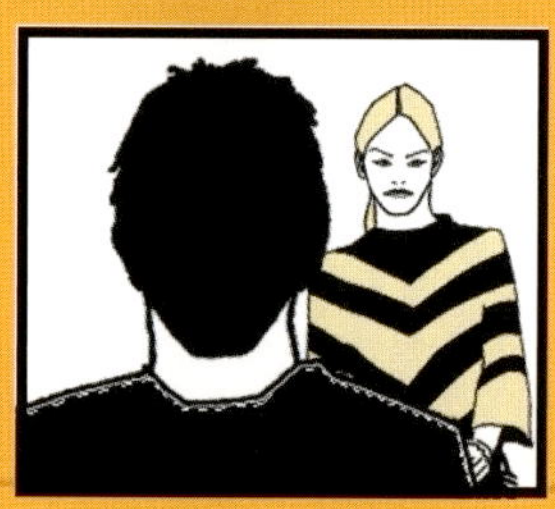

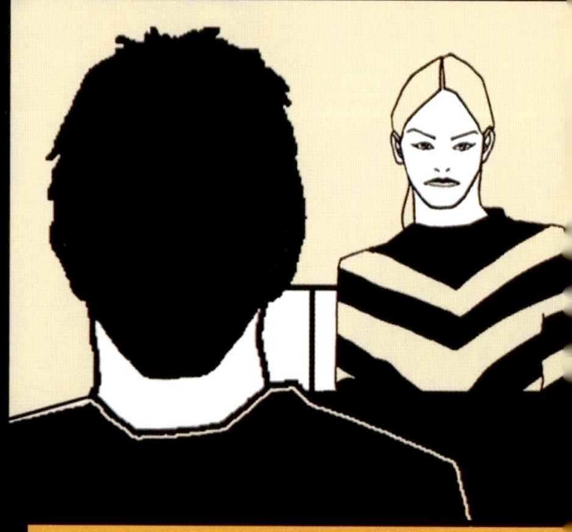

Since panel 1 is an establishing shot, showing where the story is taking place, we can in this instance use all of the Diner background.

Paddy will be to the left, but first Dinah needs to be seated at the table. She's happy to see Paddy, so the smiley face will be plopped on top of the seated Character 4 once it's been flipped horizontally. We then drag and resize the character until we get Dinah sitting neatly, with a black section of background framing her head.

Paddy should be placed so that his eye-level is higher than Dinah's, showing that he is standing, rather than sitting in an adjacent booth. Flatten, add a black border (Select>Select All; Edit>Stroke) and save.

Panel 2 takes a bit of work. We'll need to use the Cloud frame to choose part of the Park background and move it across to a blank document, in the manner shown previously (select, save, switch layers, reselect and drag). Don't forget to resize the Cloud frame to match the height of panel 1— and the width you choose— before you start.

Next, we can add the figures, remembering our plan to color them slightly differently to indicate that this is taking place some time ago, in Paddy's mind's eye. Do not flatten and save; instead, turn off the Background in the Layers palette and go to Layer>Merge Visible on the top Menu bar. Then, right click on the Background in the Layers palette and choose Delete Layer. You'll be left with a flattened, cloud-shaped image, floating on an ocean of emptiness. Which is as close to poetry as we'll be getting in this book. Save as a Tiff or PSD to preserve the new transparent non-background.

Panel 3 is even more fun, but it mainly draws on techniques we have previously explored. First, we place the walking Character 4 onto a blank background. Then we fill the face of the walking Character 1 with black so that his face now looks like the back of his head. We move him into position so that it seems like they are standing opposite each other.

As they should appear to be seated at a table, we're going to have to construct one in front of Dinah. Turning off Paddy's layer in the palette, we can use the Line tool to draw straight across Dinah's layer just where the table might be seen. This will create a new shape layer, the bottom of which can be filled with black to create our tabletop.

When we bring back Paddy, he appears to be an extremely broad-shouldered young man, as the black of his shirt blends with the table. To get around this, we resort to what is known in technical circles as "jiggery-pokery:" on Paddy's layer, we select his shirt and temporarily fill it with our background tone. We then reduce the selected area by ten pixels (Select > Modify > Contract) and fill it with black again. This gives Paddy's shirt a light outline. The outline at the side and bottom, where we don't want it, will be covered when we add a black border to our panel.

Before that final step, Dinah needs a seat. Turn off all layers except the Background. Use the Line tool to draw the seat and then use Merge Visible to combine the shape layers with the background. Bring the other layers back, add tone to the top part of the background, flatten, border, and save.

Whew! Sometimes the simplest pictures are the trickiest to complete, but there's a lifetime's learning in that one panel that can be put to further use elsewhere.

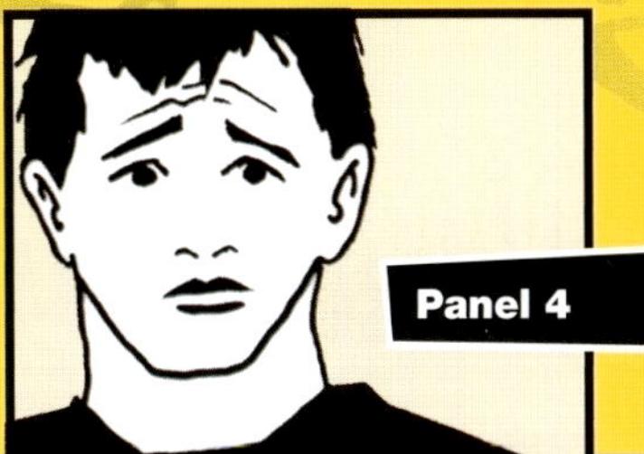

Thankfully, panel 4 is a doozy.

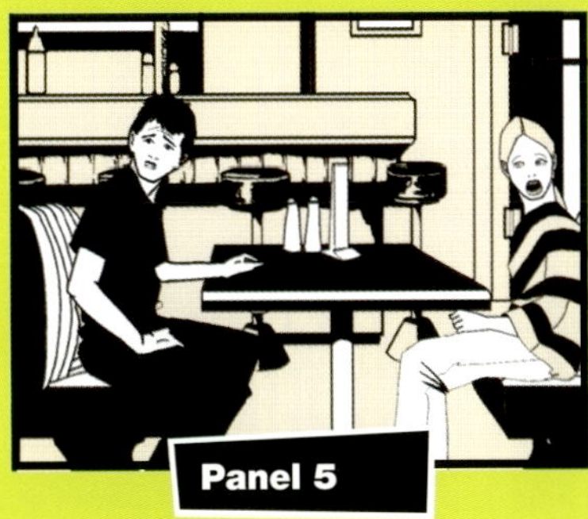

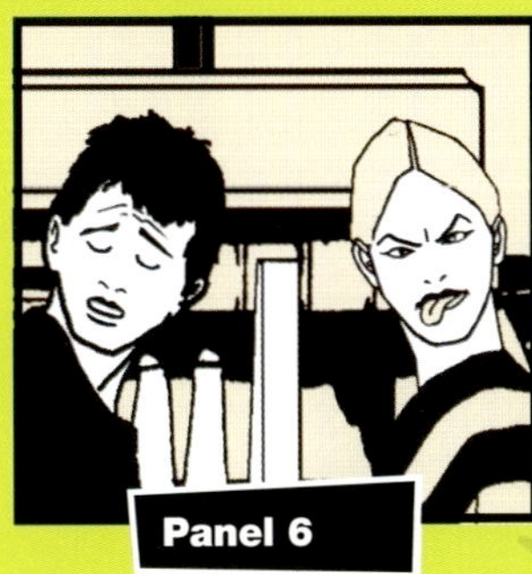

Panel 5 is put together in essentially the same way as panel 1, with some careful redrawing on Dinah's face. Likewise, panel 6 uses the same figures pushed closer together, with new faces and a dab of redrawing.

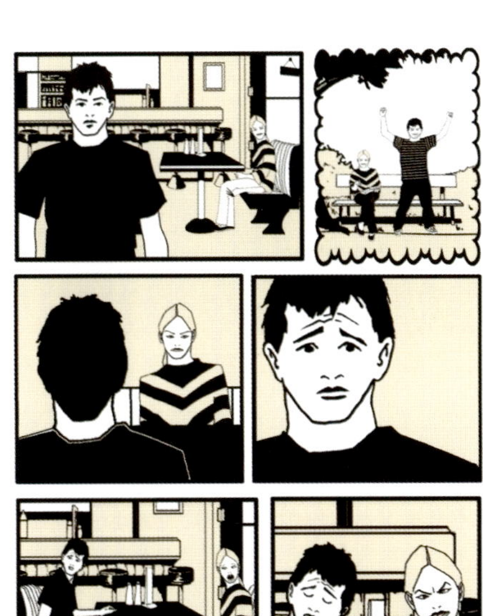

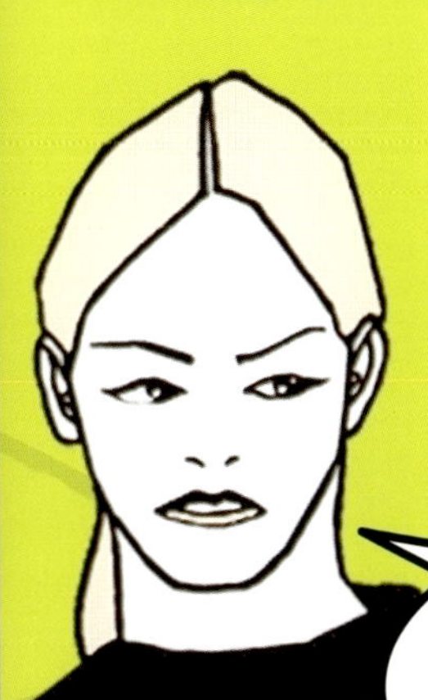

Adding Text and Balloons

The process of assembling the panels for "My Heart Belongs To Paddy" was a little complex in places, but thankfully, adding the text and balloons is fairly straightforward.

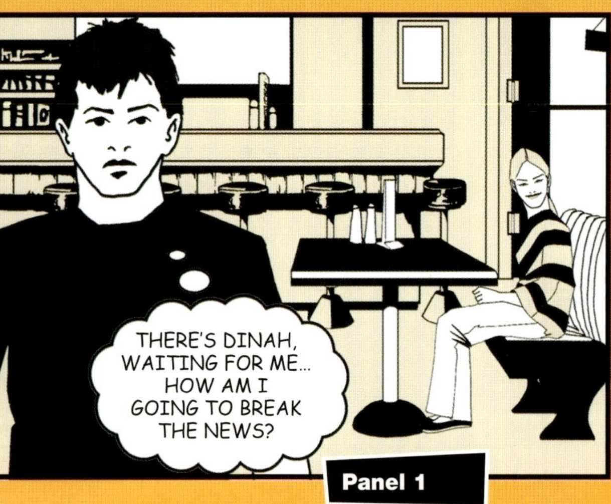

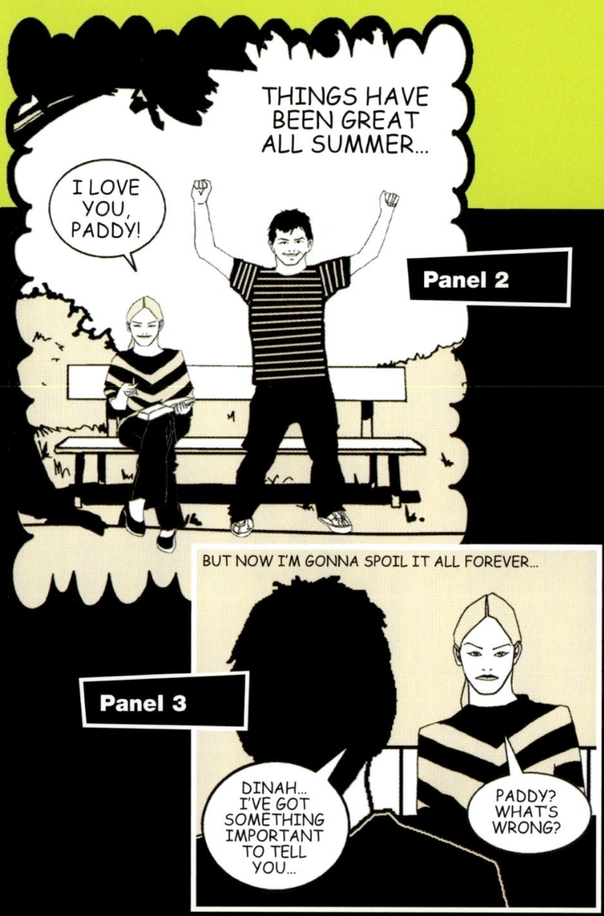

In panel 1, a thought balloon is required and it will be fairly large, despite using a font size of 4 (which is the size used on every page so far—it's not on the drop-down font-size menu, you need to type it in). Placing it near the top of the panel would obscure those important background details that set the scene, so keep it low, where it will only cover some of Paddy's torso and the floor. Don't place it directly over Paddy, else it will look like a weird T-shirt design.

A common feature of Slice of Life strips, and of the old-school romance comics from which many artists and writers take their ironic cue, is the use of first-person narration in conjunction with regular speech and thought balloons. Sometimes this will be used to serve as an introduction to the story, letting the main character set the scene. This narrative device can also be used right through a story, ensuring that the reader will tend to go along with the protagonist's view of events. Essentially, it's reminiscent of the "voice-overs" used in old gangster movies, and the original, bowdlerized version of *Blade Runner*. This technique is used in panels 2 and 3, along with conventional word balloons.

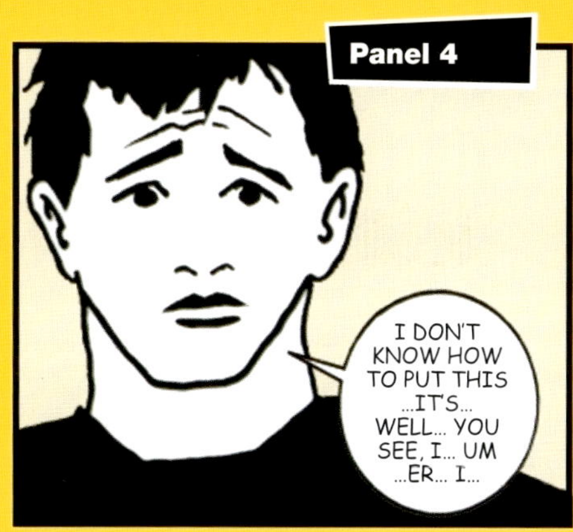

To fit the text in panel 4 in a balloon that won't obscure Paddy's face means we'll have to use the bounding box of the Move tool to squish the balloon into thinner shape, erase the pointer, and draw a new one in. All of our balloons can be modified in this way, or if you're feeling brave, you can use the Ellipse and Line tools to create your own custom shapes.

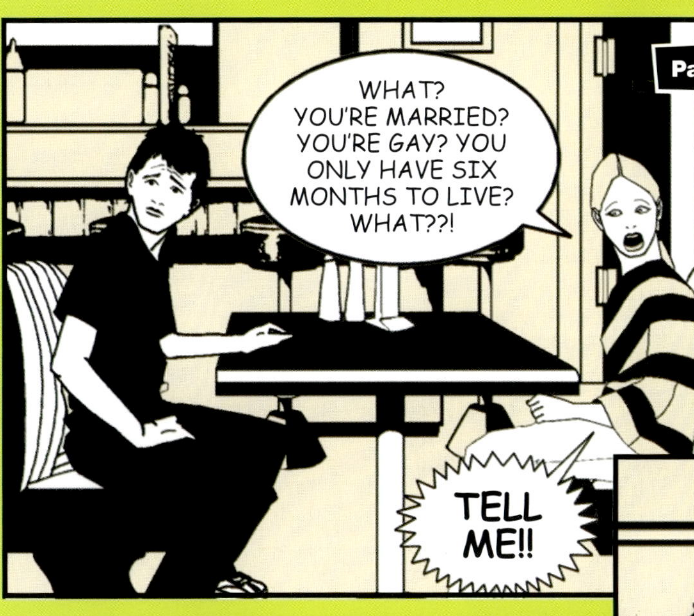

In panel 5, Dinah's speech is split into two separate balloons, serving two separate purposes: it means the first balloon won't be so large as to block out all of the background, and it also adds greater emphasis to her yelling "Tell me!" Of course, enlarging that piece of text really shows that she's shouting.

Conversely, to indicate Paddy's nervous whisper in panel 6, we can make the font size slightly smaller and then frame it in our broken-edged whisper balloon. Highlighting the word "NO!!" in Dinah's balloon and enlarging the font size gives the strip a percussive finish.

Polishing

Using your digital toolkit you can easily make those changes that make your cartoon your own. Start with the Brush tool.

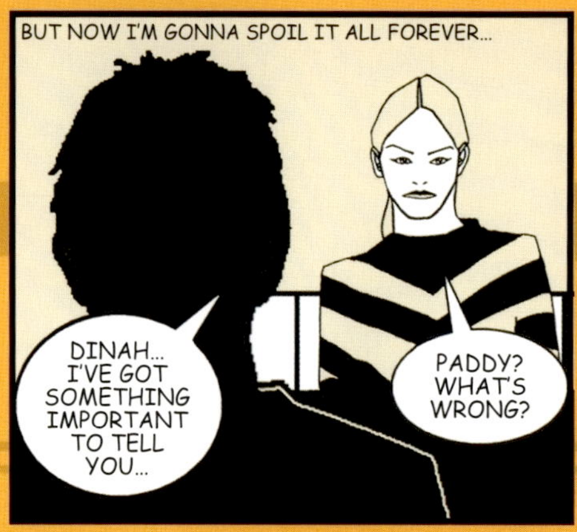

Next, in panel 3, Paddy is probably going to look better if he is rendered as a total silhouette, except for the highlight around the edge of his shirt. Now he looks like one of those guys on TV that wish to remain anonymous as they reveal some heinous crime or embarrassing exploit.

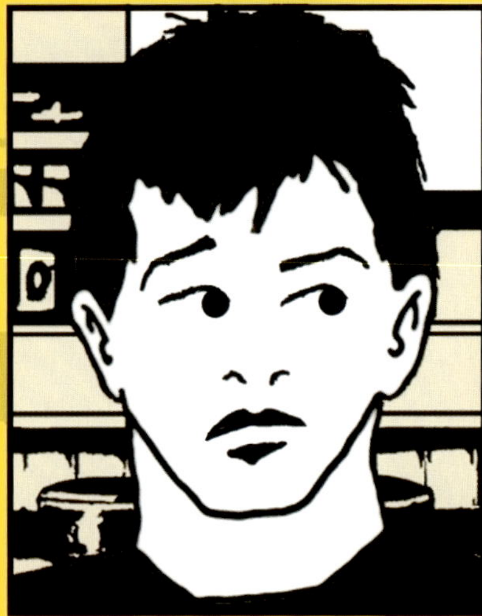

Nice and easy: the first thing we're going to do to finish off this strip is adjust Paddy's expression slightly in panel 1, so that he looks a little more concerned. All it takes is a small amount of redrawing around the eyes and mouth.

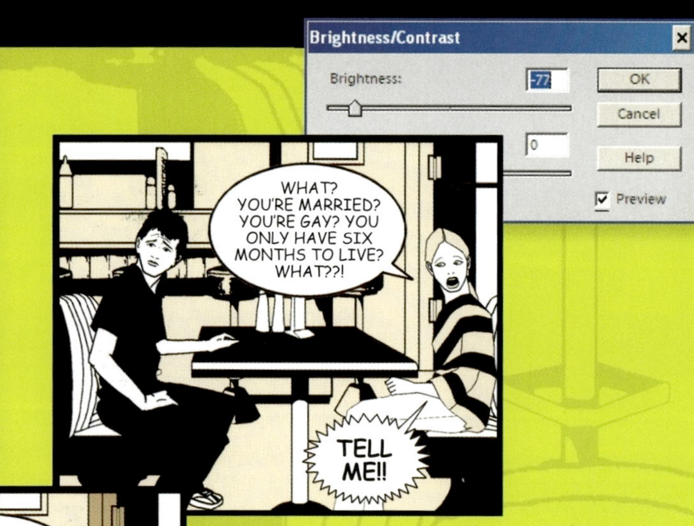

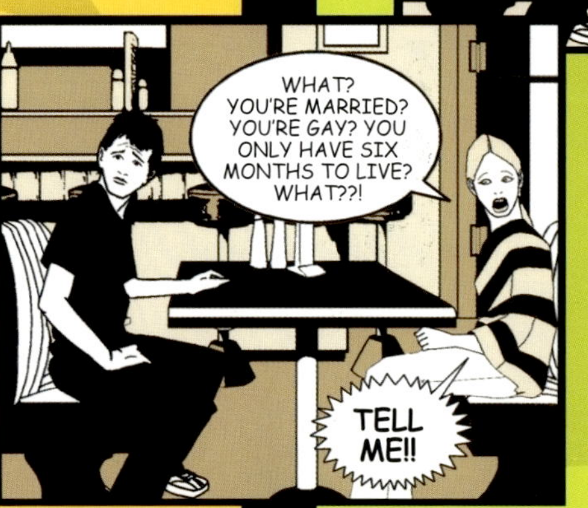

From the outset, we decided to make this an exercise in monochromatic coloring and we have used a single color to fill selected areas of each panel. The results are a little flat, but we can add variety without adding a single extra color. By selecting certain areas of color in each panel, we can alter the tone by adjusting the brightness (Enhance > Adjust Lighting > Brightness/Contrast), so we end up with a page containing two different shades of the same color.

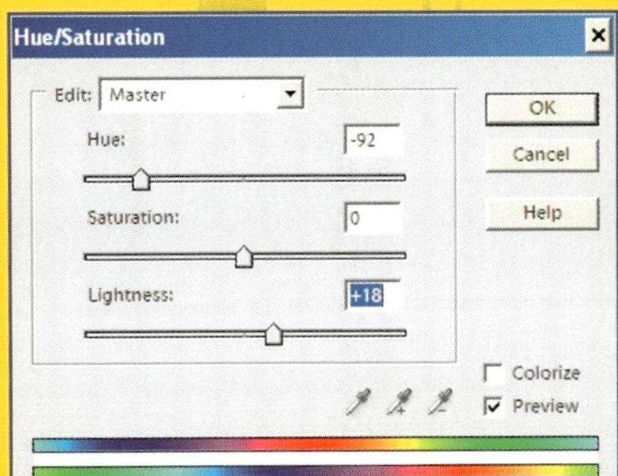

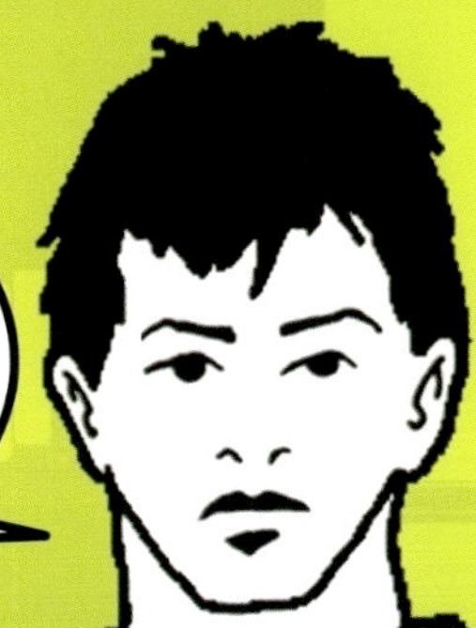

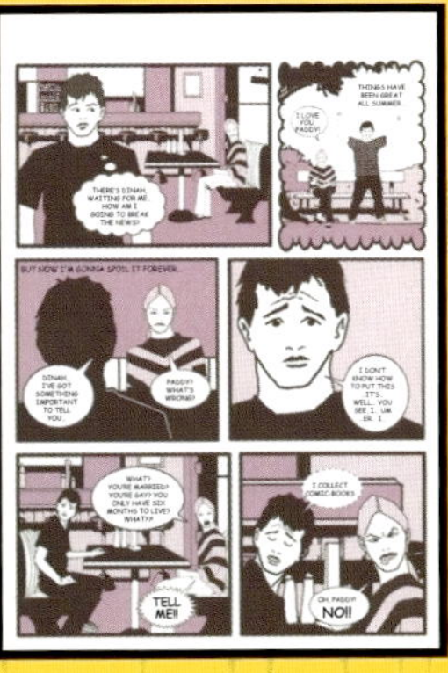

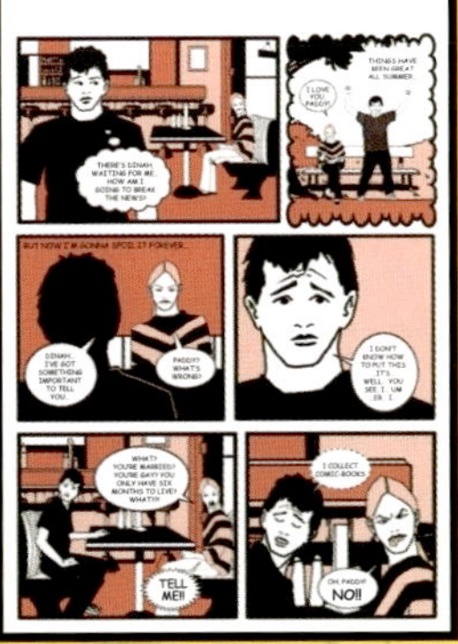

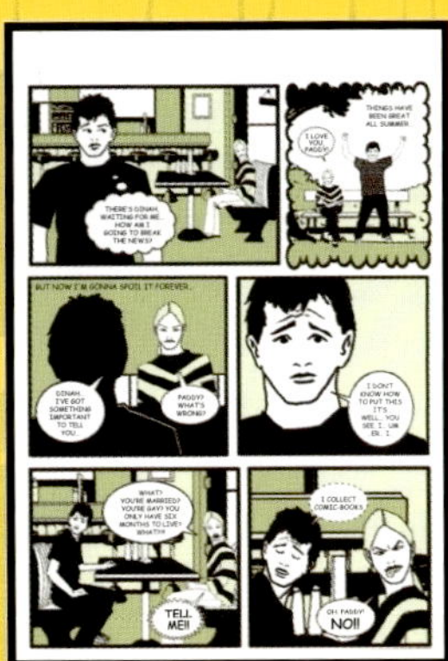

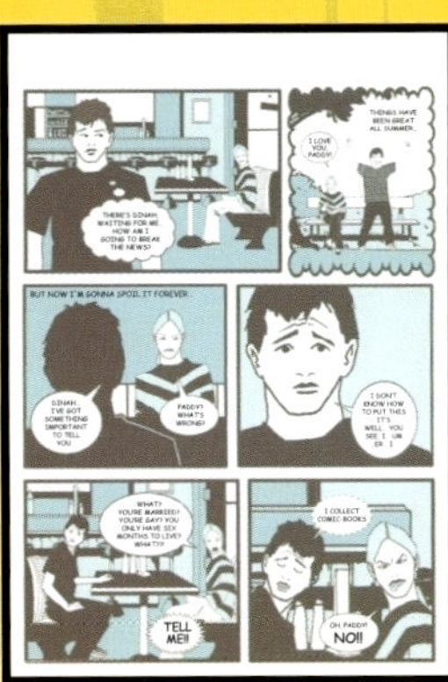

We also have the option of seeing what our page would look like if we had used shades of a different color, by heading back to Enhance on the Menu bar, and selecting Adjust Color > Adjust Hue/Saturation. By moving the Hue, Saturation, and Lightness sliders, you will instantly see the shades of color change, while retaining their relative values. Perhaps the strip would look better in shades of violet, crimson, green, or blue?

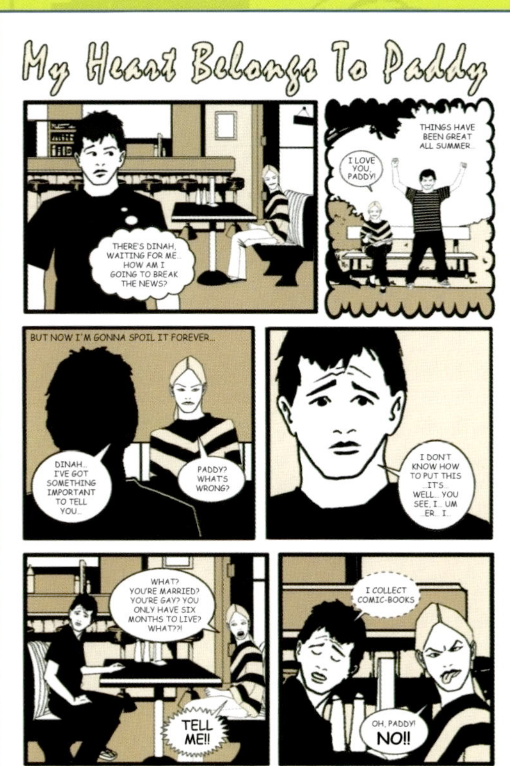

8 "That's the End of These Trousers"

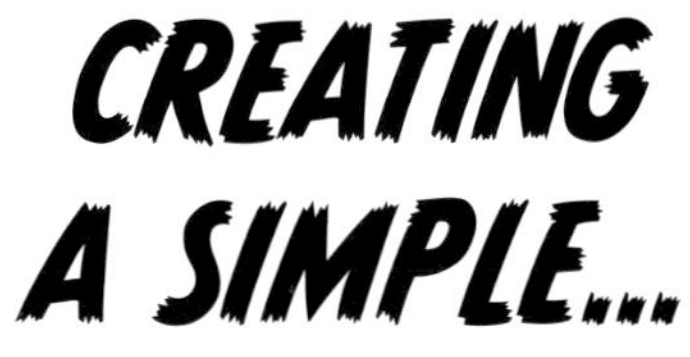

CREATING A SIMPLE...
...HUMOR OR FUNNY ANIMAL STRIP

Sample Script

Anthropomorphic animals—that is, animals who walk and talk like human beings—are a staple of Saturday morning cartoon shows and children's comics, so let's have fun creating our own version.

Although we have a whole family of cartoon cats to play with on the CD, we're going to stick with the Mom and Dad characters this time, as we plan a simple six-panel strip.

In our first panel, Katy Katt is standing outside the house; she's decided to fetch the laundry in from the line. A mysterious problem occurs in panel 2—Katy reaches the backyard to discover that her husband's trousers are missing from the hung-out laundry. Katy frets in panel 3, and in panel 4 gets the bright idea of checking the neighbor's garden to see if the trousers blew over the fence. When she climbs up the fence to take a look, we see that the neighbor's huge dog has got them and he's not giving them back. Sometime later, in panel 6, Bob Katt has got his trousers on, while Katy lies back on the armchair, covered in cuts and scratches. Bob, oblivious to what's happened and clearly not bothering to ask how his wife's day went, makes some comment along the lines of how she looks a bit rough and she should make more of an effort with her appearance. Yes, it's those old stereotypes of the clever, spirited wife, and the oafish husband… but, as a famous oafish cartoon husband once said: "It's funny 'cause it's true"….

Background: a view from outside the house.
Katy is standing outside.
K: Guess I'll go see if the laundry is dry!

Background: the garden. There is laundry on the line, but two empty clothes pegs and a significant gap where Bob's trousers used to be.
K: What the -? Where have Bob's trousers gone? I hung them there this morning!

K: Oh, there's gonna be trouble if I don't find them!

K: Maybe they blew over the fence and into the neighbor's backyard! I'll climb over and take a look!

Background: a view from the neighbor's yard. The neighbor's dog is standing over the missing trousers as Katy leans over the fence.
K: **Oh, no! Mr. Basil's dog is playing with them! Scat! Shoo!**

Background: inside the Katts' living room. Bob's got his trousers on, Katy is lying on the armchair covered in scratches and giving Bob an angry look.
B: **Darling, you should spruce yourself up a bit! You're letting yourself go!**

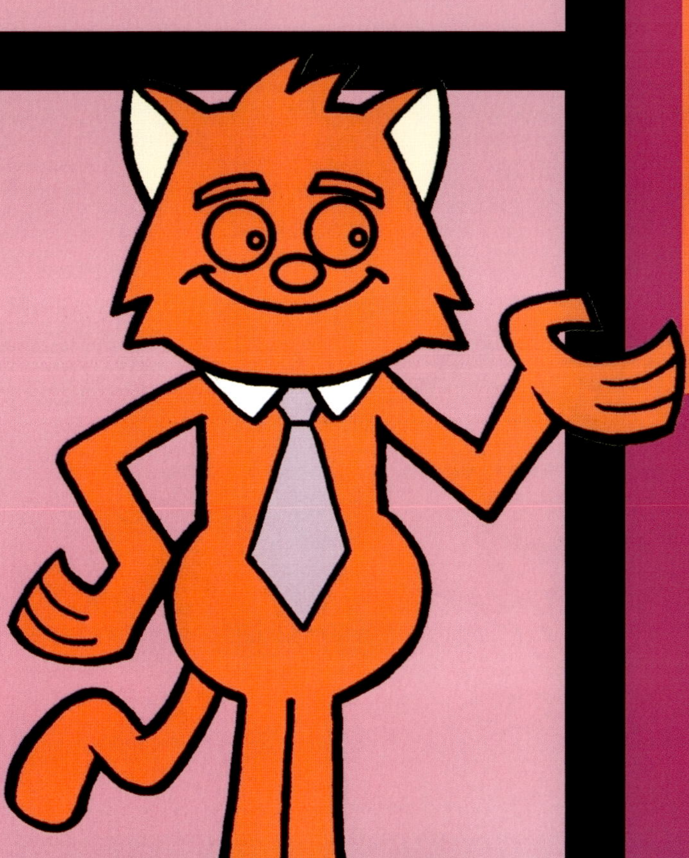

1 WHO WHERE WHAT	**2** PROBLEM
KATY KATT OUTSIDE THE HOUSE, ABOUT TO BRING IN THE WASHING	HER HUSBAND'S TROUSERS ARE MISSING FROM THE CLOTHES LINE
3 EFFECT	**4** POSSIBLE SOLUTION
KATY'S WORRIED ABOUT WHAT BOB WILL SAY	SHE DECIDES TO LOOK IN THE NEIGHBOR'S BACKYARD
5 SOLUTION ATTEMPTED	**6** CONCLUSION
SHE CAN SEE THAT THE NEIGHBOR'S DOG HAS GOTTEN HOLD OF THEM	KATY HAS OBVIOUSLY HAD A FIGHT WITH THE DOG TO GET THE TROUSERS BACK WHICH BOB IS NOW WEARING

Thumbnails

In the first panel, we need to see that Katy is outside, though it's not imperative that we see all of the house—just the window and the wall should be enough—as most of this strip takes place in the garden. Panel 2 could do with being a little bigger to give plenty of attention to the gap on the washing line. Panel 3 is a close-up of Katy looking worried. This should again allow some extra space for panel 4, where we see her marching over to the fence. We're going to need a large panel for 5, as we want the neighbor's fearsome-looking dog to take the reader's attention... in fact...

There are no dogs in the Humor section of the CD, but that shouldn't stop us looking elsewhere. There are two different dogs in the Slice of Life section (or views of the same dog), but they don't look terribly fierce and are obviously drawn in a style that's a little at odds with the style of the humor strip. We could attempt to redraw the face of one of the dogs or, if we're going to be using a different style of drawing anyway, we could switch the dog for the scary-looking creature in the Sci-Fi section. Maybe Mr. Basil has a pet raptor, or something. It'll certainly add more humor when we see Katy scratched all over in the final panel.

Also in panel 5, by flipping the Garden background and doing a bit of careful redrawing, we should be able to quickly create our view of the neighbor's garden.

Panel 6 will just need a clear view of Bob in the lounge, happy in his trousers, and Katy sprawled out on the armchair.

Already, we can see that this strip will be a little more complicated to construct than it might have first appeared. But if you have attempted the previous strips, or if Photoshop is already an old friend, it's likely that you'll have the skills needed to put the whole thing together fairly easily.

At this point, it might be worth reminding ourselves that "funny animal" strips don't necessarily have to be funny. We could have just as easily used these characters for a serious purpose and used the "cartoony" nature of the artwork as an ironic counterpoint. The most celebrated use of this was in Art Spiegelman's Pulitzer Award-winning *Maus: A Survivor's Tale*, in which he used cartoon animals to illustrate a true tale of life during the Holocaust. Spiegelman drew some inspiration from *Krazy Kat*, the 1920s newspaper strip by George Herriman, which was set in an ever-changing, surreal desert landscape, and used cats, mice, and dogs as Jungian archetypes. And it still managed to be funny!

However, our strip is more Yogi Bear than Jungy Bear, so let's take a look at the pictures we'll need to put the whole thing together.

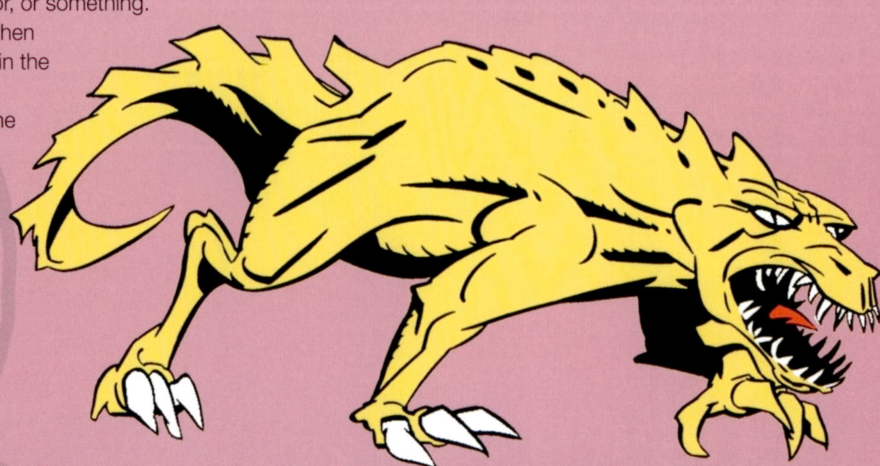

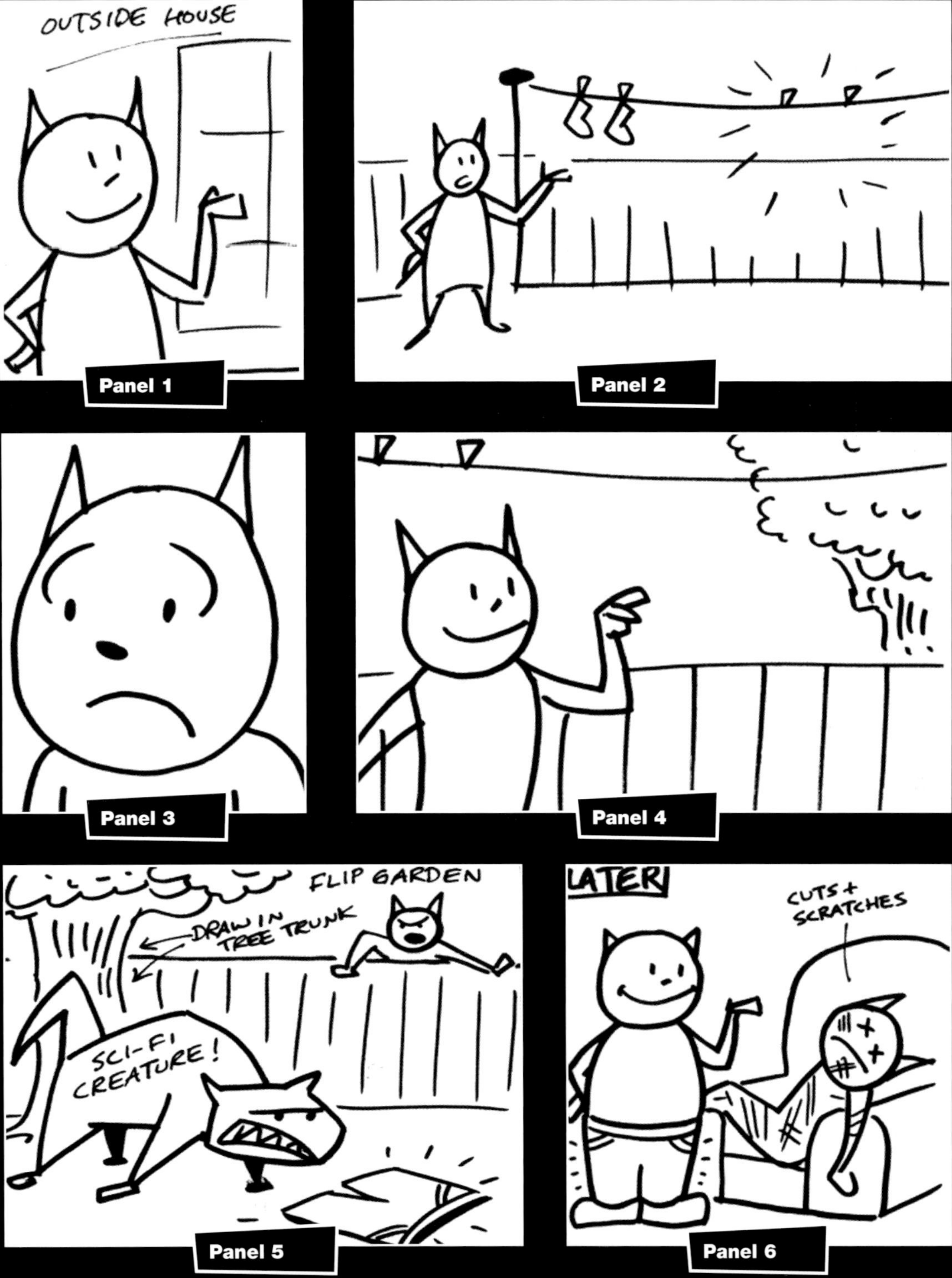

OUTSIDE HOUSE
Panel 1
Panel 2
Panel 3
Panel 4
FLIP GARDEN
DRAW IN TREE TRUNK
SCI-FI CREATURE!
Panel 5
LATER!
CUTS + SCRATCHES
Panel 6

Choosing Pictures

A mixture of bright candy colors and pastel shades have been chosen for this project, taking care to keep things consistent. This will achieve greater color harmony across the page as a whole.

Although we will only be using a very small section of the Street and Lounge backgrounds in panel 1 and panel 6, it's worth spending a few minutes coloring the whole of any background picture in case you change your mind about a panel and need to use it again later. We will be using the whole of the Garden background, and flipping it to create the neighbor's backyard in panel 5.

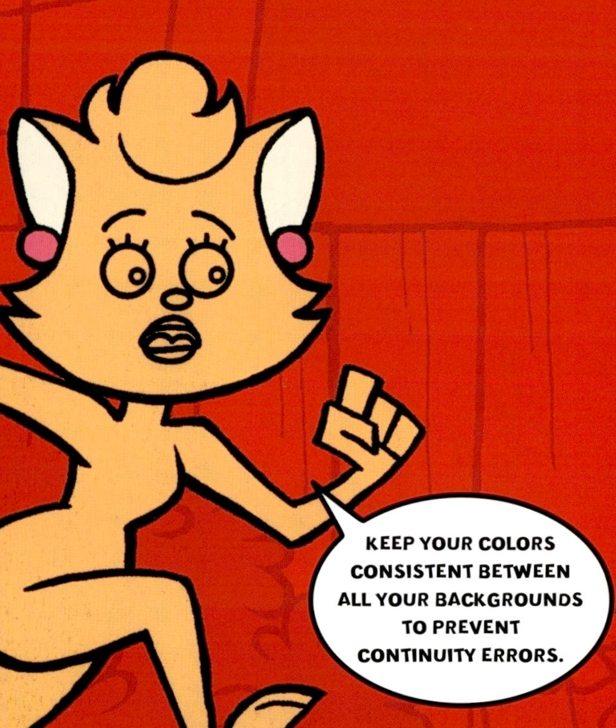

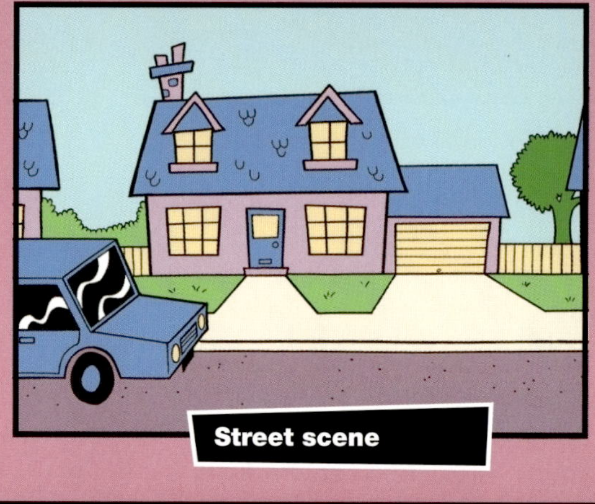

Street scene

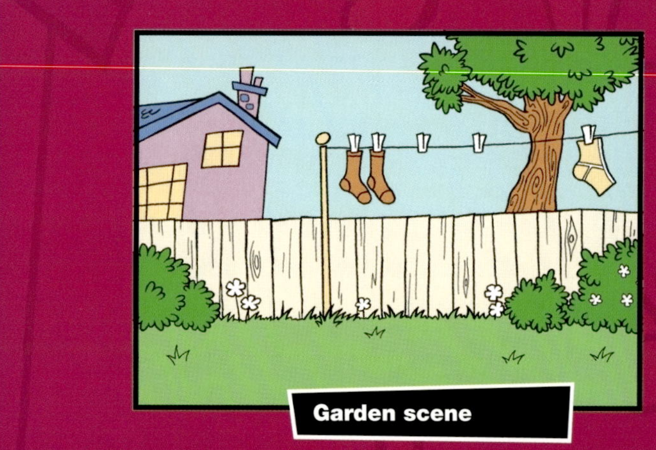

Garden scene

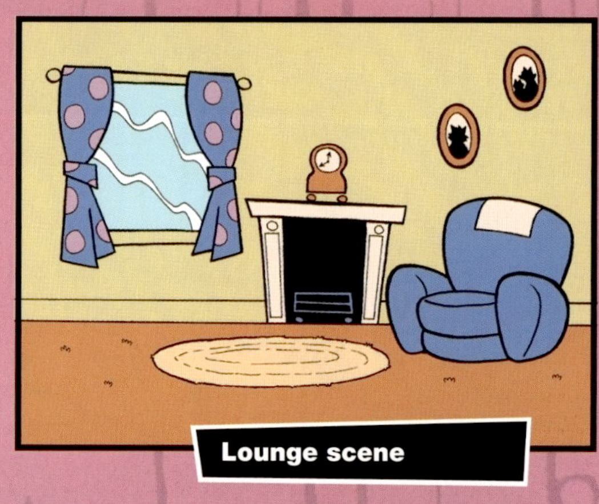

Lounge scene

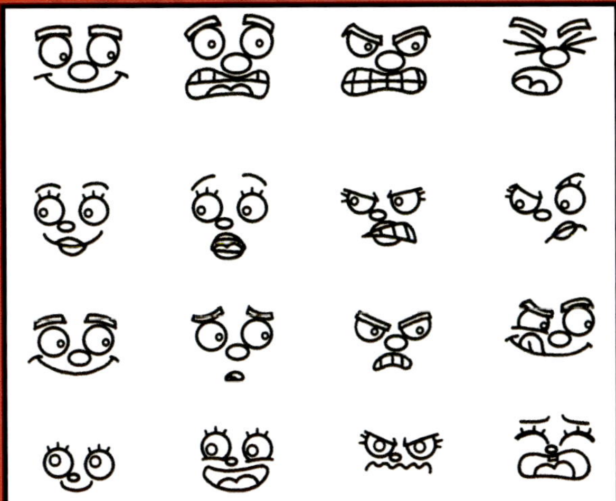

We'll be needing all of Mom's bodies, which we can flip to suit the demands of each panel. Bob only makes one appearance, and Dad 1 is tailor-made for this. Coloring the Mom bodies orange for Katy gives her an energetic appearance; conversely, coloring Bob's body deep red makes him appear somewhat older and perhaps prone to tantrums—heaven knows what he'd have done if he hadn't gotten his trousers back… perhaps there would have been a sequel featuring Katy in a sack by the canal. We have a wealth of facial expressions that can be easily dragged onto each body as required and colored to match their surroundings.

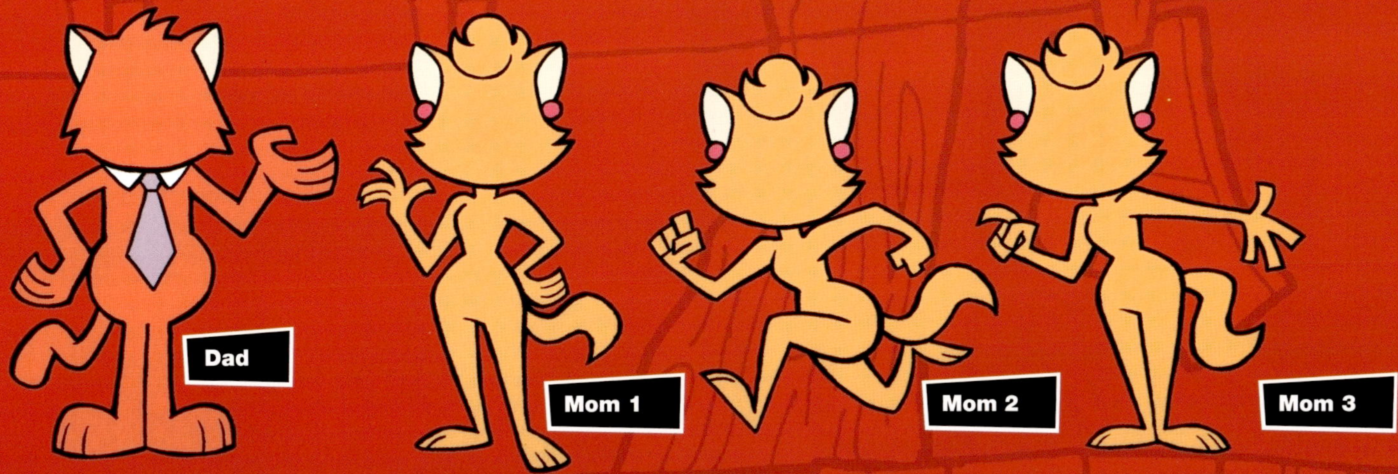

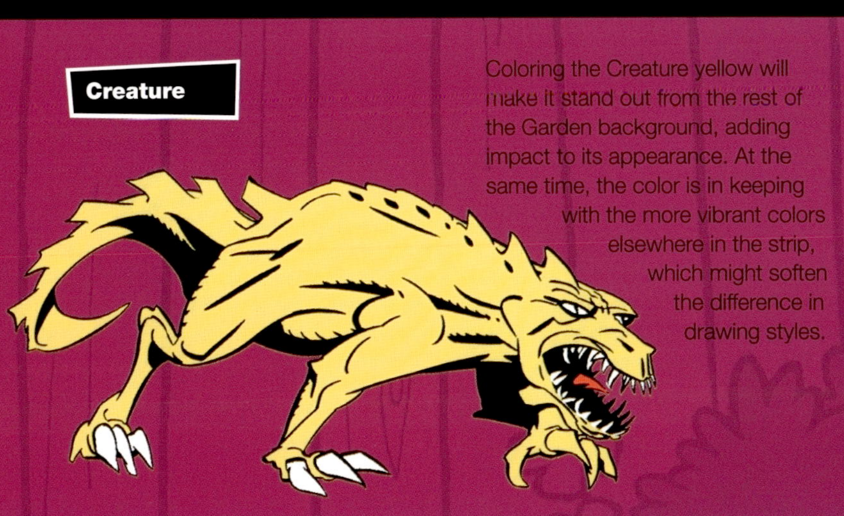

Coloring the Creature yellow will make it stand out from the rest of the Garden background, adding impact to its appearance. At the same time, the color is in keeping with the more vibrant colors elsewhere in the strip, which might soften the difference in drawing styles.

The trousers are found in the Props folder, and are colored purple to match Bob's tie. He's such a snappy dresser… too bad he doesn't wear a shirt.

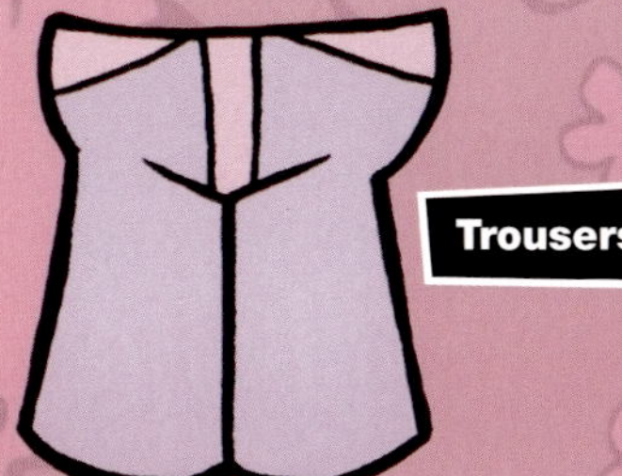

Assembling Page

Now the time has come to follow the thumbnail plan. The original wasn't terribly clear about details like what had been in the laundry basket, so we've got some room to maneuver.

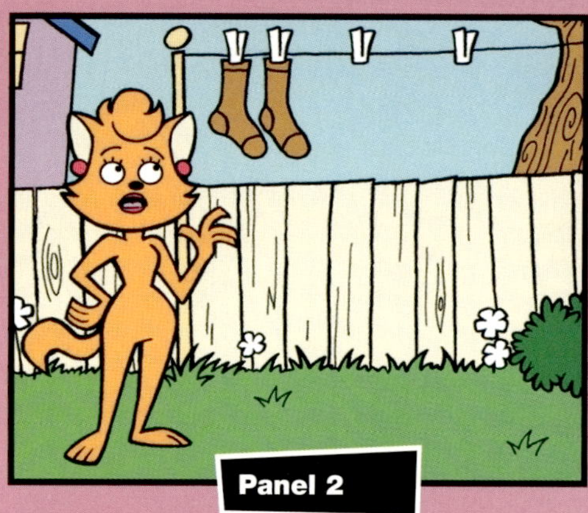

Panel 2

The first panel measures 3 x 3½ in, which means panel 2 should be slightly wider to meet 7 in, our optimum width for each tier, including a ¼-in gap between panels. Our main point of interest in the panel is the gap on the washing line, so by cropping our background with the rectangular panel border as shown, that gap is framed by the clothes line, the socks, the fence, and the tree. Choose carefully how you resize Katy for this panel; she needs to look as though she is tall enough to reach the clothes line, and that she could peep over the fence later without too much of a climb.

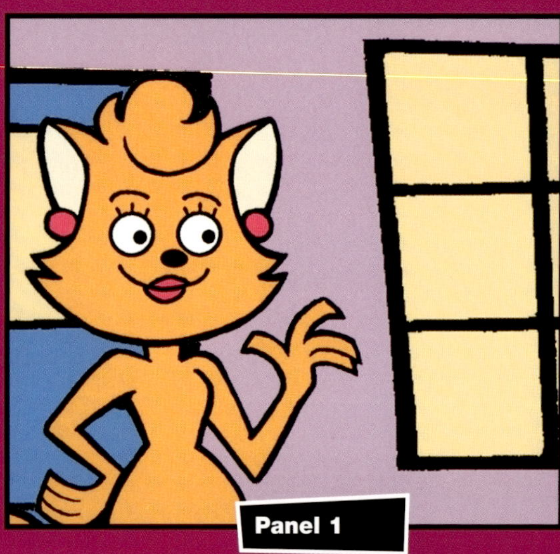

Panel 1

At the thumbnail stage, we decided that panel 1 should show Katy just outside the house. To show the whole of the house would make Katy appear very small in this first picture, so in order to give her a decent showing—and she'll be fairly small in most of the other panels—we sacrifice most of the house. This doesn't really matter, as we just need to see part of the door and window to suggest that she's outside. Using the Rectangular panel border from the CD, we can resize it to grab the section of the house we need, crop, and slot Katy into place. Choosing the smiling face from the Expressions seems apt, as she's blissfully unaware of what is to come. And maybe she enjoys doing laundry. Some people do.

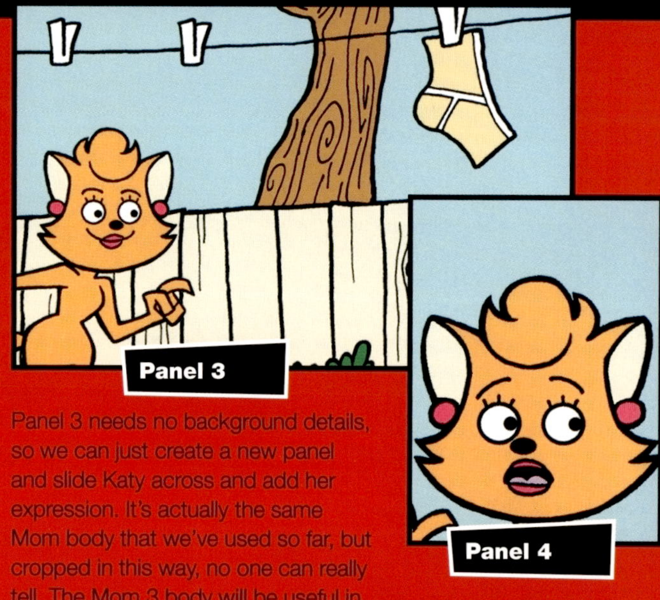

Panel 3

Panel 4

Panel 3 needs no background details, so we can just create a new panel and slide Katy across and add her expression. It's actually the same Mom body that we've used so far, but cropped in this way, no one can really tell. The Mom 3 body will be useful in panel 4, as it has a pointing finger, perfect for when Katy realizes that the trousers might have blown over the fence. Using a different part of the background adds a little variety and allows us to show the tree in the neighbor's garden, which will be an important feature of panel 5.

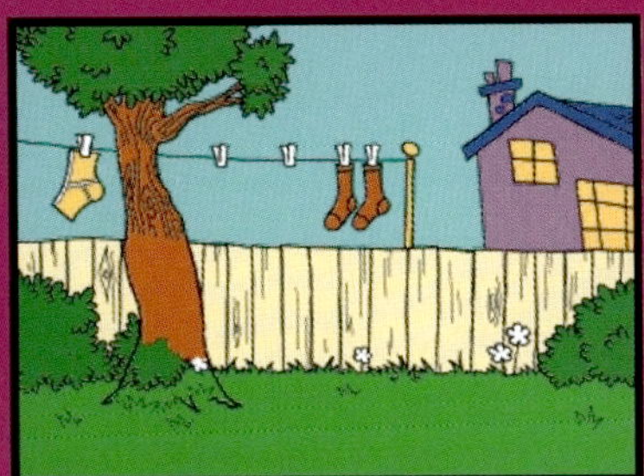

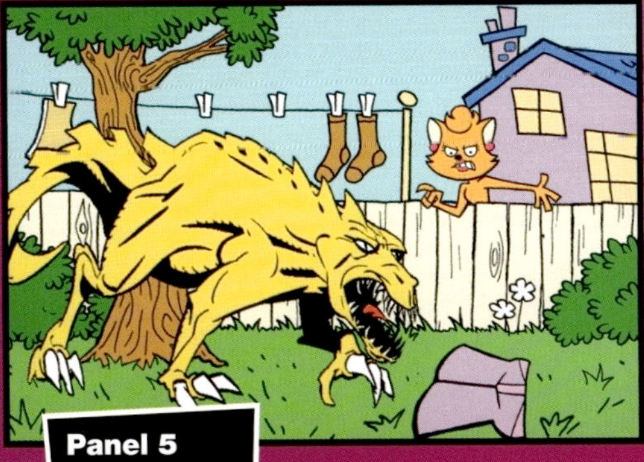

Panel 5

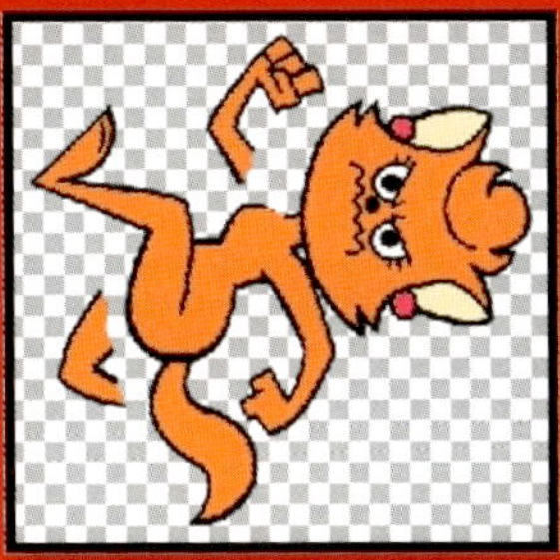

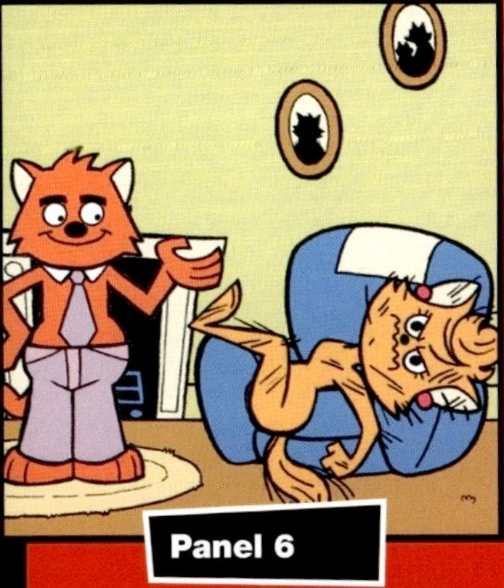

Panel 6

Choosing and cropping the background, and slipping the trousers onto Bob, are the easy parts of nailing panel 6 together. How are we going to use any of our existing Mom pictures to get Katy lying across the armchair? Here's how: crop Mom 3 from the rest, and add an expression. Then, rotate the whole image by 90 degrees (Image > Rotate > 90 Right). Next, carefully erase her arm and leg and cover her body with thin lines by zooming in and using the Brush tool. Use the Move tool to drag her onto the armchair, and it will look as though she's flopped out in exhaustion.

Flipping the full background picture gives us the starting point for panel 5, as we see what lurks next door. Before adding the Creature, we should draw in the tree trunk, as it is now meant to be seen fully against this other side of the fence. Erasing the clothesline where it appears in front of the tree completes the illusion that we are seeing a different garden. We can also draw in some extra tufts of grass near the bottom of the picture. Next, we add Katy—erasing her torso until it looks as though she is peering over the fence—and then drag the Creature across. It can be distorted slightly with the Move tool's bounding box, giving it a chunkier, slightly dog-like appearance. Lastly, we add the trousers and use Image>Transform>Distort to lie them on the ground in perspective.

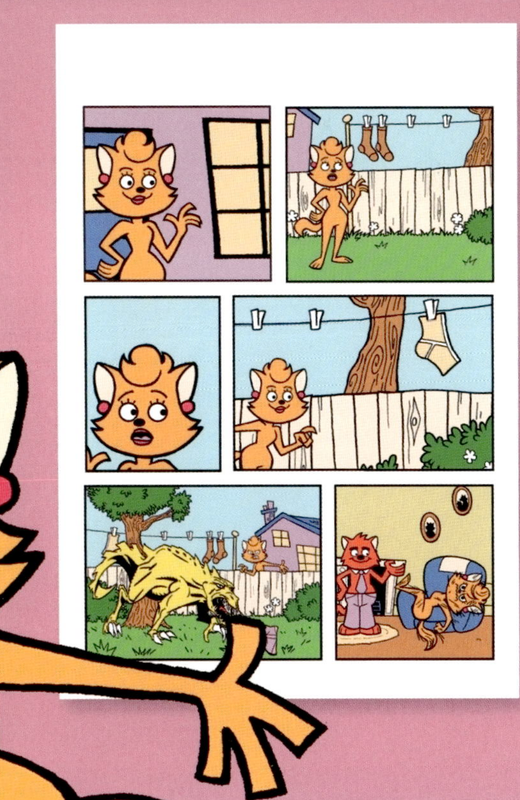

Adding Text & Balloons

Back in the day, word balloons were always written and drawn directly onto comic-strip artwork. Although this method is still used on rare occasions, the advent of computer-generated lettering allows us so much more freedom in our layout and design—if it all goes horribly wrong, we no longer have to reach for the opaque white paint or glue a patch on top. We can just start all over again. However, the letterer's skills lie not just in their neat, hand-drawn calligraphy, but in making the captions and balloons a vital but unobtrusive part of the whole panel layout, which is one reason why their skills are still much in demand in this digital age.

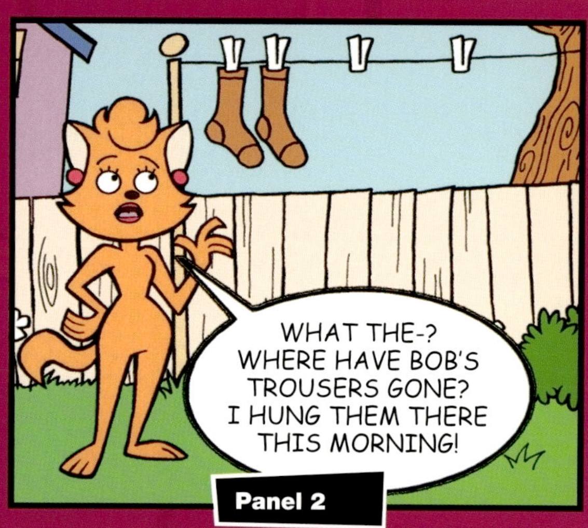

Panel 2 has lots of empty space, which is a good thing, since it's going to be quite a large balloon. Placing it in the bottom right part of the panel means it doesn't cover the nice arrangement of elements that define the area once occupied by Bob's trousers; in fact, as an element of the picture, it reinforces the framing of that area of the panel.

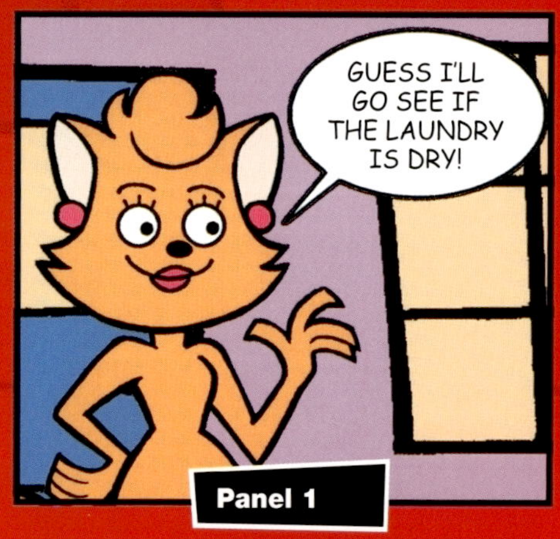

Things are a bit tight in the first panel but we can just squeeze our balloon in at the top right corner so that it doesn't obscure more of the window than is necessary. We can still see that Katy is outside the house.

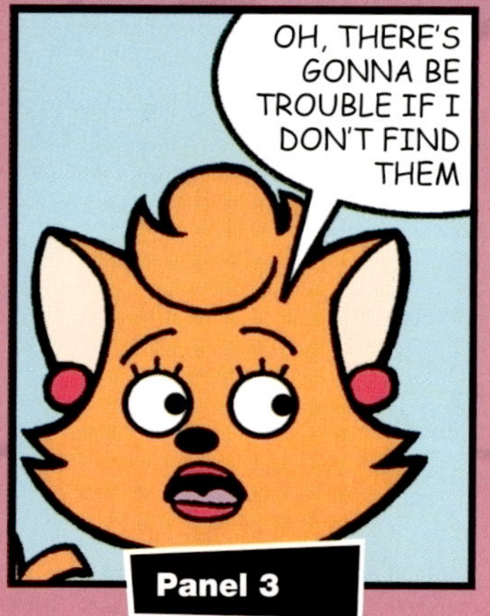

Panel 3 utilizes the "corner balloon" technique we saw in the Sci-Fi/Superhero strip; as well as looking good in the overall arrangement of the panel, it's a useful solution when there's not a lot of dead space available.

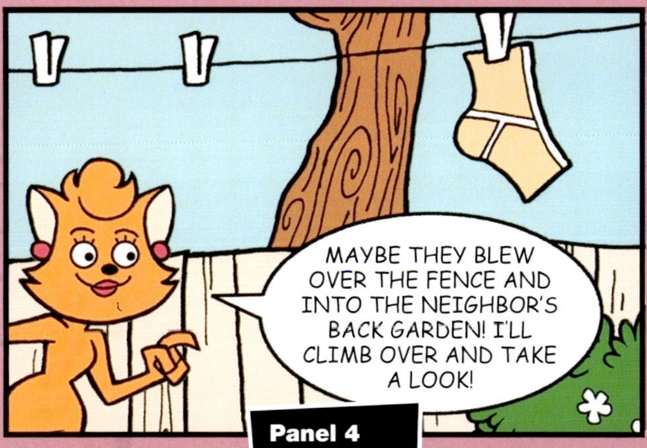

Panel 4 is very similar to panel 2, in that a large-ish balloon is needed. Once again, aiming lower-right in the panel keeps the important elements of the background clear—in this case, the tree, the area above Katy where Bob's trousers used to be, and…uh… Bob's underpants.

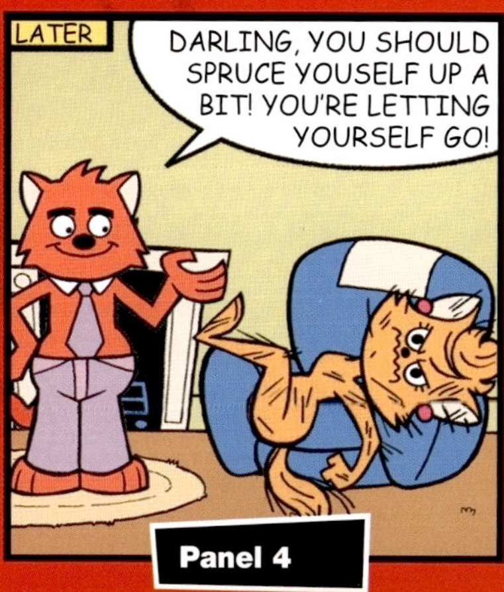

Panel 6 needs a "Later" caption in the top left corner, achieved by typing the caption first and then using the Line tool on layers beneath. Bob's word balloon is pretty big, but the old corner trick serves us well again.

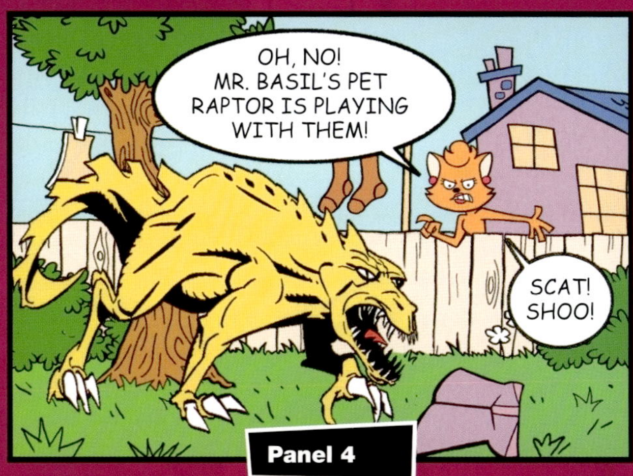

In panel 5, we certainly don't want to obscure the visual impact of seeing "Mr. Basil's pet Raptor" or the eventual resting place of Bob's trousers, so Katy's word balloon is set against the sky, with the dialogue split into a smaller balloon down in the lower right.

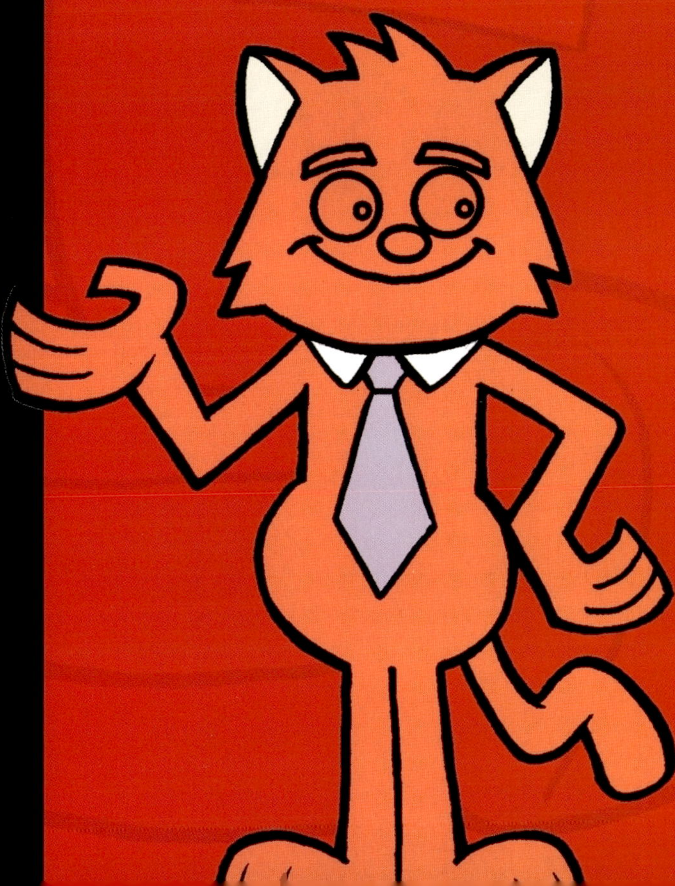

Polishing

Polishing and finishing "That's the End of These Trousers" is going to be at once one of the simplest and most complicated techniques in this book. However, it can make your work look fantastic, so here goes...

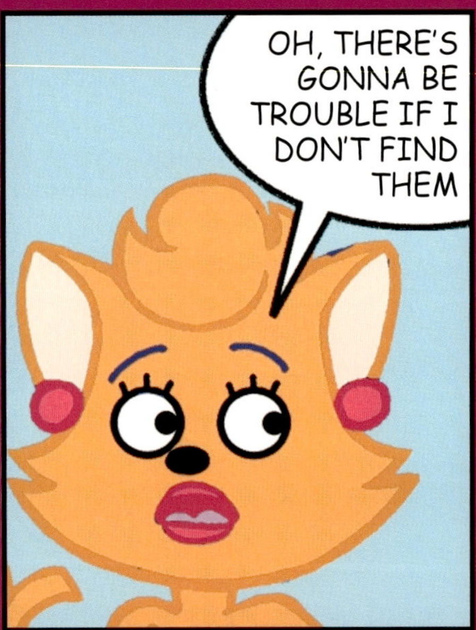

We're going to actually color the linework in each picture, using an overall color for background objects, and a darker shade of their base color for the characters. This is a technique commonly used in contemporary TV cartoons and their comic book spin-offs.

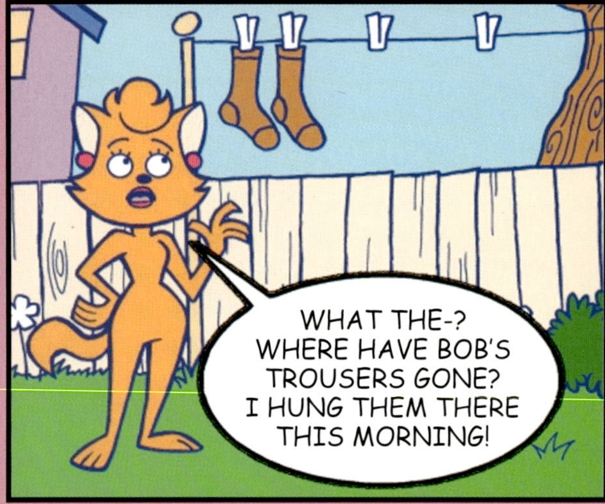

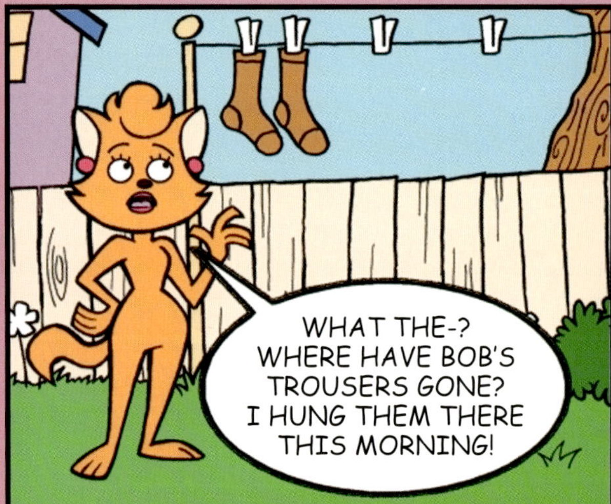

It's not a difficult process, though it can be a time-consuming one. Ensuring that you are working on the Background layer, i.e. the panels, select a black area with the Magic Wand. Go to Select > Similar on the Menu bar, and you'll see that every black area on the page is now selected. Choose a dark blue in the Color box on the Toolbar, and go to Edit>Fill. All of your black lines are now dark blue, which react nicely against the other colors and brighten up the page.

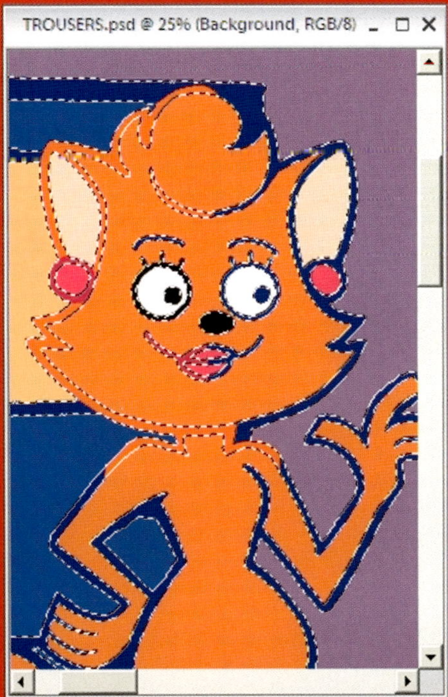

A final, artistic touch is to add a little Noise to the floor in each panel and to the wall in panel 1. When you've finished, if you have accidentally painted into the panel borders, simply tidy them up by selecting each panel with the Rectangular Marquee tool and add an inside Stroke of dark blue; your perfect panel borders return.

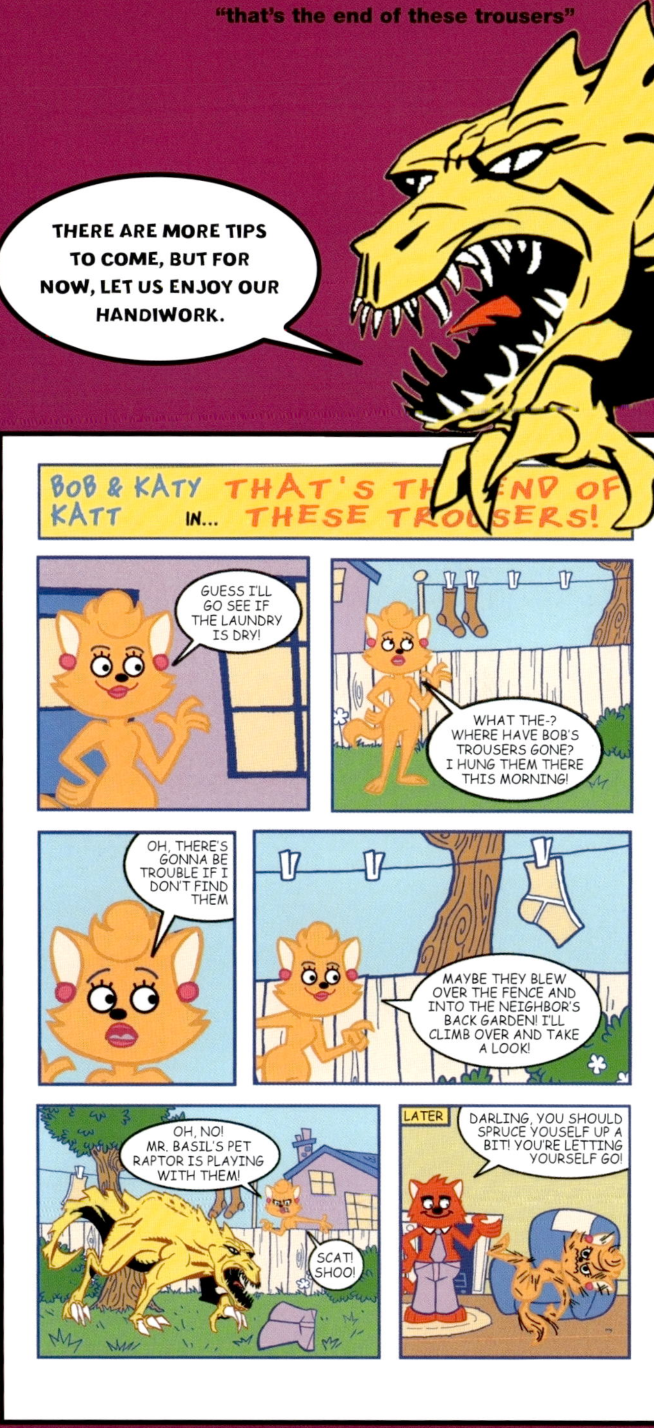

So now all we have to do is create a title block for the top of the page, choosing a suitably "cartoony" font.

That's the End of These Trousers, and the end of our four projects. If you have attempted each of them, you should now be well versed in the super-scientific technology of Photoshop Elements, and fully aware of how it can be used in dozens of different ways to enhance your cartoon imagery.

9 Mastering Your Art

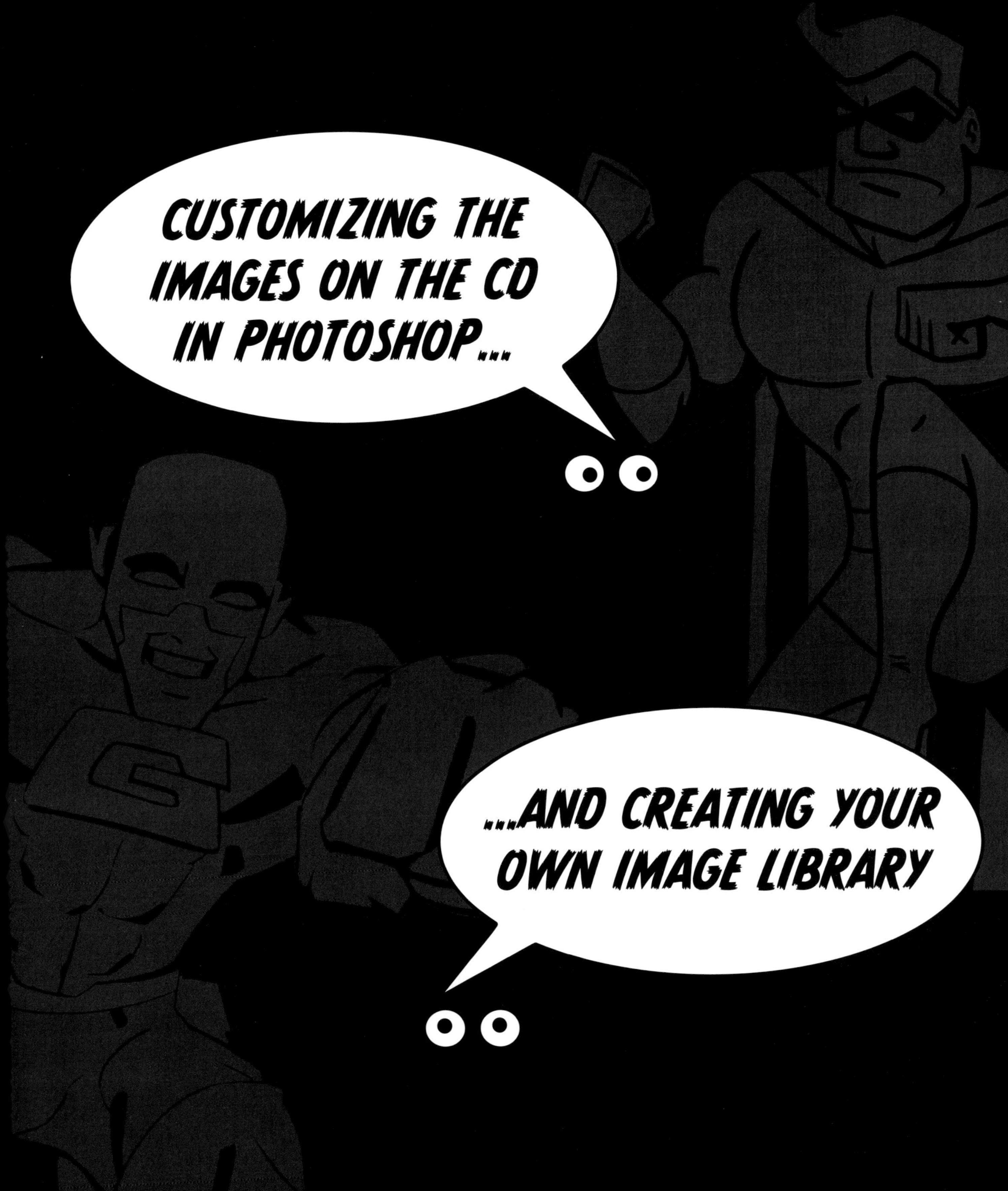

CUSTOMIZING THE IMAGES ON THE CD IN PHOTOSHOP...
...AND CREATING YOUR OWN IMAGE LIBRARY

Using Transform

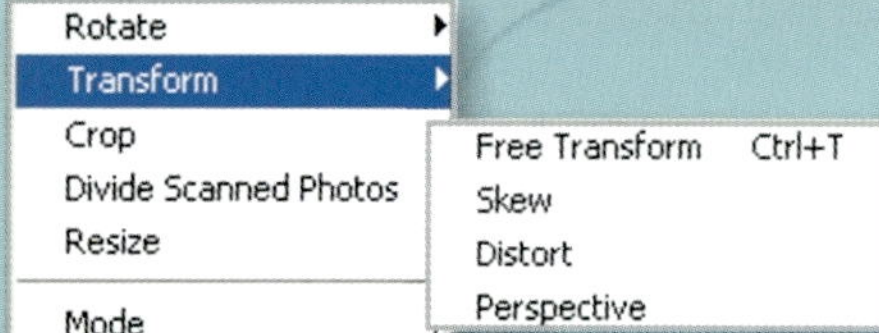

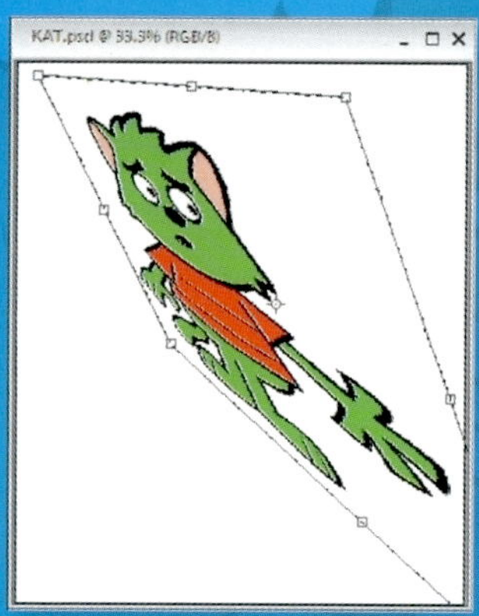

Previously, we have used the Transform tool (or its sister, the bounding box of the Move tool), for slight alterations to panel sizes or to add a touch of perspective to our view of a building. After selecting an image, in the Transform menu (Image>Transform), you will find four methods listed. Of these, Skew and Perspective work in pretty much the same way, as do Free Transform and Distort.

Using Distort, images can be twisted almost beyond recognition, which can be fun for five minutes, but this facility actually allows us to make some creative choices that can add to our image bank of characters and settings.

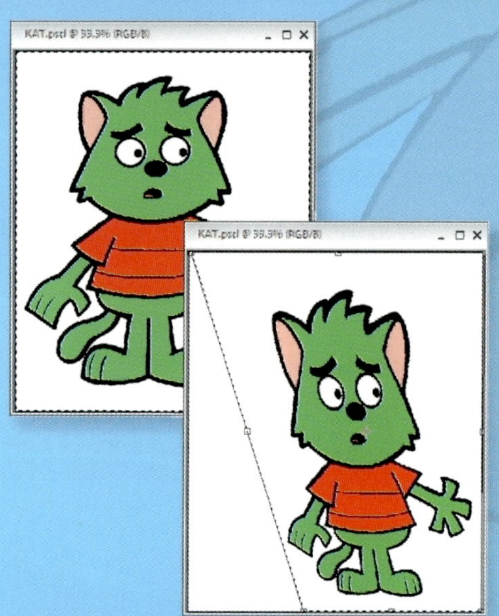

Skew and Perspective allow us to make one end of an image larger or smaller than the other; using Free Transform or Distort, we can accomplish the same effect, and a whole lot more.

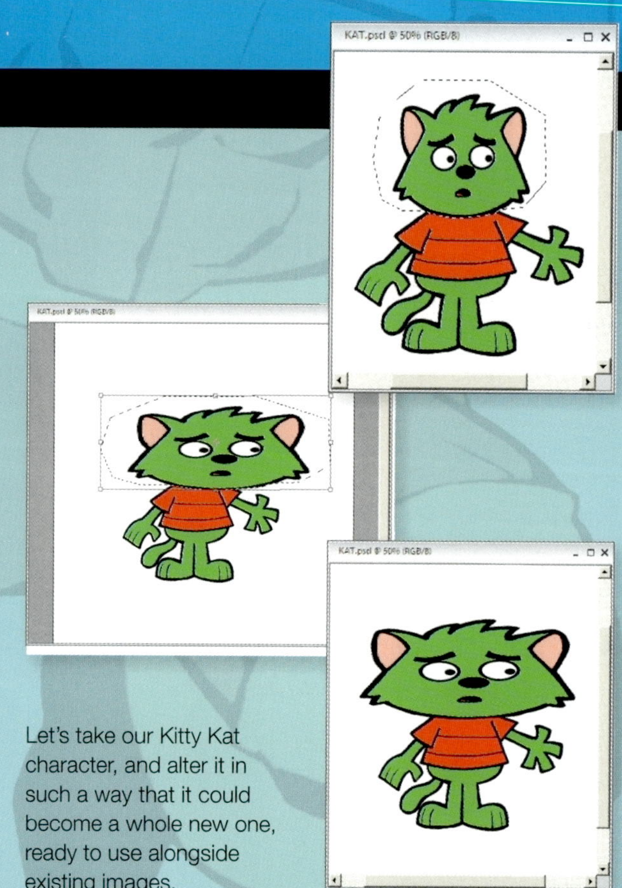

Let's take our Kitty Kat character, and alter it in such a way that it could become a whole new one, ready to use alongside existing images.

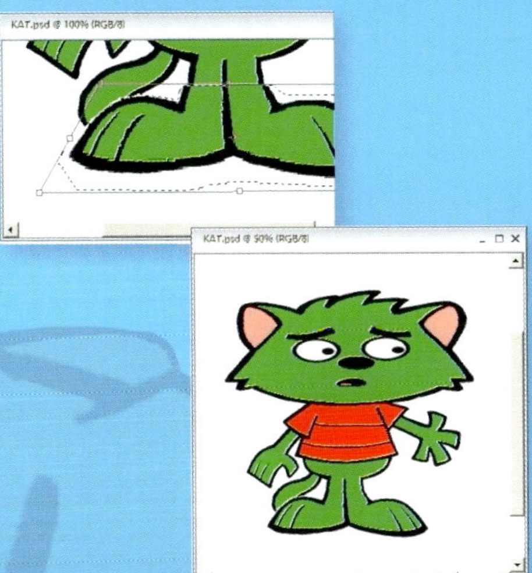

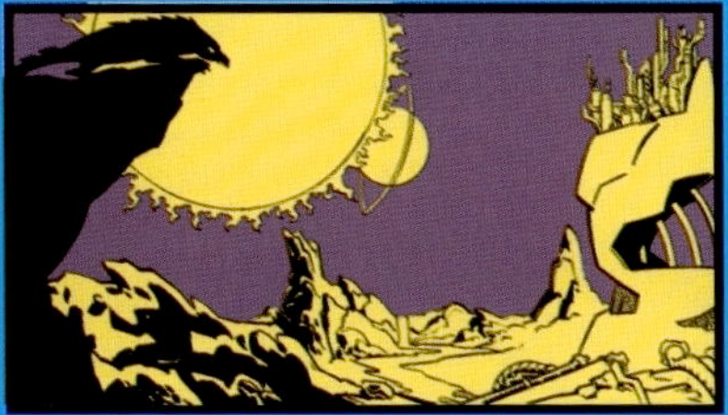

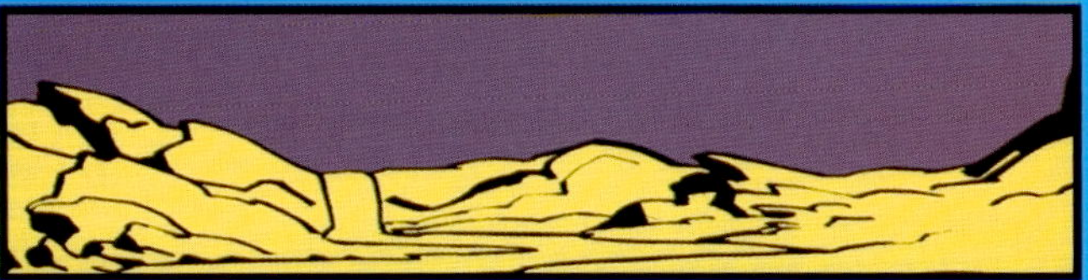

Use the Lasso tool to select the character's head, taking care around the collar area. Then choose Distort, and pull the character's head sideways using the handles of the bounding box. You'll see that it becomes wider while losing none of its height, and that it can be moved back into place on the neck, giving you a character of very different proportions. Should you choose, you can give him or her big feet, this time using the corner handles too, to get the leg lines to match the other part of the image.

Certain backgrounds lend themselves to distortion. Our Sci-Fi planet landscape can be altered merely by making it shorter and wider and cropping out a suitable section. Parts of this could then be used for a whole series of panels.

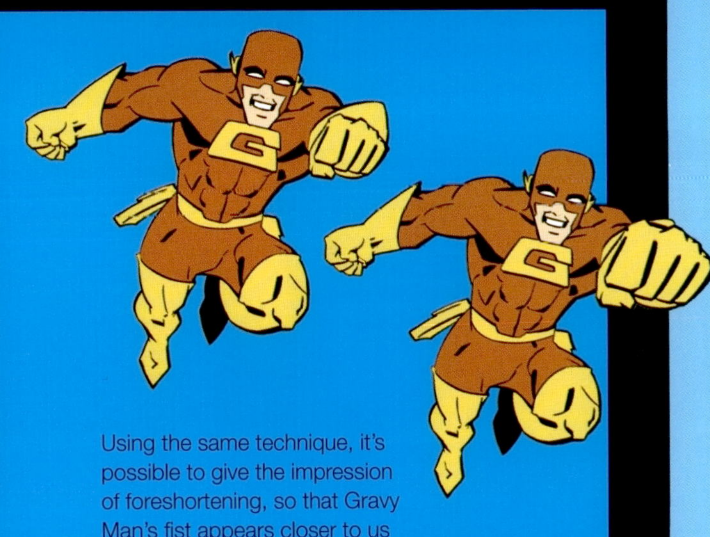

Using the same technique, it's possible to give the impression of foreshortening, so that Gravy Man's fist appears closer to us than in the original version.

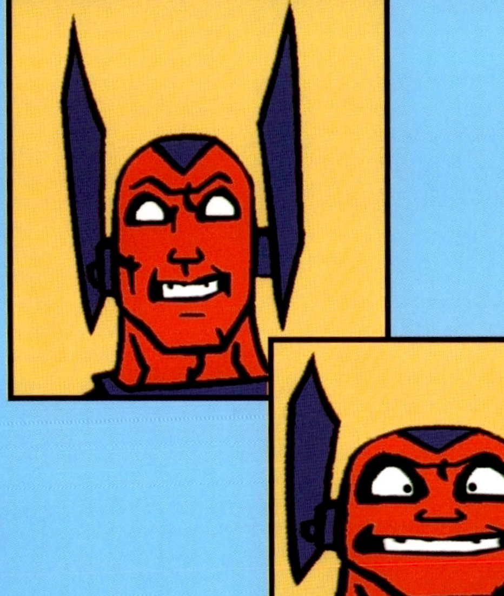

We can also distort smaller elements within an image, such as certain facial features. With practice, eyes, noses, mouths, chins, etc., can all be altered to create wild variations of our characters.

Using Filters

We've used Filters occasionally on our project pages, so you should be familiar with such effects as Noise and Clouds. There's a multitude of Filters available, some of more use than others to cartoonists, so let's take a look at those that can subtly—and not so subtly—alter the overall look of an image, rather than filling an area with texture or a special effect.

One of the most useful filters to be considered before any coloring is Artistic > Cut Out. Used at its lower settings for Levels and Simplicity, and a high level for Edge Fidelity, we can beef up the linework of a drawing and lose any tiny stray lines, giving a slightly more "cartoony" look to any picture. By lowering the setting for Edge Fidelity, the picture can take the look of a woodcut, becoming much more angular and simplified. Taken to an extreme, we can get bizarrely distorted pictures that look as though they might have been attempted by Pablo Picasso.

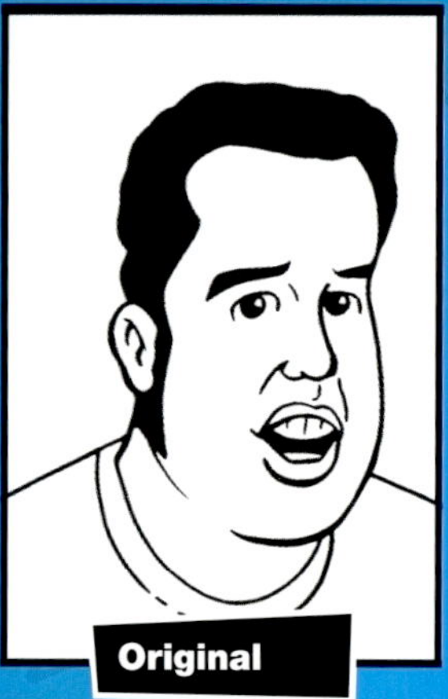

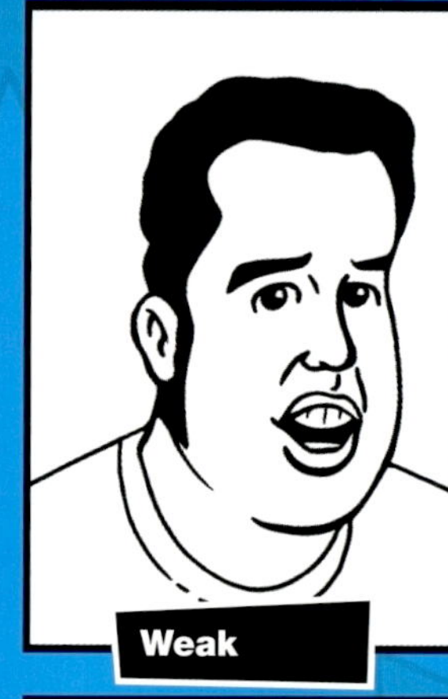

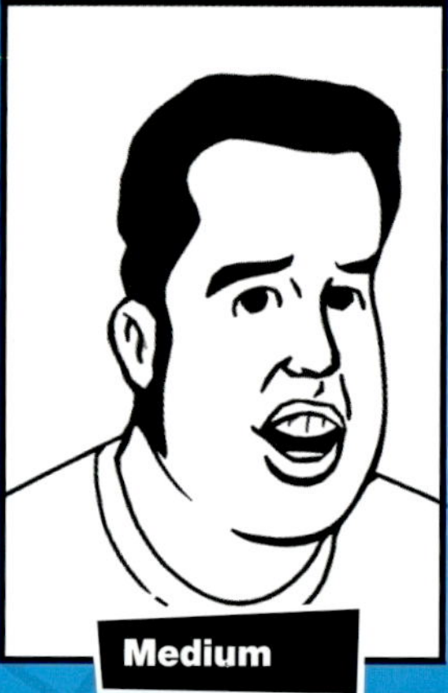

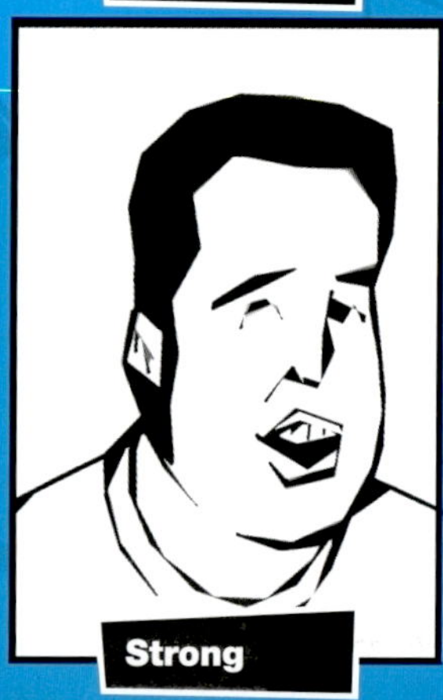

Used post-coloring, the Cut Out filter can give an image the effect of having been printed using the techniques of a hundred years ago, resembling the illustrations in old children's books. Cut Out is one of the filters most worth experimenting with in the menu.

Poster Edges will thicken up linework in a similar way to Cut Out, and Film Grain will add a very similar quality to the Noise Filter, though the effects achievable can be slightly different. Have fun trying them yourself.

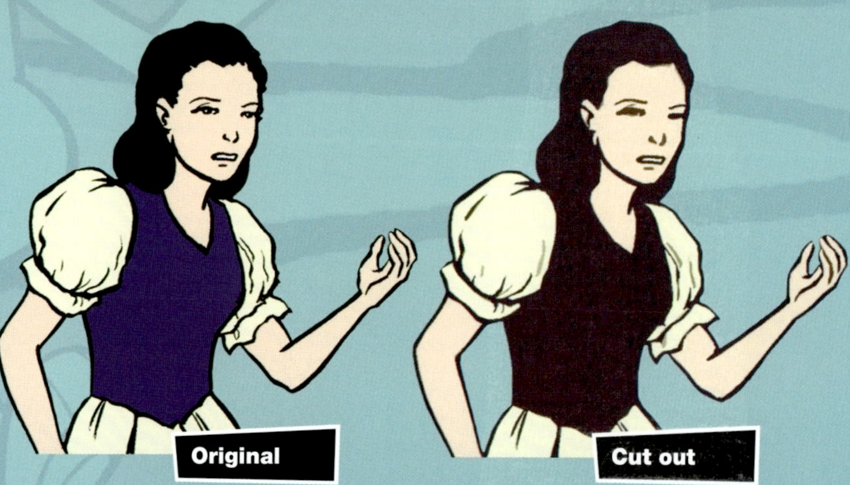

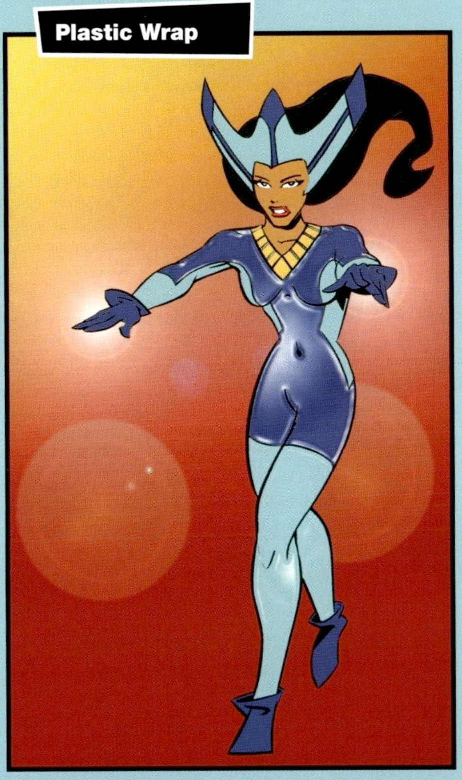

Plastic Wrap can give a kinky, rubbery look to a superhero's clothing, perfect for a crime-fighter's all-weather wear. It's seen here in conjunction with a couple of Lens Flares.

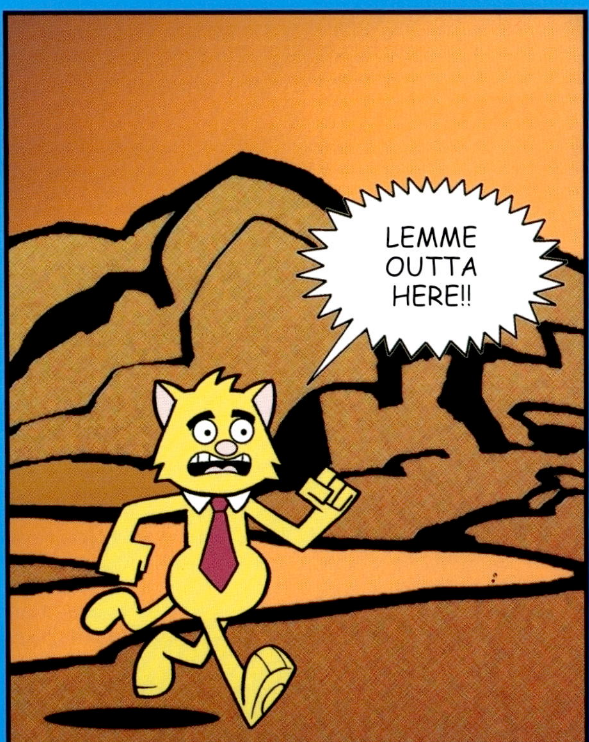

Filters can also be combined—for instance, using a Colored Pencil filter over the top of Noise softens the grain, and is useful for backgrounds.

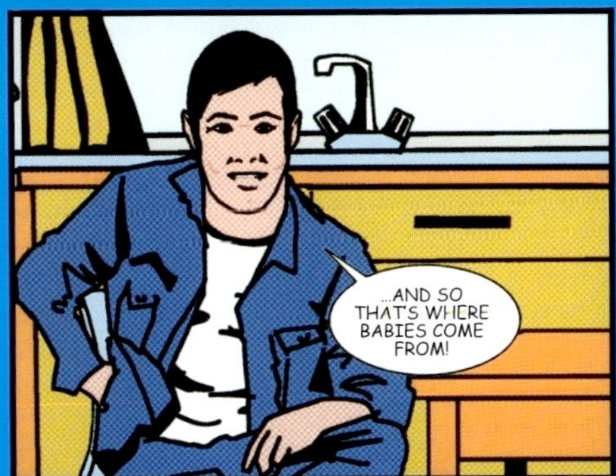

Halftone Pattern, accessible via Sketch, if used sparingly can add variety to coloring and give your images something of an "old-school" quality. Keep the slider settings low, though, or your panels could look "blob-tastic."

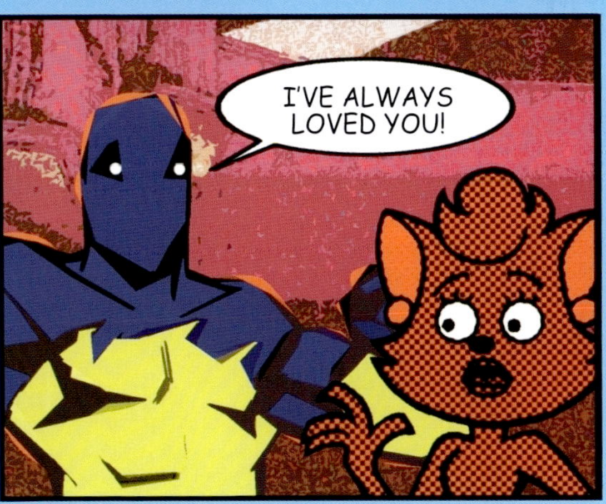

Try not to get carried away, but at the same time, stay open to new ideas!

Converting Photographs

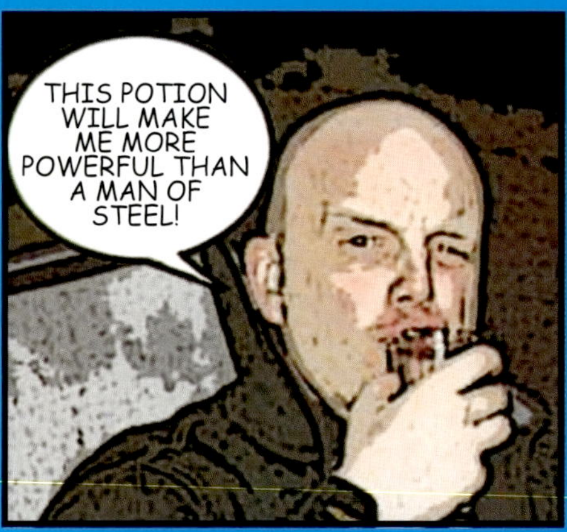

There are a number of different methods that Photoshop Elements enables us to use in order to convert ordinary photographs into cartoon images. These images can then be colored and adapted for use as comic strip panels and pages.

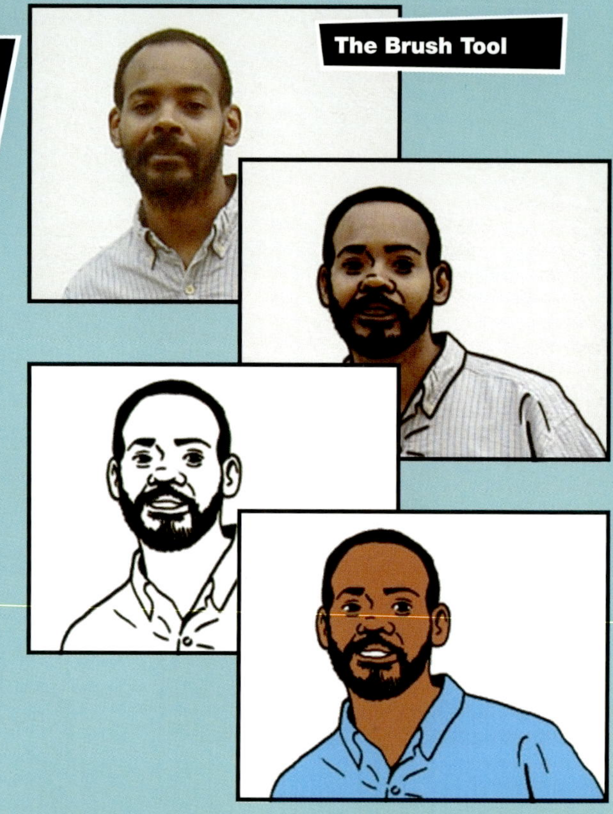

The most straightforward method is to use the Brush tool to trace the outlines of a photograph onto a new layer above the picture. When finished, delete the background layer (the photo) and fill the empty areas with white. We'll be left with a black-and-white cartoon, which can be colored however we wish.

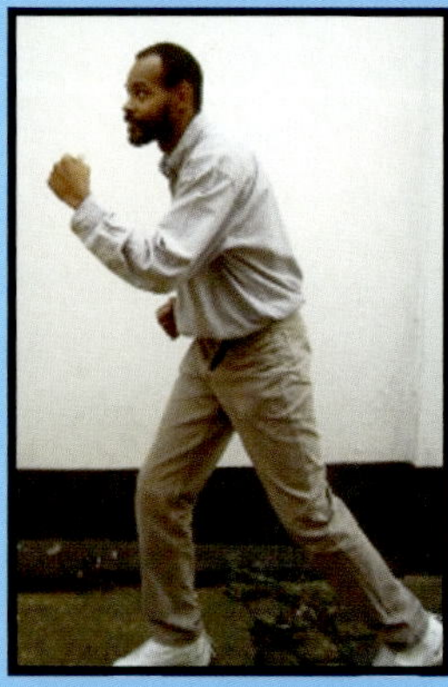
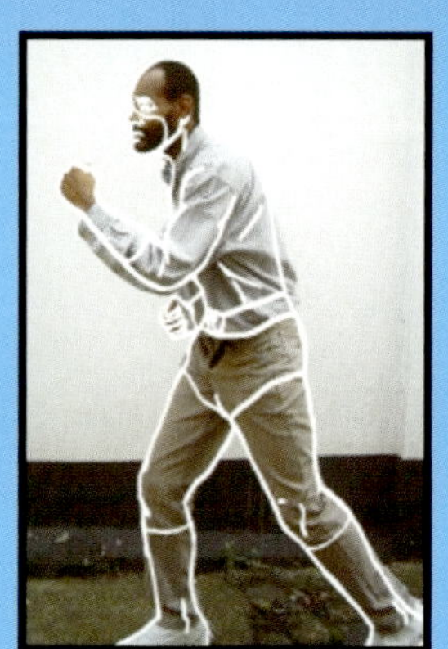
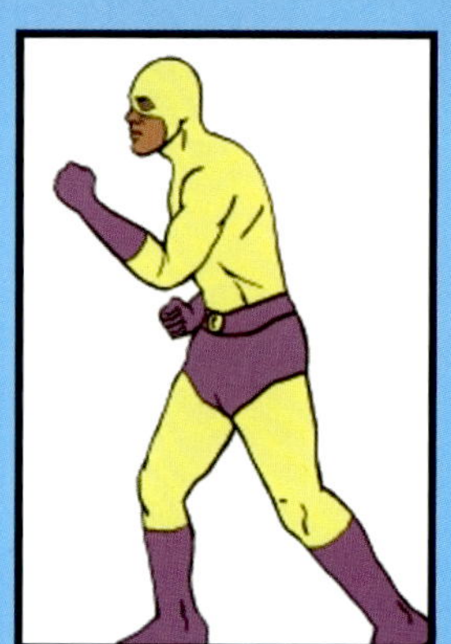

We don't have to limit ourselves to a literal tracing of the photograph; we can use it as a guide for drawing a very different kind of figure—a superhero, a princess, a monster, whatever characters we need for our comic strip.

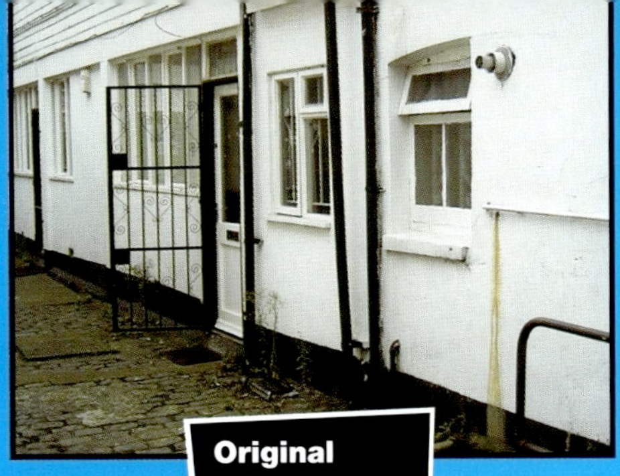

Original

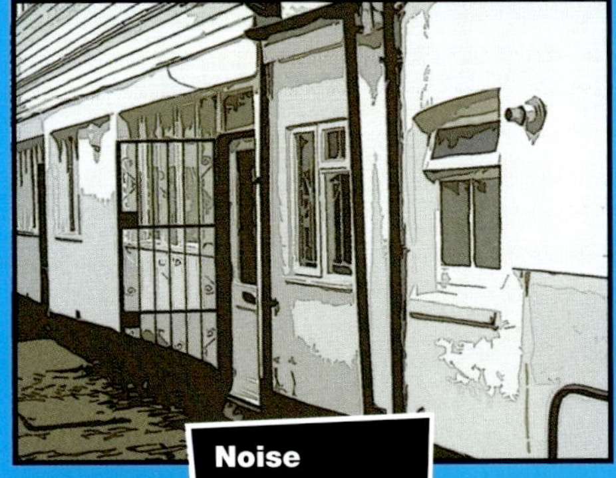

Noise

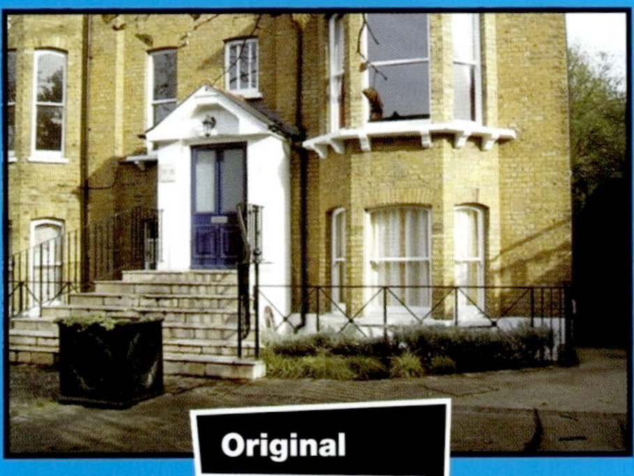

Original

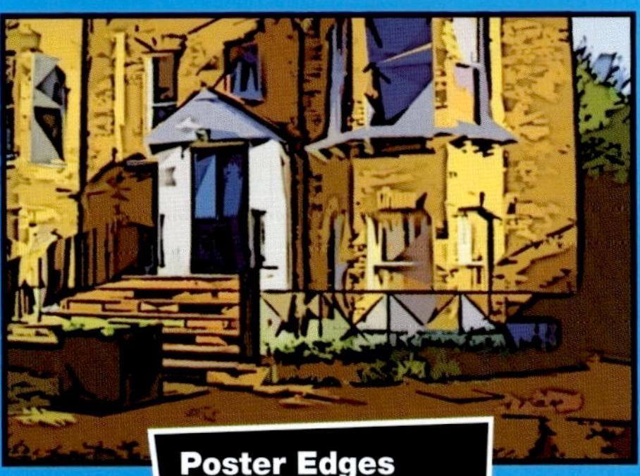

Poster Edges

We can use the same method with backgrounds and buildings, or we can combine Filters such as Cut Out, Poster Edges, and Noise to create interesting settings. Adjusting the Hue and Saturation can give a vibrant, unreal or unusual aspect to the colors.

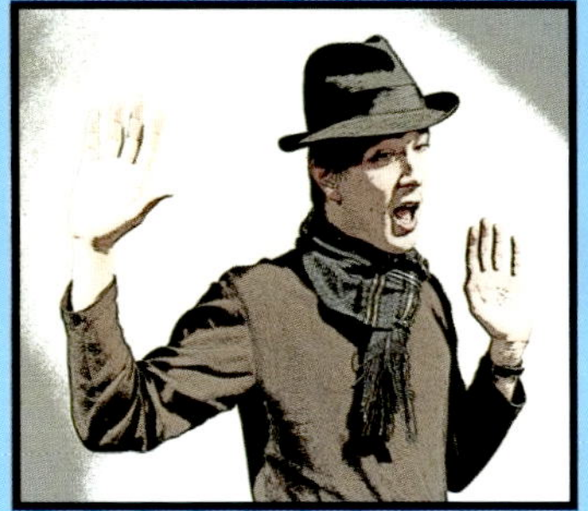

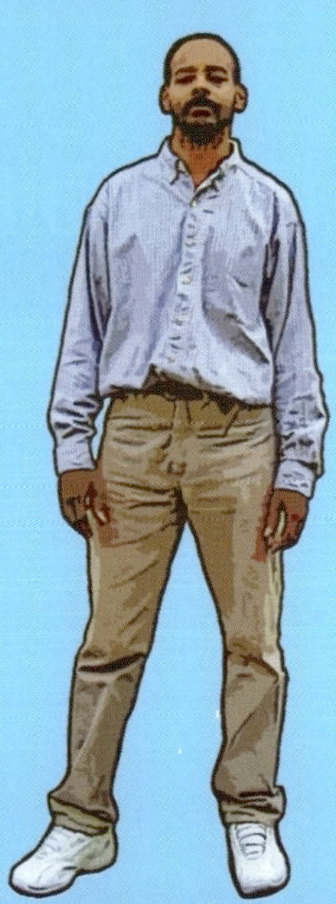

These same Filters and settings can be used on photographs of people to give them a curiously detailed but cartoonish quality. This technique is often used in comic book adaptations of movies and TV shows, when an actor has sanctioned the use of their likeness.

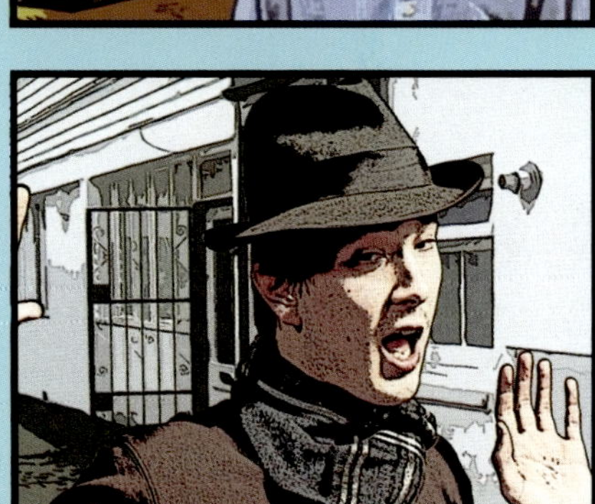

Once Filters have been applied, separating a person in a photograph from the background— so that they can be dragged into a new picture—necessitates drawing around them with black and/or white. We then carefully select every area within and including the black outline and drag them onto a new picture, or onto a blank document to save for future use; to this end, it is sometimes easier to select every part of the background, and then go to Select>Inverse on the Menu bar to be left with just the person selected. It may be necessary to slightly alter the look of the person to match the background, either with the use of the Hue and Saturation settings, or with additional Filters.

With the use of digital cameras and camera phones now commonplace, it's never been easier to build a library of images that can be used to produce cartoons and strips.

Creating Your Own Images

As well as converting photographs for use as cartoon images, readers with artistic leanings might wish to draw their own menagerie of characters to use in conjunction with Photoshop and this book.

All of the pictures on our CD were specially drawn and separated onto layers. Each separate head or expression fits exactly onto its host, ready to be placed onto a background. Background images are flat, but further objects and props can be added on separate layers. The process for creating images that can be used in this way is fairly straightforward, so let's see how it's done…

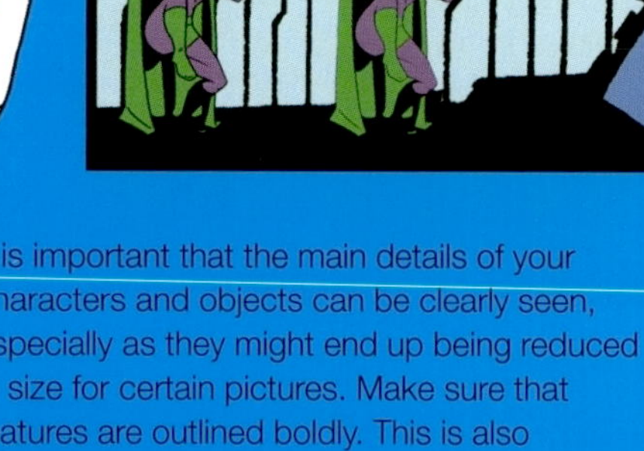

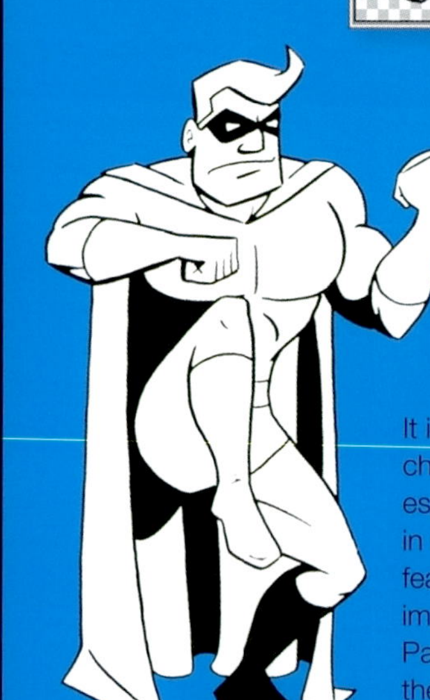

It is important that the main details of your characters and objects can be clearly seen, especially as they might end up being reduced in size for certain pictures. Make sure that features are outlined boldly. This is also important with respect to coloring; if using the Paint Bucket, colors can slightly "bleed" into the linework, obscuring details if they have been drawn too thinly.

The Pictures

Depending on the extent of your own artistic skills, this may prove to be the hardest part. You will no doubt be aware of the plethora of books available that give instruction on the rudimentary and advanced skills of cartooning, so one or two of these are a good place to start for the beginner. You might find that there are part-time classes in your area, taught by an experienced cartoonist. Or, you may already be a fairly nifty cartoonist in your own right. However, even if that is the case, there are some important factors to keep in mind.

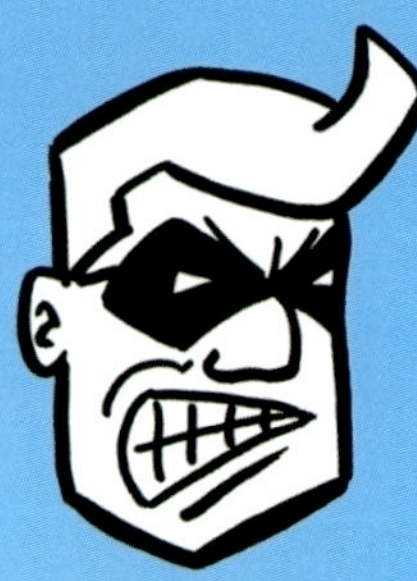

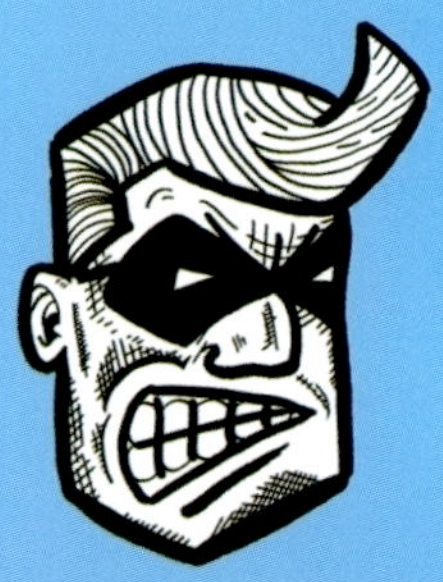

How much texture you attempt to add to a picture by shading and cross-hatching with the pen is up to you, but unless you really enjoy spending ages filling tiny areas with color, try to keep your drawings as "open" as possible. Also, your life will be made immeasurably easier if you fully enclose separate areas with line, preventing colors leaking out into other parts of the image.

Keep the details of your characters fairly symmetrical. A wristwatch or an eye-patch will appear to be on the wrong side of the body if you need to flip the image horizontally. The chest emblems of superheroes should also be symmetrical: the letter "A" looks the same either way round, the letter "S" does not.

A set of different expressions can be drawn by tracing the original head and changing the way it looks inside. This ensures that it will fit exactly onto the original image of your character.

The Process

When your drawings are complete, you will need to scan them into Photoshop, at a resolution of at least 300 pixels/inch. Once on screen, you can darken the black lines of your images, and eliminate the slightly gray cast of the paper, by heading for Enhance > Adjust Lighting > Brightness/Contrast on the Menu bar, and setting the Brightness to 20 and the Contrast to 50.

Next, you'll need to create a layered file containing your figure and different heads, ready to be dragged around with the Move tool.

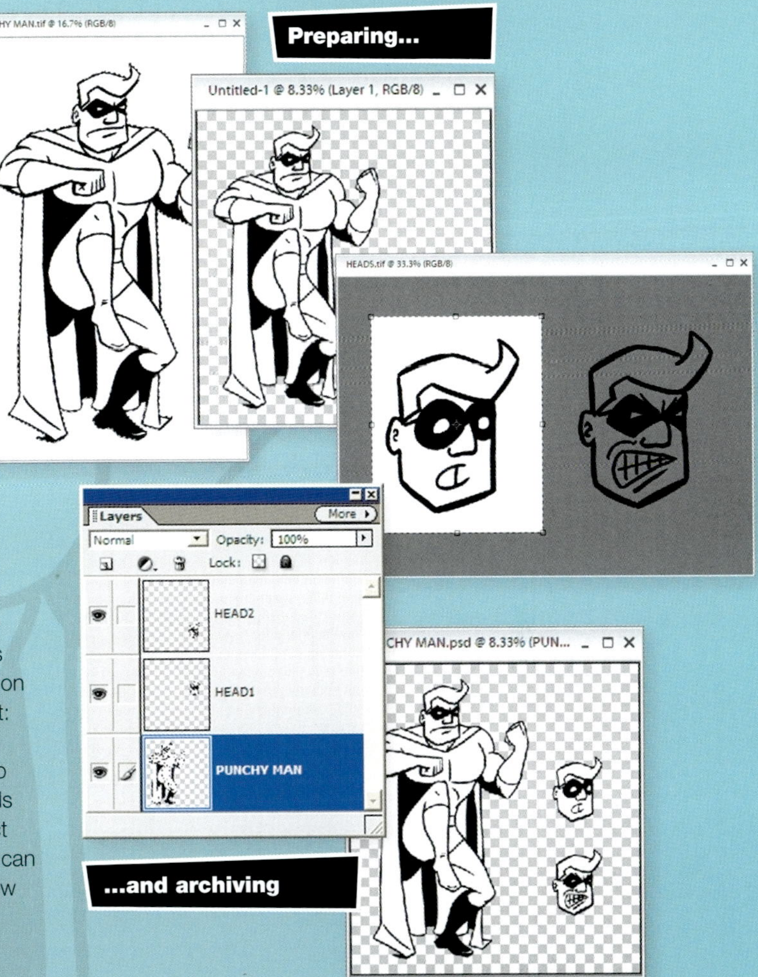

Open a new blank file approximately a third wider than the file containing your main character. Select the background of your character, go to Select > Inverse and drag the character across to the new file; you'll see in the Layers palette that it is floating on a new layer above the blank background. Here's the scary part: on your Heads file, crop around the first head. Repeat the selection process above, and drag it onto your new file, next to the figure. It, too, now floats on a new layer. Back on the Heads file, make three visits to Edit on the Menu bar, and Undo Select Inverse, Magic Wand, and Crop. Both heads return! Then you can repeat the same process to end up with both heads on the new file. By right-clicking each layer in turn in the palette, you can rename it for easy use.

All that remains is to save the new file as a PSD (Photoshop Document) or a TIFF, to preserve the layers. Your new character file is ready for use!

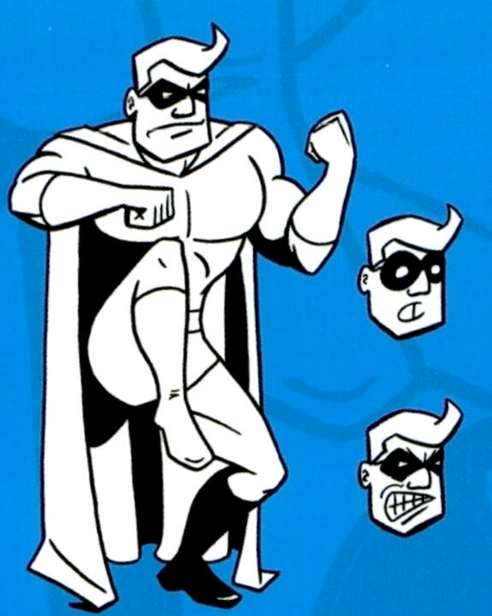

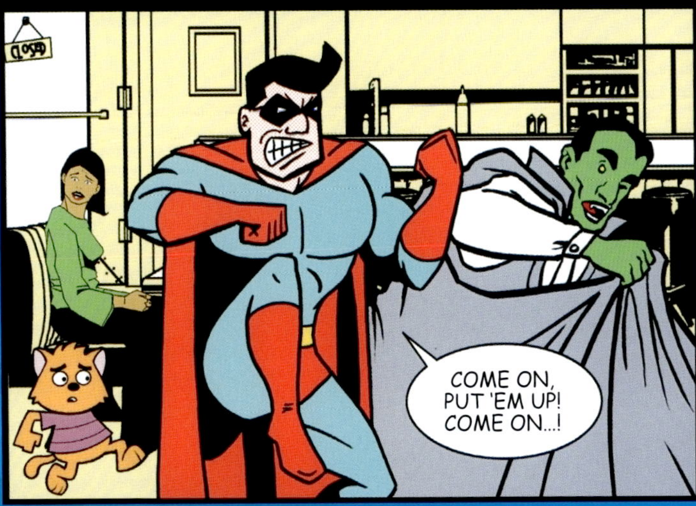

10 And Finally...

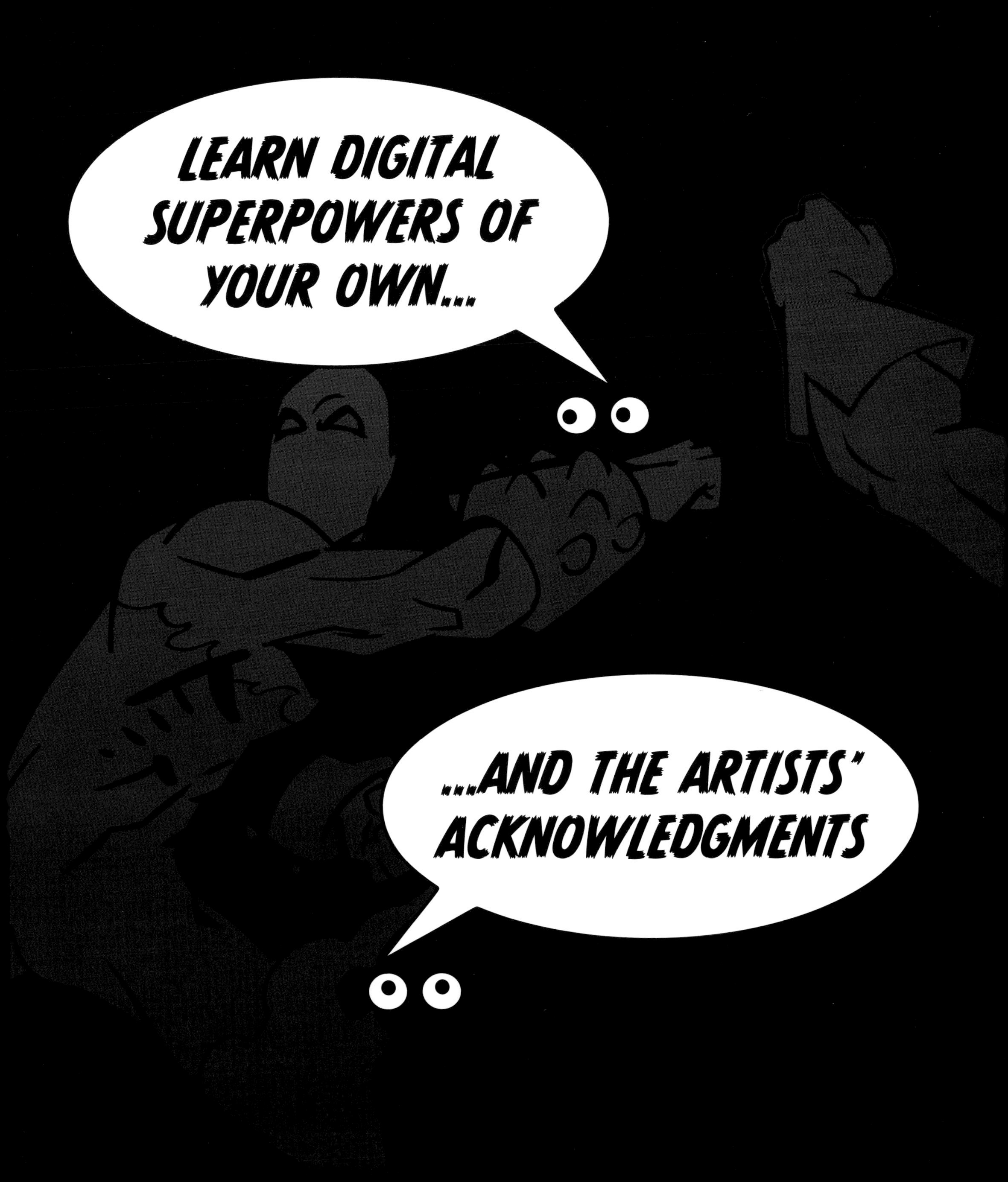

LEARN DIGITAL SUPERPOWERS OF YOUR OWN...
...AND THE ARTISTS' ACKNOWLEDGMENTS

File Formats & Image Sizes

If you have spent a great deal of time working on an image, you will want to ensure that it will eventually be seen at its best—which is why it is important to know about the most effective ways of preparing, saving, and presenting your work.

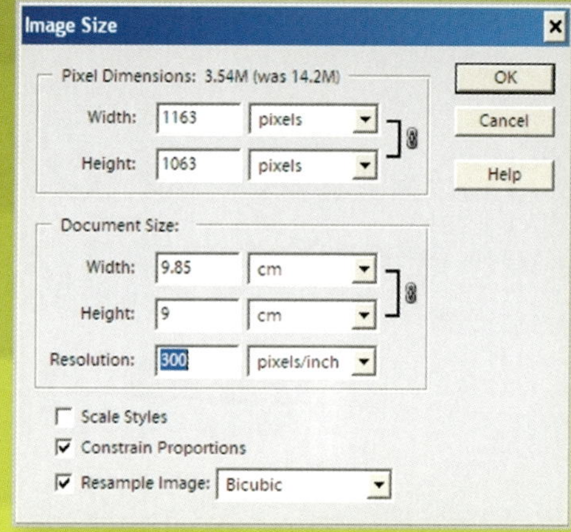

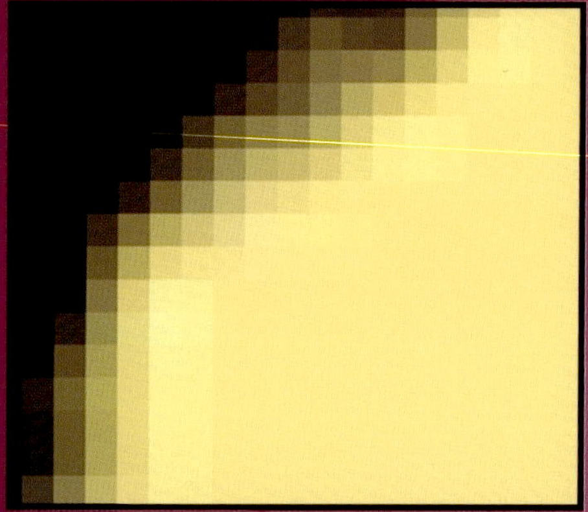

PPI (Pixels Per Inch) refers to the tiny individual points of light that make up a digital image. Zoom right in on any color image in Photoshop and you will see its individual pixels of differing hues. The more pixels used in an image, the finer it will appear. Too few, and curves will appear "pixelated"—they will have a jagged, "stepped" appearance.

The following is of most relevance if you have created your own artwork to use with Photoshop Elements.

A picture resolution of 300 ppi is pretty much the lowest you can use to ensure it will not pixelate badly if slightly enlarged. Many artists prefer to work on images of 400-600 ppi or above, but this can slow the average computer's performance to a crawl. Use your own judgment—images intended to be viewed at the size of the average comic-book page should look fine at 300 ppi; larger media, such as posters, should be 600 ppi, at least. All of this applies to scanned-in artwork, and you should be able to adjust the resolution using your scanner's own software. You can alter an image's resolution via the Menu bar (Image > Resize > Image Size), but upping the resolution will not cure pixelation, it just means that the image will use more tiny pixels to create the same jagged edges. So, always scan images at the resolution you think that you will need.

DPI stands for "Dots Per Inch" and is the factor of resolution used by printers. It refers to the number of microscopic spots of ink used to create a printed image and is a completely different factor to ppi. A 300 ppi image printed at 1400 dpi should look great, whereas a 600 ppi image printed at 360 dpi can look rough and grainy. A high ppi image printed at a high dpi on high quality paper will give you a professional-looking result.

One thing to remember: some people, even some types of scanning software, often refer to ppi as dpi, as in "Scan your work at 300 dpi." This is just lazy language. They mean "ppi." It has become a turn of phrase, as in when someone says "I could care less", when really they mean "I couldn't care less." Think about it….

Photoshop (*.PSD;*.PDD)
BMP (*.BMP;*.RLE;*.DIB)
CompuServe GIF (*.GIF)
Photoshop EPS (*.EPS)
JPEG (*.JPG;*.JPEG;*.JPE)
JPEG 2000 (*.JPF;*.JPX;*.JP2;*.J2C;*.J2K;*.JPC)
PCX (*.PCX)
Photoshop PDF (*.PDF;*.PDP)
Photoshop Raw (*.RAW)
PICT File (*.PCT;*.PICT)
Pixar (*.PXR)
PNG (*.PNG)
Scitex CT (*.SCT)
Targa (*.TGA;*.VDA;*.ICB;*.VST)
TIFF (*.TIF;*.TIFF)

Meanwhile, at the other end of the process, you might be confused by the format in which to save your finished images. Photoshop allows you to save work in a wide variety of formats, from TIFF (the most useful) to TARGA (King of the Hidden Jungle).

All of this can appear fairly confusing, so to summarize:

PPI — The number of pixels used to display an image on a monitor. The higher the better.

DPI — The number of dots used to print an image; again, the higher the better.

TIFF — A high quality and versatile format for saving your work. People will one day name their child "Tiff."

PSD — Of equally high quality, but can only be accessed via Photoshop and related Adobe programs such as Image Ready.

JPEG, GIF — These are both "lossy" formats that use digital shortcuts to save file space at the expense of detail; fine for the web, lousy for print.

OTHER FORMATS — Photoshop Elements allows you to save files in formats designed to be used with other programs because it is big and clever.

TIFFs are a universal standard. They can be used in almost all graphics packages, and can even be inserted into Microsoft Word documents. TIFFs are a "lossless" format, meaning that they save every ounce of your work. PSD format (Photoshop Document) works in the same way, but is only re-useable in Photoshop, as the name implies. However, PSDs tend to open and save faster than TIFFs, so they are ideal for saving work in progress. TIFFs can be saved using LZW Compression, which takes out extraneous information from a file and reduces its size in megabytes. At the end of the day, when in doubt, save as a TIFF and you won't go wrong.

You may, however, need to save an image at a much-reduced file size, particularly for the web or email. This is where JPEGs and GIFs come in. These file formats are "lossy," i.e. they save images at vastly smaller sizes, megabyte-wise, than others. They do this by reducing the information saved, which can affect the quality of an image.

Not a problem with an image destined to be viewed at 72 ppi on a monitor screen, but bad for a printed image. JPEGs and GIFs are used mainly for viewing on a website, because they will download faster. Compare the quality yourself: zoom in on a TIFF by 200% and it should appear fine; zoom in on a JPEG and it will appear pixelated.

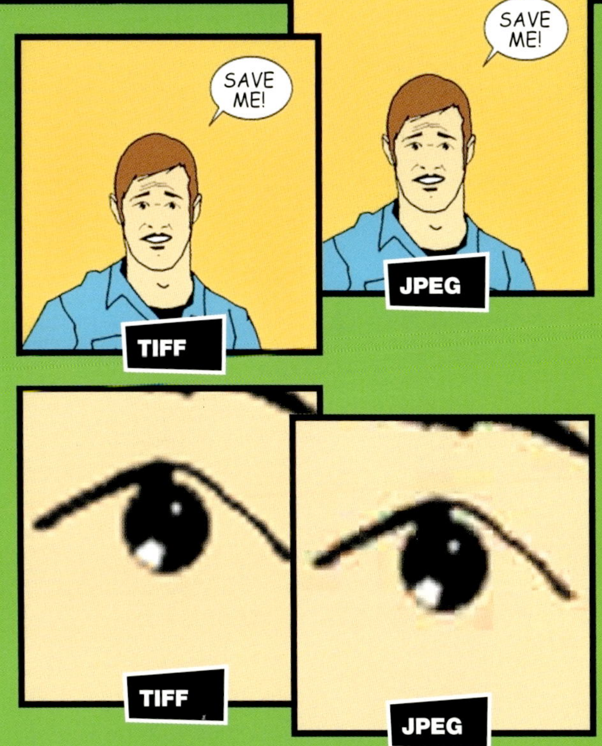

Printing etc

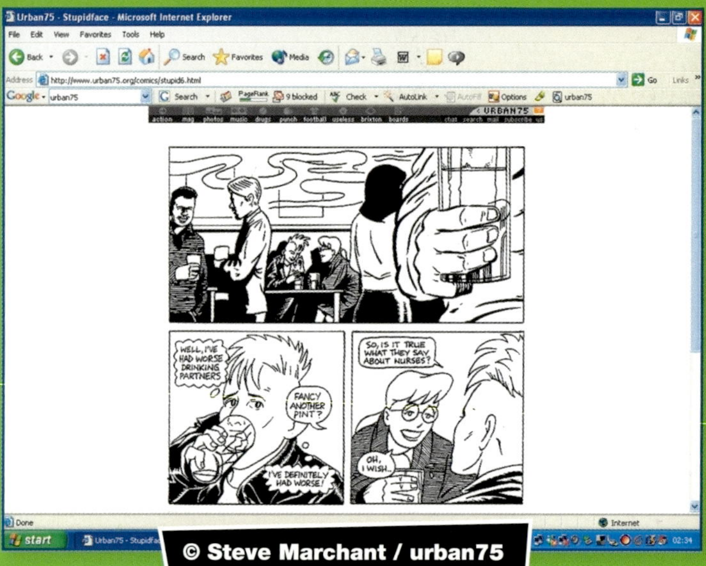

© Steve Marchant / urban75

When the time comes for you to show off your work to the world, you will most likely consider two main options: the web and the printed page. The advantage of putting your work onto a website is that people from around the world can quickly and easily enjoy your work. You can also present it in color, at no extra expense. The main disadvantage is that you need the skills and software to build your own website, but these are relatively easy to attain and there are many books, magazines, and online resources that can help you. Or, you may already know someone with a website who would like some cartoons and comic strips to add variety to its content.

For many people, the proper place for comic strips is in a printed comic book. A great many of today's most successful cartoonists began their careers by self-publishing their own work in short-run "small press" editions. The main advantage of comic books over electronic methods of delivery is that they are completely portable and can be read anywhere, from the bus to the bathroom. The main disadvantage is that printing costs money, color printing can cost a lot of money, and collating and stapling can either take you a lot of time, or add to your printing costs. However, an average home printer connected to the computer can produce decent results on quality paper (reams of 24 lb or 100 gsm paper are available quite cheaply in many stores). Alternatively, the cost of photocopying has hardly risen in 30 years, so if you don't mind presenting your work in black & white (perhaps with color covers you could print at home), your local copy shop might be a useful port of call. The most expensive route is to get your work printed professionally; though again, digital technology has made this option slightly more affordable in recent years.

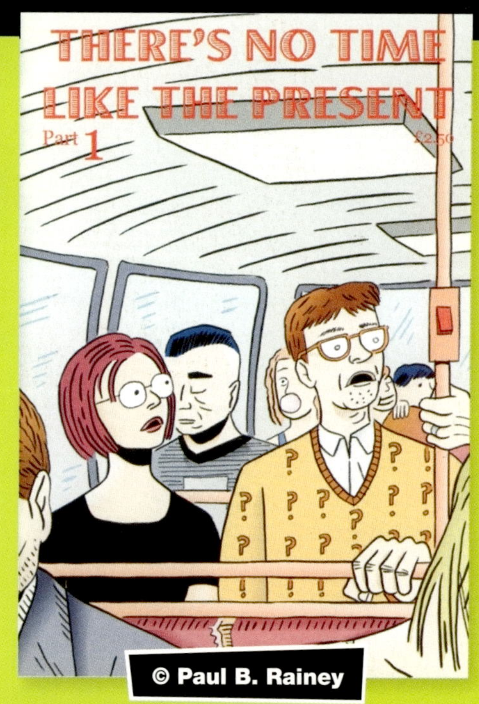

© Paul B. Rainey

By whatever means you choose, you might eventually find yourself staring at a pile of comics, wondering how you can get them into the hands of potential readers. Obviously, you'll want to give them out to friends and colleagues, but to reach beyond your own circle of contacts, you might pay a visit to your nearest comics shop. Many—though not all—of these are happy to carry self-published comics, usually for around one-third of the cover price. This is something you will have to consider when you think of how much to charge the panting public. You will have to factor in your printing costs per issue, the shop's cut, and whether or not you feel that you ought to make a small amount on top. At the same time, you shouldn't make your comic book too expensive, otherwise no one will buy it.

There are also networks of small-press distributors, aficionados who will sell copies of your work for you via the internet, mail order, or at comic marts and conventions. Search the internet for "small-press comics distribution" or check the advertisments in one of the many specialist magazines available in comics shops.

If all else fails, remember that underground comics icon Robert Crumb began his career by selling his work from an old baby carriage on a street corner…

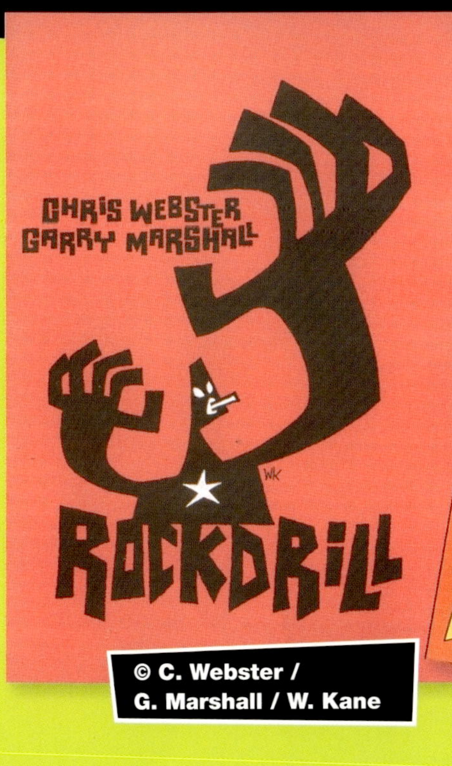

© C. Webster / G. Marshall / W. Kane

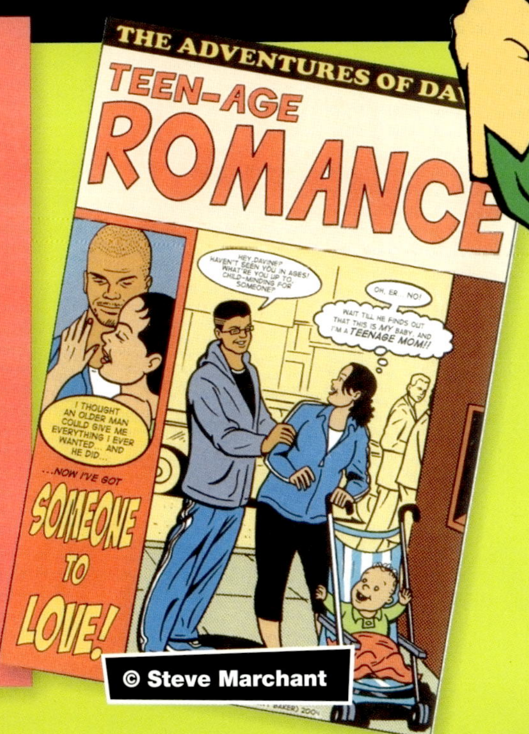

© Steve Marchant

Acknowledgments

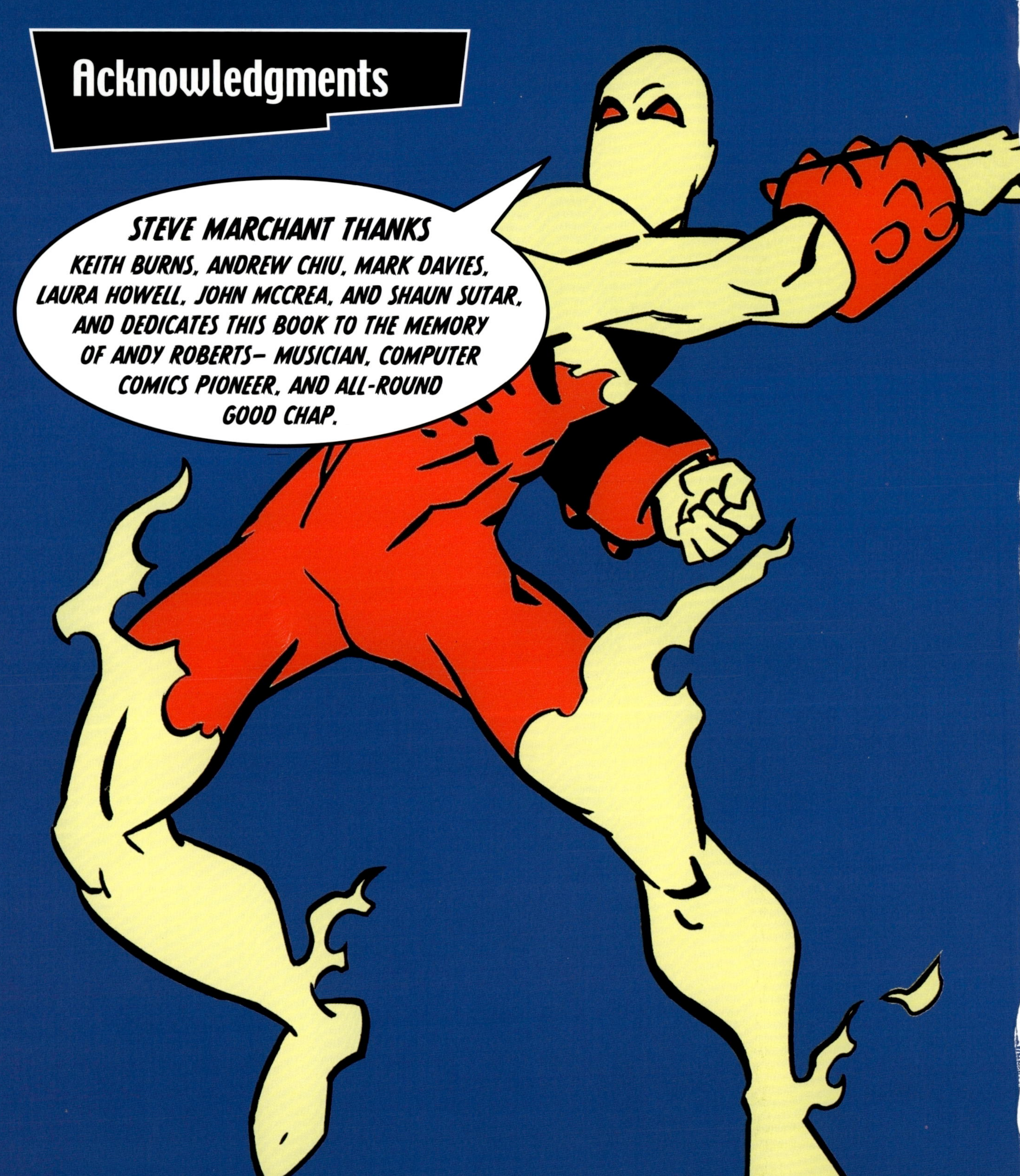